ADVANCED HOMEWORK FOR GROWN-UPS

ADVANCED HOMEWORK FOR GROWN-UPS

Old School Lessons for Clever Clogs

E. FOLEY & B. COATES

◼ SQUARE PEG

Published by Square Peg 2009

2 4 6 8 10 9 7 5 3 1

First published in Great Britain in 2009 by
SQUARE PEG
Random House, 20 Vauxhall Bridge Road,
London SW1V 2SA

www.rbooks.co.uk

Addresses for companies within The Random House Group Limited can be found at:
www.randomhouse.co.uk/offices.htm

The Random House Group Limited Reg. No. 954009

A CIP catalogue record for this book
is available from the British Library

ISBN 9780224086349

The Random House Group Limited supports The Forest Stewardship Council (FSC),
the leading international forest certification organisation. All our titles are printed on
Greenpeace approved FSC certified paper carry the FSC logo. Our paper procurement
policy can be found at www.rbooks.co.uk/environment

Mixed Sources
Product group from well-managed
forests and other controlled sources
www.fsc.org Cert no. TT-COC-2139
© 1996 Forest Stewardship Council

Typeset in Bembo by Palimpsest Book Production Ltd
Grangemouth, Stirlingshire

Printed and bound in Germany by
GGP Media, GmbH, Pößneck

⤷ CONTENTS ⤶

᥏ ASSEMBLY ᥑ

You may think you're pretty well up on your education: you know your oblique angles from your acutes, your Catherine of Aragon from your Anne of Cleves and your chiasmus from your zeugma. Now it's time to test yourselves a little further. Let's face it, the kids are getting brighter every day. It's no longer just enough to understand the laws of thermodynamics or the reasons for the rise of the Nazis, these days you're just as likely to have your little darling quiz you on the nature of Brecht's theory of *Verfremdungseffekt* or ask you to help them with their simultaneous equations. Fear not, *Advanced Homework for Grown-ups* is here to steer you through some of the more complicated elements of the curriculum and beyond.

Within these pages you will revisit the core subjects of Maths, English, Science, History, Geography, Art, Home Economics and Classics, but in much more depth. This time you will study those mysterious creatures called surds, unlock the secrets of semantics, launch yourself into the wonders of space travel, decipher the mysteries of Malthus, get to grips with sculpture, construct a beautiful Bakewell tart and learn how to curse like a true Roman. We aim to fill your eager brains to the brim with really useful information and also some excitingly esoteric material with which to impress friends, relatives and colleagues.

In addition, you will find chapters on Music, Modern Languages, Economics, Philosophy and Psychology, and Drama and Film Studies. Ever wondered what a theremin is? Always longed to be able to introduce yourself in twenty different languages? Want to equip yourself to converse on the topics of *Noh* Theatre and *commedia dell'arte*? Keen to know Nietzsche? Or familiarise yourself with Freud? *Advanced Homework for Grown-ups* will take you by the hand and lead you to the fountain of knowledge.

⌾ ENGLISH ⌾
LANGUAGE
AND
LITERATURE

The wonderful (and potentially worrisome) thing about our rich and varied tongue and its literature is their vast scope. OK, so you've mastered pronouns and relative clauses, the works of Jane Austen and Charles Dickens, but who among us has not been caught short by those tricky dinner-party conversations that seem designed to highlight our own philistinism? Well, never fear. This chapter allows us to take you further into the mysteries of grammar, to ponder the peculiar-sounding pursuits of morphology, syntax and pragmatics. We'll show you how to decipher phonetics, and unlock a world in which a word like 'ghoti' could conceivably be pronounced 'fish' and calling someone's necklace 'gaudy' could be considered complimentary. If Anglo-Saxon seems dusty, dead and buried here's where we'll bring it back to life; by taking a peep at its remarkable alphabet and at the glories of *Beowulf.* We'll also examine later literary classics, and show you how to bluff your way through even the most rigorous literary questioning, by giving you quick analyses of the more unusual poetic forms, from tankas to ghazals. Read on!

LOVELY LINGUISTICS

Have you ever wondered why the furry canine quadruped you think of as a dog is called a 'dog'? Or why a cat is called a 'cat', or a pangolin a 'pangolin'? (A pangolin is a scaly anteater usually found in Africa or Asia by the way.) Linguistics is the study of language and how it relates to thought. The term comes from the Latin word '*lingua*' meaning 'tongue'. Working in several different specialist disciplines, linguists cunningly investigate how language in general –

be it Spanish, Swahili or Swedish – works. Knowing a bit about some linguistic fields of study can be an illuminating experience, encouraging us to look at the structure and use of our own language in a new light.

- **Phonetics** is the study of how we physically articulate the sounds we use to create language, the acoustics of these sounds and how we hear them.

- **Phonology** is the study of the patterns of sound that are used to create words. Different languages obey different rules in the way they use sounds, but there are also similarities between them – all languages have syllables for example. Most languages generally use between twenty and sixty basic speech sounds, called **phonemes** (good old British English has about forty-four), but how each of these sounds is perceived and represented on the page varies. As well as investigating the sound systems of different languages, phonologists also research regional accents and dialects within the same language.

- **Morphology** is the study of the structure of words, covering such exhilarating areas as inflection, derivation and the creation of compounds. The basic units of meaning that combine to make words are called **morphemes.** You can have both **free morphemes**, which can stand alone as words, such as 'lucky' and 'cow'; and also **bound morphemes** which can only make sense attached to a free morpheme; such as 'un-' in 'unlucky' and '-s' in 'cows'.

- **Syntax** is the study of the structure of sentences. Syntax and morphology together make up what we call **grammar**.

- **Language acquisition** is the study of how children and adults learn languages. One famous theory from this field is that of **universal grammar**, which postulates that all humans have the same innate concept of the rules of language.

- **Pragmatics** is the study of how people communicate in specific contexts, often in ways that don't express their meaning directly in words. For example, if someone says to you 'Have you got the time?' you are unlikely (unless you are feeling particularly discourteous) to just reply 'yes' as if their question were literal.

- **Semantics** is the study of how meaning is expressed in language: scholars of semantics study the relationship between words and the things and ideas that they represent: for example, the relationship between an Asian or African scaly anteater and the word 'pangolin'.

SLIPPERY SEMANTICS: SEMANTIC DRIFT

Semantic drift (also known as **semantic shift** or **change**) is the process by which words change their meanings over time. Here are some examples of how semantic drift can occur:

Pejoration: This is when a word's meaning develops previously unheld negative connotations. An example of this is the history of the word 'gaudy'. It comes from the Latin verb *'gaudere'* meaning 'to rejoice' and in Middle English the word 'gaud' came to mean a rosary bead as the rosary was considered a cheery prayer. However, it gradually came to refer to the bead itself as an ornament, and finally in modern English to mean tasteless and showy.

Amelioration: This is when a word's meaning develops positive connotations. For example, the word 'nice' comes from the Latin word *'nescius'* meaning 'ignorant'. This meaning changed in Old French to 'silly' and it was this interpretation that was adopted in Middle English. Over time the meaning shifted again to mean 'agreeable'.

Specialisation: This is when a word's meaning becomes more limited and specific over time. For example, the word 'deer' in Old English just meant 'animal' but now it means a specific type of animal (a brownish grazing mammal with hooves and appealing eyes at risk of losing its mother to nasty hunters).

Generalisation: This is when a word's meaning becomes broader over time. For example, the word 'pigeon' came from the Old French word *'pijon'* which used to mean 'young dove' but now refers to any member of the dove family, even the oldest and scraggiest of those sorry excuses for avian creation that haunt our city centres.

DICTIONARY ETIQUETTE: UNDERSTANDING THE PHONETIC ALPHABET

When you peek into the treasure trove that is a dictionary (a mind-broadening exercise you should ideally undertake every day) there are arcane instructions on how to pronounce many of the words written next to the entries. Because some letters of the alphabet can be pronounced in different ways these instructions use an alphabet called the **International Phonetic Alphabet** (IPA). In this alphabet the symbols can only refer to one sound. Some dictionaries use their own phonetic alphabet but this is the most commonly recognised one.

g – got	ɛ – pet	ɔɪ – paw
tʃ – chicken	ə – ago	uɪ – too
dʒ – gin	I – pit	ʌɪ – cry
x – loch	i – busty	aʊ – how
ŋ – sing	ɒ – pot	eɪ – pay
θ – thing	ʌ – sun	əʊ – no
ð – father	ʊ – put	ɪə – ear
ʃ – ship	ɑɪ – harm	ɔɪ – toy
ʒ – pleasure	ɛɪ – air	ʊə – door
j – yes	əɪ – her	ʌɪə – hire
a – hat	iɪ – pee	aʊə – hour

The stressed syllable in a word is indicated by the mark ' positioned just before the syllable.

There are many other IPA symbols for sounds in different languages, including the symbol ǁ which stands for one of the clicking noises used in the click languages of southern Africa.

'GHOTI', PRONOUNCED 'FISH'

Since the early days of the dictionary, various campaigners ranging from Benjamin Franklin and George Bernard Shaw to the Spelling Society have sought to reform the English language by regulating the spelling of our words. Because so much of our mother tongue has come down to us from different languages and dialects over the ages, words don't necessarily look on the page the way they should logically be pronounced. English is considered one of the hardest languages to learn because there are so many exceptions to the rules of spelling and pronunciation, and some think this puts us at a disadvantage in achieving high literacy levels.

One illustration used to show the illogical nature of English spelling is the example that the word 'fish' could, obeying different rules inherent in the language, be written as 'ghoti': in words like 'cough' and 'rough' the 'gh' is pronounced as an 'f'; in 'women' the 'o' sounds like an 'i'; and in 'station' or 'nation' the 'ti' becomes a 'sh' sound.

Other languages such as Dutch and Norwegian have been modernised by government intervention but English has been left alone to grow like a wild and anarchic forest of different species of words, each of which obeys its own rules and carries the marks of its own unique history. A humorous idea of how our language might look, were reforms to be made, was explored in a piece that is often attributed to Mark Twain, although its true source is unconfirmed.

A Plan for the Improvement of English Spelling

For example, in Year 1 that useless letter 'c' would be dropped to be replased either by 'k' or 's', and likewise 'x' would no longer be part of the alphabet. The only kase in which 'c' would be retained would be the 'ch' formation, which will be dealt with later.

Year 2 might reform 'w' spelling, so that which and one would take the same konsonant, wile Year 3 might well abolish 'y' replasing it with 'i' and Iear 4 might fiks the 'g/j' anomali wonse and for all.

Jenerally, then, the improvement would kontinue iear bai iear with Iear 5 doing awai with useless double konsonants, and Iears 6–12 or so modifaiing vowlz and the rimeining voist and unvoist konsonants.

Bai Iear 15 or sou, it wud fainali bi posibl tu meik ius ov thi ridandant letez 'c', 'y' and 'x' – bai now jast a memori in the maindz ov ould doderez – tu riplais 'ch', 'sh' and 'th' rispektivli.

Fainali, xen, aafte sam 20 iers ov orxogrefkl riform, wi wud hev
a lojikl, kohirnt speling in ius xrewawt xe Ingliy-spiking werld.

DR JOHNSON AND HIS DICTIONARY

Staffordshire's lexicographical luminary Samuel Johnson was born in
Lichfield on 18 September 1709. His father was a bookseller and
Johnson himself was a great reader, which evidently helped him in
his future career as poet, critic, playwright, essayist, biographer, editor
and sparkling conversationalist. However, it is the work he undertook
between 1747 and 1755 for which he is most gratefully remembered
today. During this time Johnson relentlessly gathered together defin-
itions for 42,773 words in his *Dictionary of the English Language*, nearly
2,000 of which remain in today's *Oxford English Dictionary*. Unfortunately, 'fopnoodle' meaning 'fool' and 'dandiprat' meaning 'urchin' are
no longer included, and Johnson's lively definition for 'oats' – 'a grain
which in England is generally given to horses, but in Scotland supports
the people' – has also changed. Although Johnson's was not the earliest
English dictionary it was the first to use quotations to demonstrate
how words were used and its quality and scope meant that it remained
extraordinarily influential right up until the twentieth century. The
venerable doctor (he was made Doctor of Law's by both Dublin and
Oxford Universities) died on 13 December 1784 and is buried in
Westminster Abbey.

In homage to the great word wizard, we will now present you with
some useful, yet under-appreciated, words to enhance your vocabulary.

Ascesis: extreme self-discipline. 'Franklin is of an ascetic bent; he never
   drinks.'
Blandiloquence: flattering speech. 'His blandiloquence led me to go
   home with him.'
Caesious: bluish or greyish green. 'Her dress was a rather dull caesious
   colour.'
Deliquesce: to become liquid. 'Hurry, the cheese has begun to deliquesce.'
Ferruginous: containing iron or rust-coloured. 'His ferruginous hair
   clashed with his damson smoking jacket.'

Gallimaufry: a jumble. 'I'm afraid my CV is a bit of a gallimaufry.'

Hosel: the socket in the head of a golf club. 'Your problem is that your hosel is too big.'

Imbroglio: a complicated situation. 'I note that you have been involved in something of an imbroglio with your manager.'

Jacquerie: a peasant rebellion. 'I hear that Patty has been inciting a jacquerie in the staff room.'

Kerf: the cut made by a saw. 'Charlie's efforts at hiding his DIY projects were undone when Lucy spotted the kerfs in the kitchen table.'

Luculent: clear or bright. 'My darling, your luculent eyes have transfixed me.'

Mendicant: begging or a beggar. 'Marcie has married a mendicant.'

Nullipara: a female who has never given birth. 'Forgive my sister's insensitivity; she is nulliparous.'

Ochlocracy: mob rule. 'Patty is in some ways responsible for the current ochlocracy.'

Paillette: a large sequin or spangle. 'Sally says that paillettes are a must for the autumn.'

Quietus: death. 'Olaf's quietus was a relief for everyone.'

Redact: to edit. 'He is an excellent redactor and the newspaper would be lost without him.'

Sempiternal: eternal. 'Olaf has gone to a place of sempiternal rest.'

Thews: muscular strength. 'Charlie is somewhat lacking in thews.'

Ululate: to howl. 'We hardly had any sleep. Andy was ululating all night.'

Vesicate: to blister. 'These shoes are inclined to vesicate my feet.'

Welkin: the sky. 'The welkin is looking very blue today.'

Xeric: very dry. 'Pour me a drink; I'm feeling xeric.'

Yantra: an object used in meditation. 'Unfortunately, Violet left her yantra on the bus.'

Zucchetto: a skullcap worn by Roman Catholic clerics. 'Shermy's zucchetto looks very snazzy.'

APOSTROPHE CATASTROPHE: HOW TO USE APOSTROPHES

Surprising though it may seem, wandering around our towns and cities, there are only two uses for the apostrophe in the English language. It seems every other sign has either a plethora of the little fellows unnecessarily jostling the letters beneath, or, more commonly, there's a gaping hole where an appropriate apostrophe should be.

A greengrocer's apostrophe is a term used to indicate the over-enthusiastic misuse of an apostrophe in a plural, and refers to the handwritten signs on market stalls that are all too frequently incorrect: 'a bunch of banana's' for example, or 'six pear's for a pound'. The problem occurs because the possessive and the plural in the English language often sound the same. You must always be vigilant against making these mistakes, which have brought such calumny on the honest trade of greengrocery.

Apostrophes should be used only to indicate **contraction** or **omission** and **possession.**

Contraction/Omission

Apostrophes are inserted into words to mark where letters have been removed to shorten a word or phrase. *We'll, could've* and *mightn't* are all common examples and show that such contraction usually takes place in informal English. It can also occur for poetic effect as with *e'er* or *heav'n* in order to shorten the syllables of a word to maintain a rhythm. Logically enough, the apostrophe should appear where the relevant letters are missing.

Possession

This tends to be the area where people get confused. To signify that an object belongs to someone or something else, an apostrophe followed by an 's' is placed after the noun that is doing the possessing:

>   The chipmunk's cheeks
>   A traitor's kiss
>   The children's lollipops

If you miss an apostrophe showing possession you will be sending an entirely different message to that intended:

>   Steves Cafe

This means a place where many men called Steve have bacon sandwiches and tea, as opposed to a cafe belonging to Steve.

For singular nouns that end in 's', you can just add the apostrophe and not the extra 's' if it sounds clumsy to include it:

For goodness' sake

Plural nouns, ending in 's' add the apostrophe after the 's' but do not have an additional possessive 's'.

The cars' headlamps

ITS AND IT'S

People often get in a pickle when working out how to use apostrophes with that innocuous little word 'it'.

'It's' is a contraction of 'it is'; the apostrophe is replacing the missing letter 'i'.

'Its' is the possessive version of it: 'The dog has eaten its ball.'

TO WHOM IT MAY CONCERN: THE CORRECT USE OF WHOM, NOT WHO

The old 'who/whom' mistake is so prevalent in modern – especially spoken – English that it's almost beyond recovery, but we'll have a go.

'Who' is a subject pronoun, which means it should be used to ask or indicate which person performs an action or is in a certain condition:

Who fixed the washing machine?
Who is in a funk?

In both the above instances, the 'who' in question would be the subject of the corresponding non-interrogative sentence:

Emil fixed the washing machine.
Gustav is in a funk.

'Whom' is an object pronoun which means it is used to ask which person receives an action:

About whom are you talking?

In the answer to this question, the 'whom' would be the object of the sentence:

I am talking about Eloise.

People commonly use 'who' or 'whom' interchangeably without understanding that they have specific purposes. Mistakes are common in both direct questions such as 'Who did you go to the ice rink with?' (this is wrong because your ice-skating pal is the object of the sentence) and in indirect use such as 'Nancy expressed doubts about who she could trust' (again, the person Nancy can or cannot trust is the object of the sentence so 'whom' should be used). Sometimes people erroneously use 'whom' where a 'who' should be in order to sound more formal: 'Whom invited you to tea at the palace?'; 'He was a man whom I knew would make a good leader.'

The easiest way to make sure you're on the right track is to check whether you could substitute 'he' or 'him' in the answer to the question you're asking. Anywhere you'd use a 'he' needs a 'who' and anywhere you'd use a 'him' needs a 'whom': 'I went to the ice rink with him'; 'Nancy could trust him'; 'He invited me to tea at the palace.'; 'I knew he would make a good leader.'

TWENTY CLASSIC WORKS TO READ FOR A FULL EDUCATION

Who can say what it means to be truly well read? So many worthwhile books are published every year (and often obscured by dreadful ones) that it is impossible to keep up. What makes a book 'good' is also often a source of argument. However, you can always turn to the tried and trusted hits of the past to reassure yourself that you are spending your precious time reading only the quality shizzle. Whether you believe there should be a canon of intellectually valuable literature or not, certain classics have stood the test of time and engaged hearts and minds for generations. Below we have a selected a very partial list of the works of some authors who have continued to influence other writers and entrance readers long after their deaths.

The Divine Comedy by Dante Alighieri
Pride and Prejudice by Jane Austen

Wuthering Heights by Emily Brontë
Don Quixote by Miguel de Cervantes
Great Expectations by Charles Dickens
Crime and Punishment by Fyodor Dostoevsky
The Hound of the Baskervilles by Arthur Conan Doyle
Middlemarch by George Eliot
Madame Bovary by Gustave Flaubert
North and South by Elizabeth Gaskell
Tess of the D'Urbervilles by Thomas Hardy
The Odyssey by Homer
Les Misérables by Victor Hugo
The Turn of the Screw by Henry James
Moby-Dick by Herman Melville
Paradise Lost by John Milton
Hamlet by William Shakespeare
Dr Jekyll and Mr Hyde by Robert Louis Stevenson
War and Peace by Leo Tolstoy
Lady Windermere's Fan by Oscar Wilde

CONSTRUCTIVE CRITICISM: SOME DIFFERENT SCHOOLS OF LITERARY THEORY

Everyone loves a good natter about books – whether it be a chuckle over the latest chick-lit novel over tea and biscuits or a tutorial on the poems of Ezra Pound. When it comes to highbrow literature it's impossible to stop people talking and writing about their interpretations and evaluations of different texts: the plethora of pages that have been used up discussing the works of Shakespeare alone would fill a small cathedral. The purpose of literary theory and criticism is to approach works of literature from different angles in order to deepen our understanding of them. The results of this close scrutiny can sometimes be surprising and, over time, different schools of thought have developed which disagree over the most fruitful way to dissect texts. Although the practice of literary criticism began back in ancient times, the twentieth century saw an unparalleled breadth and depth of activity in this area, which extended to include methods of analysing culture in general. For example feminist, Marxist and psychoanalytical critical theory can be applied equally to art and film as to literature (and we investigate these schools of thought in the Drama and Film Studies chapter). It's hard to imagine what a humble sixteenth-century poet would think of a post-structuralist interpretation of his odes but this doesn't make this kind of analysis any less interesting or valid. Below we briefly summarise three of the major trends in literary theory that still influence critical studies today.

New Criticism (c.1935–1960)

This school of theory was developed by American scholars such as John Crowe Ransom who wrote *The New Criticism* (1941), which gives the movement its snappy name, and Allen Tate. It built on the work of British critics such as T. S. Eliot and I. A. Richards and advocated close-reading of the text of poems without reference to their biographical or historical context or the reader's response. The **Russian Formalists** developed similar ideas in the early 1900s, focusing on analysing the literary devices used in texts. Their work became influential in the Western world in the 1960s.

Structuralism (c.1910s–1970s)

Structuralism was not a clearly defined movement and it covered many different fields beyond literary theory, including anthropology, film studies and psychoanalysis. The central idea of structuralism was to interpret texts with close attention to the use of language in the light of **semiotics** (the study of signs and symbols in communication). The Swiss linguist Ferdinand de Saussure is commonly regarded as the founder of this school of thought, and it was developed further in the 1950s by critics such as Roland Barthes and Michel Foucault. There is some blurring of the boundaries between structuralism and **post-structuralism** which is seen to have followed it, and which includes the work of critics like the philosopher Jacques Derrida who argued that there is no stable and absolute meaning to be found in language or texts (Derrida's theories are also known as **deconstruction**).

New Historicism (1980s–)

The French thinker Michel Foucault was also influential in the establishment of the New Historicist approach to literature. New Historicism looks at texts in the light of their historical context and also investigates what literature tells us about history. Stephen Greenblatt is the most well-known New Historicist working today.

A CONTROVERSIAL CRITIC: F. R. LEAVIS

Frank Raymond Leavis (1895–1978), more commonly known as the more serious-sounding F. R. Leavis, was one of the most influential British literary critics of the twentieth century. He was born in Cambridge and then studied and worked at the university there, gaining a reputation as an original, and pugnacious tutor and critic. He was influenced by the work of I. A. Richards whose *Practical Criticism* (1929) encouraged focus on the text rather than context. In 1929 he married Queenie Roth, with whom he worked closely. In 1932 he took up the post of editor of the periodical *Scrutiny*, and published *New Bearings in English Poetry*, while Queenie published her significant work, *Fiction and the Reading Public*. Leavis passionately believed that literature was central to the cultural life of the country. He had strong and influential views on which authors were worth appreciation and study, and admired those who had a serious moral purpose. Not keen on Spenser, Milton, Shelley, Tennyson and Swinburne, he championed John Donne, Alexander Pope, Gerard Manley Hopkins, T. S. Eliot and Ezra Pound. In the field of novel writing he had no time for Laurence Sterne and Thomas Hardy (and also originally Charles Dickens although he later relented on that front) but was a fan of Jane Austen, George Eliot, Henry James, Herman Melville, Joseph Conrad and D. H. Lawrence. Many credit Leavis with elevating the study of English literature to the level of a serious and important subject for the first time.

MODERN MASTERS: TEN MODERN CLASSICS TO LOOK OUT FOR

Who knows what F. R. Leavis would make of the list below. However these ten books have been celebrated by modern critics for their originality, scope and quality of prose. They are all well worth a look.

Waterland by Graham Swift (1983)
Money by Martin Amis (1984)
Oranges are Not the Only Fruit by Jeanette Winterson (1985)

The Handmaid's Tale by Margaret Atwood (1985)
Beloved by Toni Morrison (1987)
The Remains of the Day by Kazuo Ishiguro (1989)
Possession by A. S. Byatt (1990)
Trainspotting by Irvine Welsh (1993)
Every Man for Himself by Beryl Bainbridge (1996)
Atonement by Ian McEwan (2001)

A VARIETY OF VERSES: UNUSUAL POETIC FORMS

You may know your terza rima from your sestina, and your sonnet from your villanelle, but there is a wild array of dramatically different poetic forms out there with their own elaborate rules just waiting for you to discover them. We've picked just a few below, to show you the versatility and scope of available frames upon which you can stretch out the canvas of your own creativity, should you so wish.

Form	Characteristics
Tanka	Tanka are Japanese poems involving 31 syllables. In English they tend to be split into lines of 5, 7, 5, 7 and 7 syllables. They are an ancient cousin of the more famous haiku (which consist of seventeen syllables) and originally dealt with feelings rather than nature and the seasons, as haiku do.
Pantoum	Pantoums, developed from a Malaysian verse form, are written in quatrains (four-line stanzas) with the second and fourth lines of each stanza reappearing as the first and third lines of the next.
Acrostic	Acrostics are clever-dick poems where the initial letters in each line spell out a word vertically. They pop up in the Old Testament, but their most famous creator was the ever-inventive Lewis Carroll.
Ghazal	Ghazals developed in twelfth-century Persia. They are normally short love poems written in discrete couplets

in the rhyming scheme aa ba ca da ea which usefully end with a reference to the poet's name.

Clerihew   A clerihew is a light-hearted poem of two rhyming couplets describing a person whose name makes up the first line and with a long final line. They were invented by Edmund Clerihew Bentley in the early twentieth century.

BEOWULF

Hwæt. We Gardena in gear-dagum,
þeodcyninga, þrym gefrunon,
hu ða æþelingas ellen fremedon

Lo, we have heard of the power of the Spear-Danes of olden times, and their people-kings, and how their noblemen performed great deeds.

Beowulf is the most important literary work we have from the Anglo-Saxon period. It is by an unknown poet and is thought to have been written sometime between the eighth and early eleventh centuries CE. It is composed in Old English (called *Englisc* by its speakers and Anglo-Saxon by some commentators), the language spoken in England after the arrival of the Angles, Saxons and Jutes from Denmark and Germany in the fifth century up until the Norman invasion in 1066. Over time the original Germanic language spoken by these peoples altered and took in words from Celtic, Norse and Latin, and eventually developed, via Middle English, into the language we speak today. However, on the page Old English doesn't look much like our mother tongue. Like German, its nouns and adjectives were divided into declensions and genders, and there were four main regional dialects: West Saxon, Mercian, Northumbrian and Kentish.

THE OLD ENGLISH ALPHABET

Aa	Æ æ	B b	C c	D ð	Ð ð	E e	F f	Ᵹ ᵹ	h h	I ı	L l
a	ash	be	c	de	eth	e	eff	yogh	há	i	ell
a	æ	b	c	d	ð	e	f	ʒ(g)	h	i	l

M m	N n	O o	P p	R ꞃ	S ſ ſ s	T τ	U u	P p	X x	Y ẏ	Þ þ
emm	enn	o	pe	err	ess	te	u	wynn	eks	yr	thorn
m	n	o	p	r	s	t	u	p(w)	x	y	þ

Thorn and eth are pronounced like 'th' in 'thin'.

Yogh is pronounced as a 'g', 'gh' or 'y'. Because its use declined in the sixteenth century and it looks like a 'z' it was often printed using this character, which explains why Sir Menzies Campbell's name is pronounced 'Ming-iss' and why Detective Superintendent Andrew Dalziel of *Dalziel and Pascoe* fame pronounces his name 'Dee-yell'.

Beowulf was written in the West Saxon dialect. It is 3,182 lines long and follows the traditional Old English verse form which divides each line in two with a caesura and links the two halves using alliteration. It also features many kennings, which are metaphorical reworkings of words – such as 'whale road' for 'sea'. The poem describes the adventures of the mythological hero Beowulf, a warrior and later king of the Geats, a people who lived in southern Sweden. At the start of the poem he helps out the king of Denmark by defeating a terrifying man-eating monster called Grendel who is giving him trouble, and also finishing off Grendel's mother. Later, when Beowulf has returned to the Geats, a dragon goes on the rampage and Beowulf has to fight it, eventually killing it but being mortally wounded in the struggle. The poem is a tremendously beautiful work of art, well worth poring over on a wintery afternoon, and Seamus Heaney's recent translation of it is a masterwork in its own right.

A PORTRAIT OF A POEM:
WILLIAM BLAKE'S 'LONDON'

William Blake was born in London's Soho in 1757, the son of a hosier. He began writing poetry at the age of twelve and was apprenticed to an engraver at fourteen. Blake produced a unique body of work, adorning his poems with his own engravings, which he also printed and published. His work presented a singular and potent vision, passionately attesting to the power of imagination to lead humankind back to a state of innocence and contentment founded in God and nature. Though deeply religious, Blake quickly lost faith in the organised Church and believed mankind was drifting further away from grace through the venality of modern life, the sacrifices made to industrialisation and the failure of the Church to offer succour to the increasing number of society's victims he saw in London. In addition, there was a political strand to Blake's work and he was at the centre of radical thought of his age, along with friends like Mary Wollstonecraft and Thomas Paine. As such, though impossible to categorise, he exerted a strong influence over the developing Romantic movement and has subsequently been a touchstone for generations of visionary creators. His central theme of accessing a hitherto suppressed or oppressed innocence through the imagination has had great impact on successive artists and poets ranging from Samuel Palmer to W. B. Yeats.

'London'

I wander thro' each charter'd street,
Near where the charter'd Thames does flow,
And mark in every face I meet
Marks of weakness, marks of woe.

In every cry of every Man,
In every Infant's cry of fear,
In every voice, in every ban,
The mind-forge'd manacles I hear.

How the Chimney-sweeper's cry
Every black'ning Church appalls;
And the hapless Soldier's sigh
Runs in blood down Palace walls.

But most thro' midnight streets I hear
How the youthful Harlot's curse
Blasts the new-born Infant's tear
And blights with plagues the Marriage hearse.

This poem was published in 1794 as part of *Songs of Innocence and Experience*, a collection of poems divided into two, often closely corresponding, parts representing Blake's hopes (the innocence poems) and fears (the experience poems) for humanity.

'London' is in many ways a typical example of Blake's early style, especially in its strict adherence to a simple rhyme scheme (abab) and rhythm (iambic tetrameter). In this instance, the use of these devices, along with that of repetition (particularly in the first two stanzas), not only echoes the poet's footsteps as he tramps through a dismal city, but also creates a relentlessness that complements the despairing scenes he witnesses. Blake's characteristically simple choice of vocabulary powerfully employed makes for a stark depiction of the city and adds to the growing sense of futility as the poem progresses.

In the first stanza, the 'charter'd' streets and river form a contrast to the more usual romantic view of the freedom of great cities and the boundlessness of the flowing Thames (whose 'sweet will' Wordsworth praises in 'Composed upon Westminster Bridge', for example). Here, 'to charter' refers not only to the traditional rights extended to some, though not all, city-dwellers, but was also coming to mean 'to limit' and 'to hire'. As such, the boundaries imposed by the streets and river resemble a prison constructed by figures representing authority and capitalism.

The poem proceeds to list the desperate sights of the metropolis, the claustrophobia of the city expressed in 'every ban', an allusion to government legislation limiting freedoms, while the 'mind-forg'd manacles' articulate the very Blakean sentiment of man's failure to emancipate himself by releasing the imagination.

In the third stanza, the 'Chimney-sweeper's cry' draws attention to the plight of child labourers, frequently the personification of innocence abused in Blake's poetry, while the 'black'ning Church' rather than offering relief from suffering, simply 'appalls'. The 'hapless Soldier' in the following lines is the victim of war and chaos, rather than the perpetrator, and this distinction further imbues the poem with the sense of despotic and irresponsible powers destroying guiltless lives. Indeed, the palace walls running with blood in the subsequent line is a direct reference to the upheavals and bloodshed of the French Revolution – a cataclysm that resounded across Europe and one that should have offered hope to the common man, but had by the time of this poem already degenerated into another kind of tyranny.

Worse still, the final stanza returns to another common theme of Blake's; 'the Harlot's curse' is a verbal one but refers also to the devastating spread of gonorrhoea, which caused blindness at birth, and so in being passed on to the innocent infant forms a fatal cycle of deprivation and death represented by the horrifying oxymoron of the 'Marriage hearse'. In this way, the poem builds to an ever more despairing finale and shows Blake at his most damning and apocalyptic. All very cheery.

A COMPLETE LIST OF SHAKESPEARE'S PLAYS

If you ask anyone at your local pub to guess how many plays all-round genius William Shakespeare wrote in his stellar career, the chances are they will pitch their estimate too low. Thirty-seven is the magic number, with not a dud among them, and that doesn't include the ones that scholars suspect got lost along the way.

HISTORIES

Henry VI, Part 2
Henry VI, Part 3
Henry VI, Part 1
Richard III
Richard II
King John
Henry IV, Part 1
Henry IV, Part 2
Henry V
Henry VIII, or All is True

TRAGEDIES

Titus Andronicus
Romeo and Juliet

Julius Caesar
Hamlet, Prince of Denmark
Troilus and Cressida
Othello: the Moor of Venice
King Lear
Macbeth
Antony and Cleopatra
Coriolanus
Timon of Athens

COMEDIES

The Comedy of Errors
The Taming of the Shrew
The Two Gentlemen of Verona
Love's Labour's Lost
A Midsummer Night's Dream
The Merchant of Venice
Much Ado About Nothing
As You Like It
The Merry Wives of Windsor
Twelfth Night, Or What You Will
All's Well That Ends Well
Measure for Measure
Pericles, Prince of Tyre
Cymbeline
The Winter's Tale
The Tempest

'I WILL . . . UNFOLD TO THE WORLD THE DEEPEST MYSTERIES OF CREATION . . .': MARY SHELLEY'S MONSTER

Mary Shelley was born in London in 1797. The daughter of pioneering feminist writer Mary Wollstonecraft (who died soon after her birth) and the radical William Godwin, she was raised in an intense environment of learning, literature and progressive thought. In 1814, at the age of sixteen, she fell head over heels in love with the married poet Percy Bysshe Shelley and the couple eloped to France and began an extended tour of Europe. While on their travels, during a particularly rainy stay with the poet Byron in the Alps, their host challenged his friends to a ghost story-writing competition. Mary's contribution became the basis for *Frankenstein*, which was published in 1818 to immediate critical and popular acclaim. After Shelley's wife committed suicide in 1816, Percy and Mary married. In 1822, Shelley died in a sailing accident and Mary returned to England, where she embarked on the work of editing and preparing her late husband's poetical works for publication, as well as continuing to produce novels and other books of her own. She died in London in 1851.

Frankenstein is the story of how bright, ambitious Victor Frankenstein's pursuit of knowledge goes tragically awry. The novel opens with a series of letters home from explorer Robert Walton, who is about to embark on a voyage to the North Pole. When Walton's vessel gets trapped in the floes, his journey is forestalled until the ice melts. During the wait, the crew find Frankenstein wandering hopelessly in the cold. He befriends Walton and relates his sorry tale.

Born in Geneva to a loving family, Victor develops a passion for science and while at university in Ingolstadt becomes increasingly obsessed with discovering the secret of life. Consumed by his work, Victor shuns society and eventually succeeds in creating a living eight-foot being fashioned from old body parts. Filled with horror at his hideous creation, Victor runs away in a funk. The monster, left stranded in a world he has no ability to comprehend, kills Victor's younger brother, a crime for which a family friend is executed. After this inauspicious start, the monster tracks Victor down and begs for a companion. However, just before completing the girlfriend-to-be, Victor suffers misgivings and destroys her, leading to a killing spree from his creation which leaves his best friend, his fiancée and his father dead. Victor decides to hunt down the monster and follows him north in a desperate chase, culminating in his chance rescue by Walton. After telling his tale, Victor's health deteriorates and he dies before the ship is freed from the ice. Walton finds the monster mourning over his creator's body, the only human he has been able to forge any kind of relationship with, before fleeing yet further north to die in solitude.

There are many reasons why *Frankenstein* is such a remarkable achievement. Though not yet two hundred years old, the story has assumed a mythological status and has been reinterpreted many times using all manner of media almost since the day it first appeared. Yet, while it is the book's plot and central characters that have captured the imagination of generations, it is also a literary work of bravura and brilliance, whose techniques are copied to this day. The novel is structured like a Russian doll, with Walton's narrative encompassing Victor's, Victor's narrative including that of the monster and the monster's including the subplot of Felix and Safie. This structure not only heightens tension and means the novel unfolds in an extremely sophisticated manner, but it also allows Shelley to twist and mould the narrative to a variety of viewpoints, manipulating the reader's responses to the characters and action. For example, we are given differing views of Victor, who is represented in a sympathetic light by Walton but whose ambition, self-interest and growing lack of compassion are exposed to us by the monster's narration. As well as this, the very nature of texts themselves plays a large part in the novel. The story is revealed by a series of letters, journals, diaries, notes and books, all performing a different function in the handling of the plot.

In many ways, *Frankenstein* is in the mould of other classic tragedies like *Macbeth* and *Doctor Faustus*. Victor Frankenstein is a man of benevolent motivation whose fatal flaw leads to the destruction of his ideals, his loved ones and finally himself. It is his ambition and single-mindedness that lead him to the miraculous secret of creation, but also away from everything he holds dear – his family, scientific progress, and society as a whole. As the novel progresses, he becomes more and more divorced from humanity – and so, ironically, closer to the monster – and this is symbolised by his gradual retreat into the barren wilderness of the northern ice caps.

INTERNATIONAL RESCUE: TWENTY-FIVE TWENTIETH-CENTURY CLASSICS FROM AROUND THE WORLD

When faced with bookshop shelves groaning with shiny, brightly coloured volumes, it's very hard to choose what to read next. The following list aims to give you a whistle-stop tour of some of the best books of the last century, by authors who hail from all corners of the globe. Even if you can't afford a holiday, you can always journey into one of these masterpieces of world literature instead.

Things Fall Apart by Chinua Achebe (Nigeria)
Surfacing by Margaret Atwood (Canada)
The Master and Margarita by Mikhail Bulgakov (Russia)
If on a Winter's Night a Traveller by Italo Calvino (Italy)
The Stranger by Albert Camus (Algeria)
Wild Swans by Jung Chang (China)
Disgrace by J.M. Coetzee (South Africa)
Heart of Darkness by Joseph Conrad (Congo)
The Waste Land and Other Poems by T. S. Eliot (the Waste land)
The Great Gatsby by F. Scott Fitzgerald (New York, USA)
The Prophet by Khalil Gibran (the Middle East)
Our Man in Havana by Graham Greene (Cuba)
Ulysses by James Joyce (Ireland)
Metamorphosis by Franz Kafka (Austria–Hungary)
The Leopard by Giuseppe Tomasi di Lampedusa (Sicily)
To Kill a Mockingbird by Harper Lee (Alabama, USA)
The Magic Mountain by Thomas Mann (Germany and Switzerland)
One Hundred Years of Solitude by Gabriel García Márquez (Colombia)
Nineteen Eighty-Four by George Orwell (Oceania)
Cry the Beloved Country by Alan Paton (South Africa)
Midnight's Children by Salman Rushdie (India and Pakistan)
The Prime of Miss Jean Brodie by Muriel Spark (Scotland)
The Makioka Sisters by Junichiro Tanizaki (Japan)
Voss by Patrick White (Australia)
The Voyage Out by Virginia Woolf (the Atlantic Ocean and South America)

ENGLISH LANGUAGE AND LITERATURE TEST PAPER

1. Phonology is:

a) the study of how we physically make the sounds we use to create language
b) the study of the patterns of sound that are used to create words
c) the art of faking it
d) the study of how children and adults learn languages

2. *New Bearings in English Poetry* is a work of literary criticism by:

a) Q. D. Leavis
b) F. R. Leavis
c) T. S. Eliot
d) I. A. Richards

3. Who is the author of *The Turn of the Screw*?

a) Henry James
b) Jane Austen
c) Arthur Conan Doyle
d) Katie Price

4. When a word's meaning develops positive connotations over time, this is called:

a) pejoration
b) amelioration
c) dedication
d) perspiration

5. **How many tragedies did Shakespeare write?**

a)   11
b)   13
c)   15
d)   9

6. **What are the four major regional dialects of Old English?**

a)   Celtic, Norman, Tudor and Plantagenet
b)   West Saxon, East Anglian, North Saxon and South Anglian
c)   West Saxon, Northumbrian, Mercian and Kentish
d)   Kentish, Northumbrian, Mercian and Rutland

7. **How many syllables does a tanka poem contain?**

a)   17
b)   10
c)   25
d)   31

8. **How would you write the word that 'dʒɪn' phonetically represents?**

9. **Where is *The Leopard* by Giuseppe Tomasi di Lampedusa set?**

a)   France
b)   Sardinia
c)   Corsica
d)   Sicily

10. **What is universal grammar?**

a)   a textbook by D. B. Fehler
b)   a theory postulating that all humans have the same innate concept of the rules of language
c)   the study of inflection in language
d)   a novel by E. Lathos

11. What did the Old English word 'deer' mean?

a) deer
b) cat
c) animal
d) pangolin

12. Mikhail Bulgakov's famous novel is called *The Master and*:

a) *Mary*
b) *Margarita*
c) *Millicent*
d) *Marya*

13. How would you pronounce this letter in Old English?

a) z or tz
b) q or u
c) d or p
d) g or y

14. The ghazal poetic form developed in:

a) Persia
b) Italy
c) India
d) Nigeria

15. Shakespeare's play about the Prince of Tyre is called:

a) *Coriolanus*
b) *Hamlet*
c) *Pericles*
d) *Titus Andronicus*

16. Which of the following authors was the critic F. R. Leavis dismissive of?

a) George Eliot
b) Jane Austen
c) John Milton
d) Ezra Pound

17. What does 'gallimaufry' mean?

a) breakfast
b) a jumble
c) criticise secretly
d) a horse

18. What school of literary theory is John Crowe Ransom most closely associated with?

a) New Criticism
b) New Historicism
c) Marxism
d) Formalism

19. 'Hydra Transmits' is an anagram of the title of which famous eighteenth-century novel?

20. The name of the monster Beowulf kills in Denmark is:

a) Geat
b) Gary
c) Grendel
d) Gubyon

21. How many plays by Shakespeare are still available today (excluding *The Two Noble Kinsmen* which Shakespeare is believed to have co-written with John Fletcher)?

a) 27
b) 13

c) 37
d) 104

22. In Milton's *Paradise Lost*, which archangel is the guardian of Eden?

a) Raphael
b) Gabriel
c) Michael
d) Uriel

23. The three Brontë sisters are called:

a) Emily, Victoria and Anne
b) Anne, Charlotte and Kylie
c) Charlotte, Anne and Emily
d) Jane, Lydia and Elizabeth

24. Which of the following is correct?

a) 'To whom did you give the car keys?'
b) 'To who did you give the car keys?'

25. Which of the following is a bound morpheme?

a) ab-
b) sun
c) fridge
d) kill

26. Whose last words were 'The rest is silence'?

a) Captain Ahab
b) Oliver Twist
c) Hamlet
d) The Lady of Shalott

27. What was the pen name of Samuel Clemens?

a) Samuel Taylor Coleridge
b) Agatha Christie

c)   Alexandre Dumas
d)   Mark Twain

28. What commonly recited grammatical rule does the word 'weird' break?

29. Jerry Cruncher, Harold Skimpole, Daniel Quilp and Josiah Bounderby are all characters from novels by which writer?

a)   Thomas Hardy
b)   Charles Dickens
c)   Arthur Conan Doyle
d)   Graham Greene

30. If someone described a person's eyes as 'caesious', what would they mean?

a)   puffy
b)   greyish green
c)   weepy
d)   diseased

31. Add the apostrophes in the right place:

a)   Alice, Rita and Madeline were playing catch in the garden. Aloysius ran up and stole the girls ball.
b)   The Smiths house is dilapidated. Theyre bringing down house prices in the area.
c)   Its unwise to give the baby whisky in its bedtime bottle.

32. Choose *who* or *whom* to complete the following sentences:

a)   I can't decide _____ I'm most angry with, François or Jacques.
b)   It is difficult to know about _____ Sugar Ray Leonard was more concerned, Roberto Duran or Marvin Hagler.

⌾ MATHEMATICS ⌾

We all use mathematics every day, whether we like it or not, be it to check our change at the newsagent's, work out how much lottery money we stand to win this week, estimate the percentage of our salary it is decent to spend on shoes, or double the quantity of our cake mix. Maths helps us orientate ourselves in the realms of number, quantity and space, and as such is essential to our understanding of the world around us. Some lucky souls are blessed with a natural gift for calculation and organising numerical data in their clever noggins. The rest of us have to studiously learn the laws of maths and take things step by step. This chapter aims to give you some of the ground rules of the more interesting and practical areas of mathematical study, and by the end of it you should never get stung with the bar bill after a night out, find yourself a more astute gambler and be equipped to wow your other half with a glorious pie chart to illustrate clearly how you do more than your fair share of the housework.

THE FIRST AND LAST: BODMAS AND THE RULES OF OPERATION

However anarchic and avant-garde you happen to be feeling, we all need to cultivate a sense of order every so often. There's no point getting all free-form about dressing yourself in the morning and putting your trousers on before your pants, or your socks over your shoes. Just as there is a correct way to put on your clothes for the optimum sartorial effect, there is also a correct order in which calculations should be carried out in Maths. And the result of calculating in the wrong order doesn't just leave you with people snickering at your vest-over-jumper arrangement, it gives you a totally incorrect answer.

How would you go about working out a complicated sum such as $9 + 16 \div 4 \times (8+9)^2 - 2 = $?

If you begin by adding 9 to 16 and then dividing this by 4 then we can tell you straight away that you're on the wrong track. Compare your answer to what a calculator gives you and this will be clear. This is because clever old calculators have the correct method for carrying out mathematical operations built in.

When working without a calculator, the mnemonic you need to remember is the odd word **BODMAS**. This tells you that first you calculate anything inside **B**rackets, then anything involving an **O**rder (this means the same as 'power', e.g. ^{2}, ^{3} etc.), then any **D**ivision, then **M**ultiplication, then **A**ddition and finally **S**ubtraction.

So to solve the sum above first of all you would perform the calculation inside the brackets to give you:

$$9 + 16 \div 4 \times 17^2 - 2$$

Then you would deal with the order to give you:

$$9 + 16 \div 4 \times 289 - 2$$

Then you would sort out the division part of the question:

$$9 + 4 \times 289 - 2$$

Then the multiplication:

$$9 + 1156 - 2$$

Then the addition:

$$1165 - 2$$

And last but not least, the subtraction, giving you the answer:

$$1163$$

Well done, you need never get your mathematical knickers in a twist again.

WHAT ARE THE CHANCES?: PROBABILITY

We deal with concepts of probability every day. Some things, like taxes, colds and missing the bus, are very likely to happen to us, whereas other events, like winning the Nobel Prize, finding buried treasure or running a mile in under four minutes are less probable. In Maths, so long as you are dealing with potential results that are equally possible, probability is an exactly calculable concept.

$$\text{probability of a particular outcome} = \frac{\text{the number of ways the outcome can occur}}{\text{the total number of possible outcomes}}$$

If something is impossible it scores a probability of 0 and if it is definitely going to happen then it has a probability of 1. Most events fall somewhere between the two, and in real life there are usually complicating factors that mean that any potential results are not equally possible.

For example, if you were going for a job against two other hopefuls and you were all equally qualified, equally likeable and performed equally well in the interview, then the probability of you getting the job would be ⅓, which can also be written as 0.33 if you write the fraction as a decimal, or 33% as a percentage. (When probability is expressed as a percentage, 100% means certain and 0% means impossible.)

However, this situation itself is extremely improbable; the Hamster Appreciation Society membership on your CV might be more off-putting than another candidate's recent charity work, and perhaps one of the interviewers won't like your shoes or will have recently watched his wife run off with a man who looks just like you and these factors could make the probability of you getting the job much, much less than ⅓.

SOME INTERESTING PROBABILITIES

- The probability of matching all 6 winning numbers for the lottery jackpot is $1/13,983,816$.

- The probability of drawing a diamond card from a pack of cards without looking is $13/52$ or 25%.

- The probability of getting heads when you toss a coin is $1/2$ or 50%.

These are all accurate probabilities because the number of possible results is fixed – there are only 13,983,816 different combinations of 6 numbers between 1 and 49 and there are only ever 52 cards (excluding the jokers) in a pack. However, a lot of the probabilities we see in the media are simply based on results that have been measured from previous events.

If you're told that the probability of being hit by lightning is $1/3,000,000$ and that you have a $1/11,000,000$ chance of dying in a plane crash, this is based on data that has been collected over past years about these traumatic fates. These sorts of probabilities are much vaguer and less reliable – a few random results one year can dramatically alter things, and past statistics don't necessarily match with what happens in the future. For example, increasing improvements in aeroplane safety mechanisms should mean that as time goes by the probability of this sticky end diminishes. On the other hand, if there are manufacturing errors in aircraft built in 2011 then in that year the probability of a fatal air accident might rise.

It's also worth mentioning that psychologists have recorded that human brains deal with probability measurements differently, depending on whether the news is good or bad or how it is presented. For example, if you were told you could earn £1,000 for helping to test a new medicine and that there was an 80% chance that this medicine would cause no serious side effects, then you might feel more inclined to take the cash than if you were told that there was a 20% chance that it could make you blind. Always judge statistics and probabilities carefully.

SIMULTANEOUS EQUATIONS: HOW DO YOU SOLVE A PROBLEM LIKE 2b + 4t = 34 AND 3b + 5t = 46?

An equation is simply a mathematical expression involving the equals sign. So, $2 \times 10 = 20$ counts as an equation. Quite often in life we don't have all the information we need immediately to hand, and in algebra missing values in equations are represented by letters.

There are various clever tricks to rearranging an equation with a missing value in order to solve it. Let's say you are faced with the problem of buying drinks for your friends. You order a gin and tonic and the three of them each ask for a pint of beer. You know your G & T costs £5 and the total bill comes to £14. You could work out how much each pint of beer costs by stating what you know as an equation, using the letter 'x' to stand for the cost of each pint of beer:

$$3x + 5 = 14$$

(NB When two values sit right next to each other in an equation this means that the second value is being multiplied by the first. So 'three times x' is written as '3x'.)

In order to solve this problem you can try putting random numbers into the 'x' role in the equation until you hit the jackpot or you can use the magical system of **inverses** to rearrange the equation. Basically, you undo every tricky bit of the equation by doing the inverse, or opposite, of whatever is going on in that particular part. It's very important to remember that whatever you do on one side of the equals sign you also have to do on the other.

You can make your equation above a little simpler by first getting rid of that pesky + 5. If you subtract 5 from both sides of the equation you get:

$$3x = 9$$

Then get rid of the '3' in '3x' by dividing both sides by 3. This leaves you with:

$$x = 3$$

So now you know that each pint you so generously purchased for your pals cost you £3. In order to solve equations you must always rearrange the values step by step until the unknown value is on its own on one side of the equals sign.

Equations can be made trickier by including sums that appear inside brackets, which have to be performed separately. You may also stumble across equations that involve fractions. This can mean that you end up with quite a long equation that looks pretty complicated at first glance. However, if you keep your head and take it one step at a time you'll see that things rapidly become clearer, as we'll prove by working out this ugly-looking fellow:

$$3(^{x}/_{2} + 3) - 8 = 19$$

First of all you need to add 8 to both sides of the equation so you get:

$$3(^{x}/_{2} + 3) = 27$$

Then divide both sides by 3:

$$^{x}/_{2} + 3 = 9$$

Then subtract 3 from both sides:

$$^{x}/_{2} = 6$$

Then multiply both sides by 2 to get:

$$x = 12$$

Sometimes you may have a problem where you have a set of separate equations with more than one missing value in them. These are called **simultaneous equations** because you work on all the equations together in order to find the missing values. Let's say you were trying to work out the price of a Bloody Mary (b) and the price of a Tequila Sunrise (t) from two different drinks bills. Your chum Peter has bought one round of drinks that includes 2 Bloody Marys and 4 Tequila Sunrises and your good friend Jane has then pitched in and bought a round of 3 Bloody Marys and 5 Tequila Sunrises. Peter's tab came to £34 and Jane's came to £46. In order to work out the costs of the individual drinks you can look at these equations together:

$$2b + 4t = 34$$

$$3b + 5t = 46$$

The first method for solving simultaneous equations has the sinister name of **elimination**. Ideally what you want to do is get to the point where if you add the two equations together or subtract one from the other you get rid of one of the unknown values so you can focus on the other. The easiest way to do this is to pick one of the values, let's say t, and find a way of multiplying one or both equations so that their t values are the same. As Peter's equation has 4t and Jane's equation has 5t the easiest thing to do is to get both these equations to involve 20t by multiplying Peter's by 5 and Jane's by 4. Remember that whatever you do to one side of the equals sign you also have to do to the other. If you multiply both sides of Peter's equation by 5 you end up with:

$$10b + 20t = 170$$

If you multiply Jane's equation by 4 you get:

$$12b + 20t = 184$$

If you then subtract Peter's equation from Jane's you get:

$$12b + 20t = 184$$
$$10b + 20t = 170 \quad -$$
$$=$$
$$2b = 14$$

Now simply divide both sides by 2 to get the answer b = 7. Once you know this you can work out what 't' is from the original equations by replacing the 'b's with '7's. If we take Peter's equation, it works out as follows:

$$14 + 4t = 34$$

We then solve this as normal. First take 14 away from both sides:

$$4t = 20$$

Then divide both sides by 4 to get the answer:

$$t = 5$$

This reveals that each Tequila Sunrise costs £5 and each Bloody Mary costs £7. Best to stick to the tequila.

The other way to solve simultaneous equations is to rearrange one of the equations until you get a formula for one of the unknown values and then substitute this for the same unknown value in the second equation. This sounds complicated but, using Peter and Jane's original equations, it would go like this:

$$2b + 4t = 34$$

$$3b + 5t = 46$$

First of all let's try to sort out a formula for 'b' in Peter's equation. This means rearranging the equation so that we get 'b' on its own on one side of the equals sign.

To do this we need to subtract 4t from both sides to get.

$$2b = 34 - 4t$$

and then divide both sides by 2 to get:

$$b = \frac{34 - 4t}{2}$$

Which can be simplified to:

$$b = 17 - 2t$$

Then you take Jane's equation and add the aforementioned formula into it to replace 'b':

$$3(17-2t) + 5t = 46$$

which can be simplified to:

$$51 - 6t + 5t = 46$$

and then to:

$$51 - 1t = 46$$

You can now work out this equation by subtracting 51 from both sides to get:

$$-1t = -5$$

And then dividing both sides by −1 to get:

$$t = 5$$

Well done! You've cracked it. It's just like rearranging lots of pieces of a jigsaw puzzle until they suddenly all fall into place to reveal a dazzlingly beautiful mathematical solution.

ABSURDLY SQUARE: THE WONDERFUL WORLD OF SURDS

As you will no doubt remember, if you multiply a number by itself you get its square. In Maths this can be indicated by adding a lofty little ^{2} next to the original number. So 4 squared can be written both as 4^2 or worked out as 16. **Square numbers** are numbers that have a whole number as their square root. A **square root** is the number that, multiplied by itself, gives the number you're looking at. So the square root of 16 is 4. This is written as $\sqrt{16}$. 16 is a square number because its square root, 4, is a whole number.

However, sometimes square roots do not work out to be nice neat whole numbers. For example, the square root of 7 is 2.6457513110645907. . . etc. A square root that is not a whole number is called a **surd**. Surds are known as **irrational numbers**, not because they randomly hate ice cream or are frightened of mice, but because it is impossible to express them accurately written out in figures, the numbers would just keep flowing after the decimal point forever. For this reason they are kept tidily in their square root form, e.g. $\sqrt{7}$.

Wherever you come across surds you need to simplify the life out of them to bring them down to their most basic form. To do this you need to remember the rule:

$$\sqrt{ab} = \sqrt{a} \times \sqrt{b}.$$

You can add and subtract surds with the same value just as you would normal numbers to help simplify them. For example, $3\sqrt{7} + 2\sqrt{7} = 5\sqrt{7}$ and $5\sqrt{7} - 2\sqrt{7} = 3\sqrt{7}$. However, you can't do this with surds of different values such as $3\sqrt{5} + 2\sqrt{7}$.

So, for the calculation $\sqrt{20} + \sqrt{5}$ you would first simplify $\sqrt{20}$ into $\sqrt{4} \times \sqrt{5}$. Your calculation should now look like this: $\sqrt{4} \times \sqrt{5} + \sqrt{5}$.

Ideally, you want to find a factor in the surd you are investigating that is a square number so that you can simplify it into a whole number rather than a surd. Here we have $\sqrt{4}$ which can be simplified down to just 2 (the square root of 4 is the whole number 2).

So this leaves you with $2\sqrt{5} + \sqrt{5}$ which can be added together to make $3\sqrt{5}$.

TALLY-HO!: TALLY AND FREQUENCY

Prisoners mark off each long day in prison by scratching a line for each day in the hard wall next to their beds. On the fifth day, they draw a diagonal through the preceding four lines and on the sixth day begin a new set. This method of collecting data is called **tallying**.

$$\cancel{||||}$$

For the active amateur mathematician, tallies are a useful way of counting up different sets of information in the field. If you took a survey of your child's Scout group to find out how many violent computer games each Scout owns (because you were concerned about bad influences in the pack who were more interested in teaching your little darling how to annihilate mutants in *Killer Skullpunch* than how to tie reef knots), the easiest way to collect the data is to keep tally as you ask each scout your question. When you have finished collecting the data, you can add up your tally and the final figure you have for each category is called the **frequency**.

Number of violent games	Tally	Frequency
0	||	2
1	|	1
2	$\cancel{||||}\ \cancel{||||}$	10
3	|||	3

AXES TO GRIND:
HOW TO READ CHARTS AND GRAPHS

The data collected in tallies can be expressed in different ways. Many of you will be familiar with pie charts and graphs from the boardroom, showing scarily small slivers of market share in pie format or vertiginous drops in profitability in graph format. If you were to express your Scout-spying info in the tallying exercise above in a bar graph it would look like this:

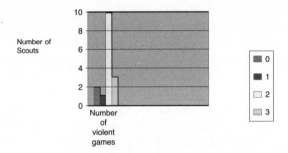

A **bar graph** (or **histogram** if you want to sound really impressive) displays information by using separate columns, or bars, arranged along the horizontal axis of the graph to represent one aspect of the data (in this case the number of violent games owned). The heights of the bars indicate another aspect of the data (here, the number of Scouts). Bar graphs are particularly useful for showing data that involves changes taking place over time. For example, a bar graph would be a good way of illustrating changes in sales of capri pants in the UK over the past five years. Each column would represent a year and the vertical axis would show the numbers of unflattering trousers bought.

Pie charts are not so useful for showing changes over time; however, they are top-notch for showing proportions or percentages. Using your original data from the Scout group, the pie chart below assumes that the 360° of the full circle, or pie, represents the total number of Scouts questioned (16). It divides this circle into different-sized pie slices that are proportional in size to the number of Scouts owning each different quantity of bloodthirsty games.

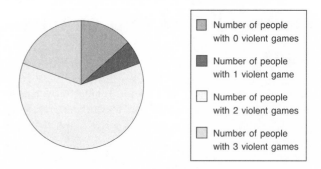

There are various other forms that graphs and charts can take but the most ubiquitous is probably the **line graph**. Line graphs show the relationship between two variable values which are measured along the two separate axes, as with the bar graph. Instead of column heights, the data is represented by separate dots that are then joined up to form a line. Line graphs are best for showing linked data so that you can easily see how one measurement varies in relation to the other. For example, if you wanted to show the pattern of purchases of marjoram from a major supermarket over a period of six months in order to check the impact of a major marjoram-awareness-raising campaign run in July then a line graph would be the perfect medium.

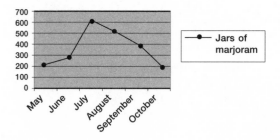

It's important to remember that graphs can be used to mislead people. Any data collected for a particular purpose can be presented to give a certain impression. Imagine you were working for the marjoram-awareness ad team. You might choose to show the same information used in the graph above as follows:

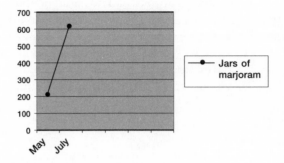

When you are looking at graphs always make sure that you check the two axes very carefully to see what information you are actually being given.

KEEP IT IN PROPORTION:
DIRECT AND INVERSE PROPORTION

If you ever come across a note from your wife that reads 'The amount I love you ∝ how often you clean the bathroom', then the clever woman is using mathematical insider jargon to impart some very important information to you. '∝' is mathlete shorthand for 'is in direct proportion to'.

Using those trusty Maths favourites for unknown values x and y, y ∝ x ('y is in direct proportion to x') means that however much x increases, y will also increase by the same proportion. So if you double x you also have to double y.

Let's say you have a recipe for marjoram and mint pea soup which makes enough for two people and specifies that you need 200g of frozen peas, 2 tbsp crème fraîche, 400ml of vegetable stock, 2 tbsp chopped mint leaves and ½ tsp of marjoram. If you want to make enough to impress 8 people at a dinner party, then the number of servings you need has quadrupled. This means you must increase the quantities of each of the ingredients by the same proportion – they must all be multiplied by 4. This means you need 800g of frozen peas, 8 tbsp crème fraîche, 1.6l of vegetable stock, 8 tbsp chopped mint leaves and 2 tsp of marjoram. The number of guests is **directly proportional** to the amounts of each ingredient.

However, if something is **inversely proportional** to another thing, it means that as one measurement increases the other must decrease by the same proportion. For example, if you were to play a lottery which involved equal prizes for each winner, the number of winners of each jackpot is inversely proportional to the amount of prize money each winner gets. The more winners there are, the smaller the prize for each.

TRYING TRIGONOMETRY: SOHCAHTOA (SINE, COSINE AND TANGENT)

Some specialist mathematical equipment is required for this section: you need a scientific calculator to immerse yourself properly in the blissful waters of trigonometry. Luckily, most computers have this facility available. A scientific calculator has buttons with 'sin', 'cos', 'tan' and 'inv' written on it (and lots of other mysterious symbols that, if pressed in the right order, may give you the coordinates of the Ark of the Covenant). 'Sin' stands for the formula sine, 'cos' for cosine and 'tan' for tangent. 'Inv' stands for inverse and is the button you press before cos, sin or tan to reverse the formula.

These formulae are very useful in the study of right-angled triangles, which also goes by the formal name of **trigonometry**. You may think this area of study is only relevant to hard-core mathmos, but trig is used all the time in areas as disparate as architecture, astronomy, engineering, cartography, computer-game development, satnav systems and chemistry. Naturally, you will know that triangles have three sides and three angles. In a right-angle triangle the side opposite the angle you're concerned with is called the **opposite**, the **adjacent** is adjacent to it and the **hypotenuse** is the side opposite the right-angle.

Sin (angle) = the length of the opposite side divided by the length of the hypotenuse
Cos (angle) = the length of the adjacent side divided by the hypotenuse
Tan (angle) = the length of the opposite side divided by the adjacent

The easy way to remember these formulae is to remember the word **SOHCAHTOA**, which sounds like the volcano Krakatoa, another triangularly significant entity.

These formulae mean that if you are given certain measurements of a right-angled triangle, you can work out the unknown measurements.

For example:

If you have a right-angled triangle where you know that one of the angles is 60° and the length of the hypotenuse is 34cm, you can work out the length of the opposite side.

Because you have the hypotenuse measurement and you want to find out the opposite measurement, you need to use the function which involves both the O (opposite) and the H (hypotenuse). If you break down SOH CAH TOA you can see that the function you need is sin (SOH).

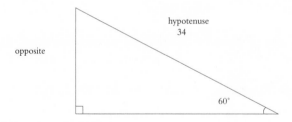

Once you've identified the function you need, write it out including the measurements you know.

$$\sin 60 = \frac{O \text{ (opposite)}}{34 \text{ (hypotenuse)}}$$

Then you get busy with your calculator: type in 60 and then press the sin button. Add this into your working:

$$0.87 = \frac{O}{34 \text{ (hypotenuse)}}$$

Now you can rearrange this formula, like any other equation, to find out the unknown measurement O. Just to remind you, whatever you do to the values on one side of the equals sign you have to do to the other side.

So to get O on its own you need to multiply both sides by 34. 0.87 × 34 = O = 29.58. So the length of the opposite side is 29.58 cm.

If you end up with an equation where your unknown quantity is the divisor, e.g.:

$$\sin 60 = \frac{29.58}{h}$$

you need to go through two steps to get h on its own. Multiply both sides by h and you get:

$$h \times \sin 60 = 29.58$$

then divide both sides by sin 60 to get:

$$h = \frac{29.58}{\sin 60}$$

Using your calculator you can write this out as:

$$h = \frac{29.58}{0.87}$$

This means h = 34.

To calculate the angle when you know the length of two sides, you use the inv button with sin, cos or tan.

Let's say you have a right-angled triangle with the hypotenuse measuring 34cm and the opposite side measuring 29.58 cm

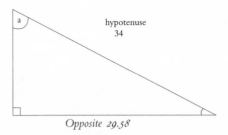

Opposite 29.58

Remembering SOHCAHTOA, you can see that because you have the O (opposite) and H (hypotenuse) you need to use the SOH part of the mnemonic and the function sin.

$$\sin a = \frac{29.58 \ (O)}{34 \ (h)}$$

So, sin a = 0.87

To work out a, use your calculator and type in 0.86 then press the inv button and then the sin button. The answer will be 60.45. So the angle is 60.45°.

Depending on how many decimal places you use in your calculations, your answer may vary by a degree or two. Don't get too het up about this – it's still great detective work.

A BINARY BON MOT

Maths enthusiasts are not the boring, bespectacled boffins you might expect. They know how to have a good time just as much as the rest of us, as the following witticism proves: 'There are only 10 types of people in the world – those who understand binary, and those who don't.' This is funny because if you are a layperson the figure '10' means 'ten' so the statement seems nonsensical. But if you are a mathematics insider or computer whizz then you can also read '10' as a binary expression meaning 'two'. This is because the binary number system only uses combinations of the two figures '1' and '0' to represent all other numbers (e.g. 3 is written as '11', 4 as '100' and 7 as '111'). Digital devices like computers use binary codes to store all their information because they are essentially made up of lots of switches that can either be on (1) or off (0). What larks!

HOW TO COUNT FROM ONE TO TEN IN BINARY

0000 = 0

0001 = 1

0010 = 2

0011 = 3

0100 = 4

0101 = 5

0110 = 6

0111 = 7

1000 = 8

1001 = 9

1010 = 10

∽ MATHEMATICS ∾
TEST PAPER

1. Simplify $\sqrt{20} + \sqrt{125}$.

2. If Eric bets Harry that he will roll an even number, using a six-sided die, what is the probability that Eric will win the bet?

3. What is the answer to the calculation $10 - \frac{8}{2,000} \times (6+2)^3 - 3$ to two decimal places?

4. If you are asked to pick one card from a full pack, what is the probability that the card you pick will be a queen?

5. A surd is
a) an imaginary creature from a Lewis Carroll poem
b) the square root of 16
c) a square root that is not a whole number
d) an angle greater than 90°

6. If Pat bought 5 individual apples and they cost her £1.65 in total and Isabel bought a bag containing 6 apples for £1.89, which sister shopped most economically?

7. Solve the following equations:

$8x + \frac{y}{9} = 27$
$3y + 5x = 96$

8. What is the radius of a circle with a diameter of 24cm?

a) 12cm
b) 6cm
c) 24cm
d) 8.76cm

9. What is ⅓ expressed as a decimal (to two decimal places)?

10. If you have a party for 20 friends and between them they bring 28 bottles of wine, what is the mean number of bottles of wine brought by each person?

11. What is −4 + −4?

12. How many thousands are there in a million?

13. What do 271, 401, 541, 607, 647 and 709 have in common?

14. What is −5 − −7?

15. What is the word used to describe a quadrilateral with two pairs of parallel opposite sides?

16. What is the difference between an isosceles and an equilateral triangle?

17. In an effort to detox, you have bought two packs of blueberries, three packs of spinach and one pack of flax seeds costing an extortionate £8.99. Your bill at the checkout comes to £15.86. Unfortunately, you are so hungry that you eat all the blueberries and one pack of spinach in one go and have to go back to the shop to buy two more packs of blueberries and one pack of spinach, which comes to £4.29. Write out your shopping as equations, using 'b' to stand for each pack of blueberries, 's' for spinach. Then work out how much each pack of blueberries and each pack of spinach cost you.

18. What is a reflex angle?

19. If Hermione's edition of *War and Peace* is 1,296 pages long and she has 3 weeks and 3 days until her reading group meeting, how many pages does she need to read each day in order to finish it in time?

20. If your bedroom wall is 5m high and 8m wide, what is its area?

21. If Todd successfully completes 15 out of 20 of the 'required objectives' on his performance review form, what percentage did he achieve?

22. What is the square root of 36?

23. If there are 6.35kg to a stone and Patty weighs 11 stone and Susie weighs 68kg who is heaviest?

24. What is $\frac{4}{7} \times \frac{3}{8}$, simplified down as far as possible?

25. What is the area of a triangle with a base of 12cm and a height of 6cm?

26. How many sides does an octagon have?

27. If the recommended calorie intake for a man is 2,500 calories a day and Roland's favourite chocolate bar contains 530 calories, how many whole bars can he eat each day (assuming he eats nothing else) before he goes over the recommended limit?

28. What is the value of x in the following formula?

$$x = 3(7 + 6)$$

29. If your WI cake sale sells 50 cupcakes and 25 of them are chocolate-flavoured, 11 of them are carrot and 14 are lemon sponge and you are asked to present this information to the next meeting in a pie chart, how many degrees of your pie would you allocate to the chocolate wedge?

30. If Ziggy owes his brother £25 and Robbie owes Ziggy £7, Julie owes him £2.50 and Fay owes him £3, how much does he need to find to pay his brother once his friends have paid him back?

Ꮧ GEOGRAPHY Ꮧ

Geography is the study of our ever-fascinating Earth's features, and covers the spectrum of its characteristics, be they political, physical, or to do with its resources and populations, so banish thoughts of it as a dry and dull subject. In fact, in this chapter we'll take you even closer to unearthing the mysteries of the ground beneath your feet: we'll be looking at that most sparkling of treasures, diamonds – a girl's best friend – and showing you how to make your way through the mine-field of cut, colour, clarity and carat. Ever wondered who Malthus was? Find out why his Malthusian catastrophe has particular resonance in these days of rapidly expanding population and ever-decreasing food supplies. We'll examine the seasonal equinoxes, and get right down to the nitty-gritty of how we organise the hours of the days, weeks and months. We'll also meet Beaufort and his wonderful wind scale, examine storm surges and tropical cyclones, and see why we're more at risk now than ever from natural disasters. Even better, we'll reveal just what a willy-willy is (we know you've been worrying about it).

COUNTING THE HOURS: THE CALENDAR

We humans have always liked a bit of organisation, and since time immemorial we have been finding ways to structure our time. There are different types of calendar but the most widely used is the Gregorian. This is a solar calendar, which means that it is based on the movement of the Earth round the sun. The Gregorian calendar was instituted by Pope Gregory XIII in 1582 to replace the less accurate Julian calendar which was introduced by Julius Caesar in 45 BCE and used throughout the Roman Empire. The Gregorian calendar made adjustments to the Julian calendar to make sure that the calendar didn't drift out of sync with the seasons.

Years

The Gregorian calendar is divided into years made up of 365 days with an extra day added every four years as 29 February to keep the calendar in line with the movement of the Earth round the sun. Back in the bad old days women were only supposed to ask their beloved to marry them on 29 February and the rest of the time it was up to the gentlemen. These special years with 366 days are called **leap years**.

Months

The Gregorian calendar subdivides the year into twelve months, originally based on the time it takes for the moon to orbit the Earth.

January	31	July	31
February	28 (29 in leap years)	August	31
March	31	September	30
April	30	October	31
May	31	November	30
June	30	December	31

There are two easy ways to remember how many days fall in each month.

The first one is by clenching your fists and holding them up next to each other in front of you. Running from left to right, with the first knuckle representing January and the first dip between knuckles representing February, you can remind yourself that all the months that fall on knuckles have thirty-one days. All the rest have thirty apart from February.

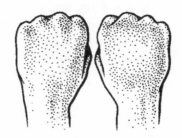

There is also the famous rhyme:

> Thirty days hath September,
> April, June and November;
> All the rest have thirty-one;
> Except February alone
> Which hath twenty-eight days clear,
> And twenty-nine in each leap year.

Weeks

There are fifty-two weeks in the year and the subdivision of months into seven-day weeks was based on the Book of Genesis where, after six days of making oceans and snowdrops and giraffes, God takes a rest on the seventh day of Creation. The Ten Commandments made this example holy law – 'Keep the Sabbath day holy'.

Days

A day lasts the amount of time it takes for the Earth to rotate on its axis. For the sake of simplicity this is always considered to be twenty-four hours, even though the time actually varies slightly. In English the days of the week are named after a mixture of heavenly bodies and the Norse gods of the Vikings.

Sunday – the Sun's day
Monday – the Moon's day
Tuesday – Tiu's day (god of war and the sky)
Wednesday – Woden/Wotan/Odin's day (king of the gods)
Thursday – Thor's day (god of thunder)
Friday – Freya's day (goddess of fertility)
Saturday – Saturn's day

The Seasons

The year is not just divided into months, weeks and days but also into the four seasons, each of which is associated with particular weather conditions, temperatures, and times of sunrise and sunset (and pizza toppings). The seasons occur because the Earth is tilted on its axis in relation to the sun, so as it orbits the different hemispheres are exposed to more or less sunlight. Whatever the season in the northern hemisphere, it will always be the opposite in the southern hemisphere. Of course, in these times of global ecological catastrophe, Mother Nature's seasonal activities are being compromised: who ever thought we would see daffodils in January?

The astronomical division of the year into seasons follows these dates if you live in the northern hemisphere:

Spring begins around 21 March on the **vernal equinox**.
Summer begins around 21 June on the **summer solstice**.
Autumn begins around 22 September on the **autumnal equinox**.
Winter begins around 22 December on the **winter solstice**.

The summer solstice is the longest day – this is when the North Pole is closest to the sun so it is light for the longest time in the year. In Iceland they have sunlight for almost twenty-four hours a day around the summer solstice. The winter solstice is the shortest day.

The equinoxes have equal hours of daylight and darkness.

The southern hemisphere has its summer and winter solstices the other way round and that's why our Antipodean brethren are able to have Christmas on the beach.

PEOPLE ALL OVER THE WORLD: POPULATION

With the world's population weighing in at a staggering 6.9 billion souls, and that figure expected to rise to 9.1 billion by 2050, it's no wonder geographers are interested in mapping how mankind colonises the planet. Population is measured by comparing **density** – the number of people per km^2 – and **distribution** – the way in which people are spread across an area. Density is calculated by dividing the total population by the total land area in km^2, and can be measured on a local, regional, national and global scale. Population density is highly variable; factors such as climate and economics will have a huge influence on how populated an area is. The Scottish Highlands, for example, although unsurpassed in beauty and spirit, are sparsely populated – vertiginous mountains and unforgiving weather repel all but the most hardy and brave settlers.

There are three main factors influencing population change: **birth rate**, **death rate** and **migration rate** (the rate at which people move in and out of an area). The difference between the birth and death rate – usually measured per 1,000 pop. (members of the population) – is called the **natural increase**, and the **growth rate** is calculated by dividing the natural increase by 10. It is given as a percentage. For example, if the birth rate per 1,000 pop. is 17, and the death rate per 1,000 pop. is 9, then the natural increase is 17 − 9 = 8 per 1,000 pop., which is a growth rate of 0.8%. Growth rates vary across the world, but generally **MEDC**s (more economically developed countries) such as the UK and Germany have a lower growth rate than **LEDC**s (less economically developed countries) such as Mozambique and Brazil.

The exciting-sounding **demographic transition model** demonstrates how population changes over time, especially how birth rate and death rate affect the total population of a country. First dreamed up by the American demographer Warren Thompson, in essence it shows how, after standards of living and life expectancy grow, family sizes decline, because of a desire for fewer children (brought about by industrialisation, urbanisation, increased literacy and declining infant death rates), leading to a stable population growth rate.

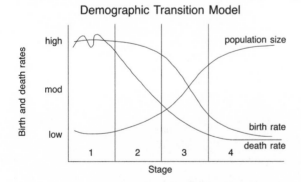

The model can be divided into four stages:

Stage 1: the total population is low but, because of high birth rates and high death rates, it is balanced.

Stage 2: the total population begins to rise as death rates fall, but birth rates remain relatively high.

Stage 3: population is still rising rapidly, but the gap between birth and death rates narrows. The natural increase is high.

Stage 4: population is high, but balanced because of a low birth rate and a low death rate.

As a country passes through the demographic transition model, the total population rises. LEDCs are normally at stage 2 or 3 (with a growing population and a high natural increase), while MEDCs are at stage 4.

Population structures (i.e. the composition of a population) are often shown using **population pyramids** – not quite as gasp-inducing as those as Giza, we'll grant you, but fascinating nonetheless. Population pyramids show the make-up of a given population (be it a school, village, town, city or country) in terms of age and gender. The length of each horizontal bar represents the number of people in an age group, and each bar is divided into segments for the numbers of males and females. In most populations the proportion of older people is much smaller than that of the younger, so the chart thins towards the top to become triangular, like a pyramid.

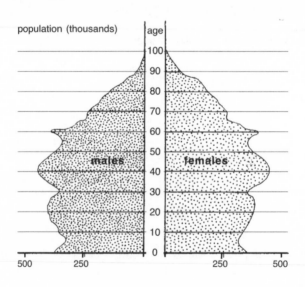

The population pyramid above, showing British society today, reveals some fascinating data in its 'bulges': for example, the life expectancy of men and women is pretty much equal until we get to old age, where women begin to outlive men. The low birth rate of the 1970s is reflected in the shrinking of the population between the ages of thirty and thirty-six, and you can also see the bulge of the 1960s baby boom. If the country being examined had a very high birth rate and a low life expectancy (as many LEDCs do), the graph would look more steeply triangular.

MARVELLOUS MALTHUS: A POPULATION THEORY THAT CHANGED THE WORLD

Thomas Malthus (1766–1834) was born into a well-off family near Dorking in Surrey and educated at home until he went to Jesus College, Cambridge, in 1784, studying a wide range of subjects before becoming Professor of History and Political Economy at the East India Company's college at Haileybury in 1805. A supremely clubbable chap, he was elected a fellow of the Royal Society in 1819, a member of the Political Economy Club in 1821 and a member of the Royal Society of Literature in 1824. As if all this clubbing didn't keep him busy enough, he also found time to write a work in 1798 that would change the way we think about population growth.

The unwieldy title of *An Essay on the Principle of Population as It Affects the Future Improvement of Society, with Remarks on the Speculations of Mr Godwin, M. Condorcet, and Other Writers* masked a simple but extraordinary argument: that population increases geometrically (1, 2, 4, 8, 16, etc.) while the resources on which it depends increase arithmetically (1, 2, 3, 4, 5, etc.), so population will always tend to outgrow production. This revealed that the eighteenth-century Poor Laws, which encouraged large families on the basis that a large population led to national wealth, would in fact prove disastrous for mankind, which, Malthus argued, was instead doomed to the **Malthusian catastrophe** (famine, epidemics and general misery) if allowed to run unchecked.

In fact, Malthusian catastrophe on a global scale has, happily, so far not come to pass. Malthus failed to anticipate the agricultural revolution, and the world's food supply has thus far kept up with population growth. But to match the predicted rise in population, the world's farmers need to produce more food in the next forty years than they have in the past two hundred, so perhaps Malthus will finally be proven right.

WHICH DIRECTION IS EAST?

The easiest way to remember the points of the compass is by using the rhyme 'never eat shredded wheat'.

If you are careless enough to have left home without your compass, you can salvage the situation and work out roughly which direction is east by the position of the sun in the sky. If it's morning the sun will be in the east, and in the afternoon it will be in the west. One of the few reliable things in this life is that the sun always rises in the east.

**BATTERED AND BUFFETED:
THE BLUSTERY BEAUFORT SCALE**

This wonderful piece of Aeolian analysis was created in 1805 by Commander Francis Beaufort of the British Navy to observe and classify wind force at sea. It was originally based on the effect of the wind on a full-rigged man-of-war, and in 1838 it became essential to log entries on all ships in the Royal Navy. It was taken up in 1874 by the International Meteorological Committee for general use and tweaked to include observations of phenomena on land as well as at sea.

FORCE	EQUIVALENT SPEED km/hour	DESCRIPTION	SPECIFICATIONS FOR USE ON LAND
0	0–1	Calm	Smoke rises vertically.
1	1–5	Light air	Direction of wind shown by smoke drift, but not by wind vanes.
2	6–11	Light breeze:	Wind felt on face; leaves rustle; wind vanes move.
3	12–19	Gentle breeze	Leaves and small twigs in motion; wind extends light flag.
4	20–29	Moderate breeze	Raises dust and loose paper and moves small branches.
5	30–39	Fresh breeze:	Small trees in leaf begin to sway; crested wavelets form on inland waters.
6	40–50	Strong breeze	Large branches in motion; whistling heard in telegraph wires; umbrellas used with difficulty.
7	51–61	Moderate gale	Whole trees in motion; difficulty in walking against wind.
8	62–74	Fresh gale	Breaks twigs off trees; generally impedes progress.
9	75–87	Severe gale	Slight structural damage occurs (chimney pots and slates blown off).
10	88–101	Storm	Trees uprooted; considerable structural damage occurs.
11	102–118	Violent storm	Very rarely experienced; causes wide-spread damage.
12	119+	Hurricane	Rarely encountered outside tropical revolving storms.

The shipping forecast is broadcast four times a day every day on the BBC and gives the Beaufort level of winds in all the major shipping areas around the United Kingdom (which are blessed with magnificent names such as Dogger, Viking, Malin, Forties, Fastnet and German Bight).

ICE, ICE BABY: HOW GLACIATION SHAPED OUR WORLD

Glaciers are masses of ice formed high up in the mountains that move very slowly downhill, affecting the landscapes around them in a process called **glaciation**. Glaciation works in various ways: through **erosion**, through **transportation** and through **deposition**. Erosion causes dramatic changes in landscapes, as the huge masses of ice carve out U-shaped valleys (as opposed to V-shaped valleys created by faster-occurring river erosion). **Corries** (also known as **cwms** and **cirques**) are valleys created by the movement of glacial ice, and a **tarn** is a lake that has formed in a corrie. When two corries form close together, over time they gradually move together, forming a high ridge between them known as an **arête** or **knife-edge ridge**. **Pyramidal peaks** are formed when three or more corries form together (think of Mount Everest).

WHEN NATURE TURNS NASTY: ENVIRONMENTAL HAZARDS

Bounteous and beautiful though our wonderful world is, nature can also be awesomely terrifying and dangerous. Below is a list of some menacing hazards posed by our environment that you should try to avoid on holiday.

Avalanches: Avalanches are very fast (an average of 40km/h) movements of snow, ice and rock, which can occur naturally because of changes in temperature, snowfall or wind direction, or can be triggered by other causes such as loud noises (be careful when yodelling from mountain tops). In both cases, stress on the snow exceeds the tensile strength where it touches the ground, causing it to move.

Drought: Agricultural drought occurs when the water supply falls short of meeting the demands of livestock and crops. Droughts can be devastating: between October 1984 and April 1987, for example, it is estimated that a million people died from drought and food shortages in North Africa.

Earthquakes: Earthquakes occur because of a build-up of pressure in the Earth's rocks, which is then quickly released, leading to secondary hazards such as **soil liquefaction** (which causes buildings to collapse), landslides and tsunamis. Earthquakes are not confined to the San Fernando Valley or Italy's Apennine mountains; even our humble shores are prone to seismic activity. In February 2008 an earthquake measuring 5.2 on the Richter scale shook teacups from shelves as far apart as Plymouth and Edinburgh.

Flooding: Usually triggered by dramatic rainfall, the effects of flooding depend on the surrounding landscape: for example, a steep-sided river channel or lack of surrounding vegetation will lead to very fast **surface run-off** (when soil becomes so saturated water flows over its top instead of sinking in), which is why over-farming can have devastating effects on the land's ability to cope with flooding.

Storm surges: These occur when water is pushed towards the shore by the force of winds swirling around a storm. The surge combines with normal tides to create the terrifying **hurricane storm tide** which can increase the water level by four metres or more. Our American cousins are particularly at risk from storm surges, because much of their coastline lies less than three metres above sea level.

Tropical cyclones: Also known as **hurricanes**, **typhoons** or **willy-willies**, tropical cyclones are hugely powerful and destructive circular winds that are thought to cause more deaths than any other natural hazard. They spark to life over the Atlantic and Pacific oceans, most often in autumn when ocean temperatures are highest. There is some evidence to suggest that their frequency and severity is increasing as a result of global warming.

Volcanic eruptions: A volcanic eruption takes place when magma from the Earth's interior makes its way to the surface, via a vent. Some catastrophic eruptions include a Bronze Age eruption at Santorini in Greece which destroyed an ancient and highly developed culture, possibly inspiring the myth of Atlantis; Vesuvius, in Italy (79 CE); and the devastating eruption of Krakatoa in Indonesia (1883 CE), in which four enormous explosions occurred that were heard over 4,800 kilometres away. Each explosion produced huge tsunamis, measuring over thirty metres in some places, 36,000 people were killed, and most of the island was destroyed. The gases and ash produced by Krakatoa were held responsible for producing intensely multicoloured sunsets all over the world for three years after the eruption. Norwegian painter Edvard Munch's famous picture, *The Scream*, is thought to feature a Krakatoan sunset.

THAR SHE BLOWS!:
THE WORLD'S MOST ACTIVE VOLCANOES

Volcanoes are embodiments of Mother Nature at her most lethal and lovely: producing pyrotechnics to take the breath away, and destroying the lives of those who venture too close. Below is a list of the ten most active volcanoes.

1. Etna, Italy, active for over 3,500 years
2. Stromboli, Italy, active for over 2,000 years
3. Yasur, Vanuatu, active for over 800 years
4. Ambrym, Vanuatu, active since 1935
5. Tinakula, Solomon Islands, active since 1951
6. Langila, Papua New Guinea, active since 1960
7. Erta Ale, Ethiopia, active since 1967
8. Semeru, Indonesia, active since 1967
9. Bangana, Papua New Guinea, active since 1972
10. Manam, Papua New Guinea, active since 1974

DON'T BE IGNORANT, KNOW YOUR IGNEOUS!

When volcanoes erupt, they spew forth molten rock in a flow that is sometimes runny, and sometimes dense, but both types are equally deadly and gloriously dramatic. Igneous rocks are made when the flow cools down and becomes hard. The type of igneous rock produced depends on the lava flow and how quickly it has cooled: igneous rock is made of crystals which are small if the flow has cooled quickly and large if the flow has cooled slowly. Here's a handy table to help you remember the most prominent types:

	Made from lava that is runny	Made from lava that is dense
Made from small crystals	Basalt	Rhyolite
Made from large crystals	Gabbro	Granite

We really shouldn't have to include this; after all, our sceptred isle is hardly huge. However, it is amazing but true that a surprising number of people seem in a permanent state of confusion about our eighty-six counties: unable to pinpoint where Shropshire actually is or whether Fife is in Ireland or Scotland. No, it is not 'East Angular' and it's not abroad, and the 'home counties' are not necessarily the ones nearest your house. Take your time to study this map: your country needs you!

A GIRL'S BEST FRIEND: DIAMONDS

Who hasn't imagined themselves dripping head to toe in delectable diamonds? Apart from being quite the most beautiful accent to any evening gown or smoking jacket, the physical properties of diamonds are enthralling in themselves.

Diamond is the hardest material known to man or woman, and they can only be cut or scratched by their own kind. The word diamond derives from the ancient Greek word '*adamas*' meaning 'unconquerable'. Their dense mysteries are formed between 100 and 200km below the Earth's surface and brought up to us by volcanic movements. In prosaic terms, they are made of carbon that is compressed by the weight of the rock piled on top of it. However, only the perfect pressure, temperature and chemistry leads to diamond crystals forming.

IS YOUR DIAMOND GOOD ENOUGH?

Diamonds are valued according to the four critical Cs: **cut, colour, clarity** and **carat**. The cut of a diamond is the work of a highly skilled technician and is responsible for making the diamond sparkle. In terms of colour, the most valuable diamonds are colourless – your everyday diamonds probably have tinges of yellow, brown or grey muddying their crystal waters. The clarity of a diamond is defined by how many flaws (also called **inclusions**) are present in the diamond. And finally the carat of a diamond simply refers to its weight. One carat is equal to ⅕ of a gram.

The Cullinan

The largest rough diamond ever recorded is the Cullinan, which was discovered in South Africa in 1905 and weighed 3,106 carats. The Cullinan was split and part of it is mounted on a sceptre which forms part of the British monarch's Crown jewels, and which any commoner good for the price of an entry ticket can see on display in the Tower of London.

WATER, WATER, EVERYWHERE!: THE WORLD'S TEN LARGEST LAKES

NAME	LOCATION	VOLUME
1. Caspian Sea	Azerbaijan, Iran, Kazakhstan, Russian Federation, Turkmenistan	78,200km³
2. Baikal	Russian Federation	23,600km³
3. Tanganyika	Burundi, Congo (Democratic Republic of), Tanzania, Zambia	18,900km³
4. Superior	Canada, United States of America	12,100km³
5. Malawi	Malawi, Mozambique, Tanzania	8,400km³
6. Michigan	United States of America	4,900km³
7. Huron	Canada, United States of America	3,540km³
8. Victoria	Kenya, Tanzania, Uganda	2,750km³
9. Great Bear Lake	Canada	2,236km³
10. Great Slave	Canada	2,090km³

MORE WATER, WATER EVERYWHERE!
THE WORLD'S TEN LONGEST RIVERS

	NAME	LOCATION	LENGTH
1.	Nile	Africa	6,695km
2.	Amazon	South America	6,516km
3.	Yangtze	China	6,380km
4.	Mississippi	United States of America	5,969km
5.	Ob	Russia	5,568km
6.	Yenisei/Angara	Russia	5,550km
7.	Yellow River	China	5,464km
8.	Congo	Zaire	4,667km
9.	Rio de la Plata	South America	4,500km
10.	Irtysh	Asia	4,440km

THE COUNTIES AND REGIONS OF THE UNITED KINGDOM

1	Cornwall	36	South Yorkshire
2	Devon	37	Greater Manchester
3	Somerset	38	Cheshire
4	Dorset	39	Merseyside
5	Hampshire	40	Lancashire
6	Wiltshire	41	North Yorkshire
7	Avon	42	Cleveland
8	West Sussex	43	Durham
9	East Sussex	44	Cumbria
10	Kent	45	Tyne & Wear
11	Surrey	46	Northumberland
12	Greater London	47	Gwent
13	Berkshire	48	South Glamorgan
14	Oxfordshire	49	Mid Glamorgan
15	Buckinghamshire	50	West Glamorgan
16	Hertfordshire	51	Powys
17	Essex	52	Dyfed
18	Suffolk	53	Gwynedd
19	Norfolk	54	Anglesey
20	Cambridgeshire	55	Clwyd
21	Bedfordshire	56	Dumfries & Galloway
22	Northamptonshire	57	Borders
23	Warwickshire	58	Tayside
24	Worcestershire	59	Strathclyde
25	Gloucestershire	60	Fife
26	Herefordshire	61	Lothian
27	West Midlands	62	Highland
28	Shropshire	63	Grampian
29	Staffordshire	64	Down
30	Derbyshire	65	Londonderry
31	Leicestershire	66	Fermanagh
32	Nottinghamshire	67	Antrim
33	Lincolnshire	68	Tyrone
34	Humberside	69	Armagh
35	West Yorkshire		

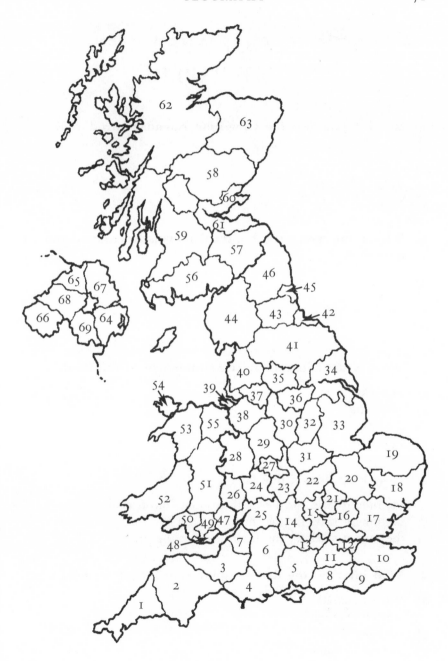

GEOGRAPHY TEST PAPER

1. In what year was the Gregorian calendar introduced?

a) 1582
b) 1682
c) 1482
d) 1782

2. What is the carat weight of the Cullinan, the largest diamond ever found?

a) 306
b) 3,106
c) 33,106
d) 333,105

3. What is the approximate circumference of the Earth?

a) 13,076km
b) 40,076km
c) 60,076km
d) 73,076km

4. How long does a day last?

a) the time it takes for the Earth to rotate on its axis
b) the time it takes for the moon to orbit the Earth
c) the time it takes for the Earth to orbit the sun

5. Who invented the demographic transitional model?

a) Warren Buffet
b) Warren Hastings
c) Lorraine Warren
d) Warren Thompson

6. **Approximately, what is the Earth's population?**

a) 3.5 billion
b) 4.5 billion
c) 5.5 billion
d) 6.9 billion

7. **How often does an extra day need to be added to our year, creating a leap year?**

a) every 2 years
b) every 3 years
c) every 4 years
d) every 5 years

8. **Which stretches further north, Lancashire or West Yorkshire?**

9. **Which of the following does NOT directly affect population change?**

a) the birth rate
b) the marriage rate
c) the death rate
d) the migration rate

10. **In what year was Thomas Malthus born?**

a) 1666
b) 1677
c) 1766
d) 1777

11. **In the northern hemisphere, when is the vernal equinox?**

a) around 22 December
b) around 22 September
c) around 21 June
d) around 21 March

12. **Where did the Bronze Age eruption that may have inspired the myth of Atlantis take place?**

a) the Bay of Naples, Italy
b) Santorini, Greece
c) Rhode Island, USA
d) Cardigan Bay, Wales

13. **What is a Malthusian catastrophe?**

a) the hypothetical situation in which a population will outgrow the resources it depends on
b) the hypothetical situation in which population growth outstrips the birth rate
c) a type of volcanic eruption
d) a type of landslip

14. **In what year was the Beaufort scale invented?**

a) 1800
b) 1805
c) 1905
d) 1907

15. **In geographic terms, what is density?**

a) the intelligence level of a population, as measured by GCSE fail rates
b) the number of people per km^2
c) the way in which a population is spread over the land

16. **At which force on the Beaufort scale are you likely to see large branches in motion, hear whistling in telegraph wires and only be able to use your umbrella with difficulty?**

17. **In what year and in which country did the catastrophic eruption of Krakatoa take place?**

a) 1745, Sri Lanka
b) 1783, Japan

c) 1883, Indonesia
d) 1845, China

18. What is the capital city of Madagascar?

19. Anglesey is in:

a) England
b) Ireland
c) Scotland
d) Wales

20. What are the four critical Cs of diamonds?

a) cut, colour, clarity, carat
b) cost, colour, carbon content, carat
c) cut, cost, clarity, carat

21. Which of the following counties does NOT have a coast?

a) Stirling
b) East Lothian
c) Moray
d) Fife

22. Where could you catch a glimpse of part of the Cullinan diamond?

a) the Palace of Versailles
b) the Tower of London
c) Buckingham Palace
d) Holyrood Palace

23. Which is the shorter day, the winter solstice or the vernal equinox?

24. What is the sum number of days for April, May, June and July?

a)   121
b)   122
c)   123
d)   124

25. Which is the longest river in the European Union?

a)   the Rhine
b)   the Danube
c)   the Seine
d)   the Po

26. The most valuable diamonds are generally:

a)   yellow
b)   colourless
c)   white
d)   grey

27. Which is larger, the Atlantic or Arctic Ocean?

28. What is a solar calendar?

a)   one that is powered by the sun
b)   one that organises units of time based on the movement of the Earth round the sun
c)   one that organises units of time based on the movement of the moon round the Earth

29. In geographic terms, what does the acronym MEDC stand for?

a)   mountainous, empty and dramatic country
b)   more economically developed country
c)   medically and economically developed country
d)   marshy, enormous and damp country

30. What is a willy-willy?

a) a tropical cyclone
b) a volcanic eruption
c) a storm surge
d) a very naughty boy

❧ HISTORY ❧
AND
POLITICS

Think you know History? That you're primed in Politics? You might have finally mastered the fates of Henry VIII's unfortunate wives and got to grips with the calamitous death of Archduke Franz Ferdinand, but in this chapter we'll be delving in more depth into certain key areas of British and world history that pop up in school lessons and also provide opportunity for greater understanding of all different elements of today's world – from how it is that Britain has so many good curry houses to understanding the background to cowboy films. We'll be asking if the Dark Ages were really that dark, following the rise of Protestantism round Europe, introducing ourselves to some significant (and significantly naughty) popes, taking to the seas on famous ships and meeting some of the fruitier figures of America's Wild West. We'll also be looking at the legacy of good old Queen Vic and her Empire and dancing our way through the Roaring Twenties, getting déjà vu about the Wall Street Crash, dodging whiz-bangs in the trenches of World War I and investigating the reasons behind the Vietnam War.

In the Politics section of this chapter we'll tell you what democracy actually means and how it didn't actually seem terribly democratic in its early years in ancient Greece; we'll explore political movements, and look in detail at British prime ministers. Do you know who our only Jewish prime minister was? Or which prime minister was the first to invade Afghanistan? Or who the only prime minister born outside Britain was? Or which prime minister fought a duel on Putney Heath while in office? Turn the page and prepare to be enlightened.

THE BARBARIANS ARE COMING: THE FALL OF THE WESTERN ROMAN EMPIRE

Early in the fourth century, faced with invaders from both the east and the west, the Christian Emperor Constantine I ordered the building of a modestly monikered new capital called Constantinople (now Istanbul) to better defend the Roman Empire's eastern borders. The Roman Empire could now be said to be comprised of two parts: the Western Empire, whose seat was Rome, and the Eastern Empire, ruled from Constantinople. The Eastern Empire successfully resisted the menace of the marauding Persians and evolved into the Byzantine Empire, which survived as a beacon of civilisation for a thousand years. In contrast, within a century the Western Empire and Rome had fallen victim to barbarian hordes from forests beyond the Rhine. So how did the proud and power-hungry city of Rome fall so fast and so fully? The answer lies in a series of invasions culminating in the sack of Rome in 476 CE. Here are some key dates tracing the rack and ruin of the eternal city:

- **200s CE**: Goths begin a period of repeated attacks on Roman territories by barbarian tribes.

- **285**: Emperor Diocletian divides the empire into two areas of control, and then later into four.

- **306**: Constantine is proclaimed emperor by the legions in Eboracum (York) in Britain and takes over the whole empire. He ends the persecution of Christians and Christianity becomes the major force in the Roman Empire.

- **300s**: Constantinople is built as the new capital of the Roman Empire.

- **395**: After the death of the Emperor Theodosius, his sons divide the empire into East and West and the two territories are never again reunited.

- **404**: The capital of the West Roman Empire moves to Ravenna.

- **410**: Rome is sacked by Alaric, the king of the Visigoths, a tribe from what is now East Germany. The last Roman legions leave Britain.

- **426**: The Vandals, another Germanic tribe, begin to conquer much of Spain and North Africa. (The name Andalusia is thought by some to be a memento of their presence.)

- **442**: The Roman Empire recognises the Vandal kingdom as an independent state.

- **451**: Attila and his Huns are defeated by an alliance between Romans and Germanic tribes led by the Roman commander Aëtius.

- **452**: Attila invades northern Italy but dies the next year, leaving his sons to partition his territories.

- **455**: The Vandals sack Rome so enthusiastically that their name has since become synonymous with wilful destruction.

- **474**: The Visigoth king Euric refuses to recognise the Roman Emperor's supremacy and begins to conquer Roman Gaul.

- **476**: The German barbarian chief Odoacer deposes the last Western Roman emperor, Romulus Augustus, and proclaims himself king over Italy.

JUST HOW DARK WERE THE DARK AGES?

The Italian scholar Petrarch, famed for his lovesick sonnets, also left us a key phrase when, writing in the 1330s, he described the six hundred years after the fall of Rome as 'The Dark Ages'. For Petrarch, it was a dingy period because the ideals of classical antiquity had vanished and, as he saw it, civilisation had come to an end. For historians since, these centuries were shady because so little was known about them, though modern methods of historical research have penetrated the gloom somewhat. Despite the constant disorder as warring tribes across Europe fought for supremacy and the generally nasty nature of life for ordinary people, we know that light did shine during what historians now rather more tactfully call 'The Early Middle Ages'.

A BEACON OF LIGHT: THE MONASTERIES

In the chaotic, changeable Europe of the fifth to eleventh centuries, the Church was the strongest unifying force, and religious faith dominated every aspect of life. Some individuals chose to withdraw from the world in order to serve God better through contemplation and prayer. One, the comfortingly named Benedict of Nursia, is considered the father of Western monasticism. He founded the great abbey of Monte Cassino in Italy in around 520 CE and set down the principles of monastic life in the famous 'Rule of St Benedict'. Throughout Europe, abbeys and monasteries became oases of scholarship, learning and knowledge as monks were usually the only educated people in a community. The preservation of many important ancient Greek, Latin and early Christian writings can be ascribed to hard-toiling monastic scribes who produced such works of art as the Lindisfarne Gospels (c.715 CE) and the Book of Kells (c.800 CE). And then of course there is the incalculable gift to civilisation they left in the form of Buckfast, the fortified wine of champions even today.

ANOTHER BEACON OF LIGHT: THE CAROLINGIAN RENAISSANCE

Charlemagne

Charlemagne (c.742–814 CE), son of Pepin the Short and first Holy Roman Emperor, was originally king of the Franks, a Germanic tribe who gradually conquered what is now France, Belgium and the Netherlands, eventually ruling most of Western Europe. Even though he was illiterate, Charlemagne initiated a period of great flowering in education and the arts that began in his reign (768–814 CE) and continued for a century. His aim was to create a new culture in Europe that would combine Christian, Roman and Frankish elements. Among the many great academic achievements of this period were:

- The development of a standard version of Latin which allowed new words to enter the language while preserving the grammar of the classical form. This medieval Latin became the common language of scholarship and the liturgy of the Church at a time when Vulgar (ordinary people's) Latin was evolving into the various Romance languages.

- The establishment of an educational curriculum of the seven liberal arts: the **trivium** (grammar, logic, rhetoric) and the **quadrivium** (arithmetic, geometry, astronomy and music).

- The introduction of the **Carolingian Minuscule** – a standard script which was the first to use lower-case letters and was the precursor of all later forms of Western writing.

. . . AND ANOTHER BEACON OF LIGHT: THE INFLUENCE OF ISLAM

Islam was founded by Muhammad who was born in around 570 in the city of Mecca in what is now Saudi Arabia. Shortly after the death of Muhammad, the First Islamic Empire began to expand beyond the Arabian Peninsula to rule eventually over a huge swathe of territory including most of West Asia, North Africa, India, Indonesia and Spain. Damascus in modern-day Syria was for a time its administrative capital while Baghdad was its intellectual centre.

For five centuries, Islam was the leading civilisation of the world, a tolerant and enlightened colonist that allowed religious freedom and preserved the knowledge of countries under its sway. Scholars translated the works of the ancients such as Aristotle, Socrates, Ptolemy, Pythagoras and Euclid into Arabic, and medieval Europe owed much of its knowledge of science, medicine, mathematics and philosophy to them. In the ninth century the Arab mathematician, al-Khwarizmi, working in the House of Wisdom in Baghdad, laid down the foundations for calculation that centuries later resulted in computer chips. Via Muslim Spain, Christian Europe discovered algebra, algorithms, trigonometry, geometry, chemistry, cosmology, astronomy, medicine and optics. And if this all seems a little cerebral, the art of distillation was learned from Arab chemists and taken on by monasteries which made medicinal drinks from herbs and berries – some, like lip-smacking Benedictine liqueur, still survive today. But perhaps the most important Islamic innovation at the time was the introduction of the numerals now in use every day (1, 2, 3, etc.) which put an end to those unwieldy Roman Xs and Vs.

PRODIGIOUS PONTIFFS: THE POPES

The real inheritors of the Roman Empire were the popes, who, as supreme leaders of the Catholic Church, were able to assume the moral and divine authority once held by the emperors. There have been 266 popes since the first, Jesus' right-hand disciple, St Peter. Over its long history the papacy has at times been perceived as greedy and corrupt but it has also carried out many good works. Many popes have distinguished themselves by making contributions to history, or just by being bad to the bone. Here are some of the more colourful characters:

440–61: Leo I's claim to fame is that he met the invading armies of Attila the Hun outside Rome virtually alone and convinced them to turn back.

590–604: Gregory I, later canonised, built schools and hospitals, mounted the successful defence of Rome against a new German barbarian invasion, sent missionaries to England and, best of all, reputedly invented Gregorian chant.

891–96: Formosus was so loathed that nine months after his death, his corpse was dug up and placed on a throne in full papal vestments to be tried for a variety of offences. Bizarrely, he was then sentenced to death.

955–64: John XII was a thoroughly bad lot who was accused of sacrilege, perjury, murder, adultery and incest. His answer to those annoying accusations? He excommunicated his enemies.

1088–99: Urban II instigated the First Crusade to recapture the Holy Land from Arab occupation in 1095.

1154–59: Born in St Albans, Adrian IV is famous on our shores as the only English pope in history so far.

1227–41: Gregory IX is the only person ever to expect the Inquisition, as he established it to root out heresy.

1492–1503: Alexander VI was father of the murderous Lucrezia Borgia and possibly the most venal pope in history despite stiff competition.

1534–49: Paul III made his two teenage grandsons cardinals but also led the Counter-Reformation and authorised the foundation of the Society of Jesus (Jesuits) under the leadership of St Ignatius of Loyola.

1846–78: Pius IX saw Rome become the capital city of a reunified Italy and instituted the concept of 'papal infallibility', which means that when the Pope speaks *ex cathedra* (with the authority of his position) on questions of faith and morals he cannot be wrong.

1939–58: Pius XII campaigned for peace during World War II but has been accused of failing to do enough to stand up to the Nazis.

1978–2005: John Paul II was the first non-Italian pope for over 450 years and became the most travelled and most popular pope in history. He was also apparently a great goalkeeper in his youth.

RESHAPING RELIGION: THE REFORMATION

The Reformation was born out of a deep resentment of the Roman Catholic Church, which, thanks in part to some of the pontiffs we've discussed, was seen by some as tyrannical and corrupt. Christians in Northern Europe particularly longed for a more spiritual religion that was based on justification by faith, a personal relationship with God and the authority of the Bible, not Rome. Educated people were appalled by the Church's mercenary practices such as the sale of **indulgences** where sins could be forgiven for a fee. Matters came to a head in 1517 when the friar Johann Tetzel was sent to Germany by Pope Leo X to raise money for the rebuilding of St Peter's in Rome by hawking indulgences. Word reached Martin Luther, then an obscure Augustinian monk who taught at the University of Wittenberg. His response was one of the most significant acts in European history – the nailing of the **Ninety-Five Theses** on the nature of faith and contemporary Church practice to the door of the Castle Church in Wittenberg.

Luther had no intention of breaking with the Church, but in 1521 Pope Leo excommunicated him. The Holy Roman Empire's **Diet of Worms** supported the Pope but Luther refused to recant. (We wish there was a more thrilling explanation for this preposterously named meeting, but the truth is that 'Diet' means 'council', and Worms was a small town in what is now Germany.) Instead, Luther appealed to the German princes who held great political influence. Many agreed with him and also saw an opportunity to have a go at the Holy Roman Emperor Charles V and make themselves rich at the expense of the Church. Conflict between the Protestant princes and the emperor lasted for the next thirty-five years until the **Augsburg Settlement** of 1555, which left the German princes free to decide the religion of their subjects.

Henry VIII of England proclaimed himself head of the Church in direct opposition to the Pope in 1534, and then asserted his authority over Rome by seizing the property and land belonging to the Catholic Church. Between 1536 and 1540 he closed down over 850 monastic houses, sold off their assets and claimed the money for the Crown – a period known as the **Dissolution of the Monasteries**.

During this period Protestantism spread throughout Northern Europe. The ensuing struggle between Protestants and Catholics was the cause of roughly two centuries of bitter religious wars. The newly Protestant Dutch rebelled against their Spanish Catholic masters and eventually drove them out; the French experienced eight civil wars in which Catholics fought Protestants; and the Thirty Years War (1618–48) involved much of Western Europe.

In 1685 the French King Louis XIV revoked the **Edict of Nantes** (1598) that had proclaimed religious and civil liberties for French Protestants. He expelled the leaders of the Huguenots (as French Protestants were known) and around 200,000 Huguenots followed them into exile.

In England the wars between the two sides officially ended when the Catholic Stuart King James II was defeated at the **Battle of the Boyne** in Ireland by the forces of the Protestant Dutch King William III in 1690 (this event is still controversially commemorated in Northern Ireland by the Orange Marches). Since this time British monarchs have all been Protestants.

A LIFE ON THE OCEAN WAVE:
SIX SHIPS THAT CHANGED THE WORLD

The *Santa Maria* was the flagship of the first expedition funded by Spain and led by Italian explorer Christopher Columbus, which sailed west across the Atlantic Ocean in search of a new route to the East. On 12 October 1492, Columbus landed on an island in the Caribbean, and, thinking he had arrived in the Indies, didn't realise he had discovered a new continent.

The *São Gabriel* was the carrack captained by Vasco da Gama, the great Portuguese explorer and navigator, and the first person to attempt to reach India from Europe by sea via the Cape of Good Hope in southern Africa. He arrived on the western coast of India in 1498 and established a Portuguese presence that gave Europe direct access to the wealth of the East, particularly the valuable spice trade.

Golden Hind

The *Golden Hind* was the only vessel to come back from Sir Francis Drake's epic voyage around the world, which left Plymouth Sound in Devon, in 1577. Three years later Drake returned and was knighted onboard the ship by Queen Elizabeth I.

The *Mayflower* was the salvation of the Pilgrim Fathers who escaped persecution by sailing from Plymouth in September 1620 to settle in America, anchoring near what is now Provincetown, Massachusetts, on 11 November.

HMS *Endeavour* is the ship in which Captain Cook set out to find the great southern continent *Terrae Australes Incognitae* or 'unknown lands in the south'. In October 1769, Cook became the second European to reach New Zealand after Abel Tasman who visited in 1642. Later, in 1770, he surveyed the eastern coast of what was then known as New

Holland (now Australia) and, on 22 August 1770, claimed this territory for Great Britain.

HMS *Beagle* carried out marine surveys in South America and along the coast of Australia between 1826 and 1843, carrying Charles Darwin with it between 1831 and 1836. In 1835 the *Beagle* anchored in the Galapagos Islands where Darwin began to formulate his ideas of natural selection based on his observations of the wildlife there.

WHERE THE SUN NEVER SETS: QUEEN VICTORIA AND BRITISH IMPERIALISM

After the American Revolution (1775–83) the international territories ruled by Britain consisted of Canada, parts of the Caribbean, and various scattered trading posts. However, after the Napoleonic Wars (1799–1815) Blighty found herself with no serious international rival and the second great age of British imperialism began, with vast territories like Australia and New Zealand formally apropriated by the Crown. During the reign of Queen Victoria (1837–1901) the British Empire became the greatest the world had ever known: industrial innovation at home and dominance of the great ocean routes had made Britain the world's foremost trading nation. Prime Minister Disraeli and others promulgated a strategy of economic expansion abroad, linked to the idea of Britain as a civilising influence which could bring Christianity to the heathen masses. For many reasons – mercantile, political, philanthropic – by the time of her death in 1901 over one-quarter of the world's population acknowledged Victoria as head of state and her domain included Canada, Australia, India, New Zealand, large chunks of Africa and many countries in the Far East and the Caribbean. Covering 14 million square miles and stretching from east to west in every time zone, the sun literally never set on British rule.

THE JEWEL IN THE CROWN: INDIA

Britain's long love affair with India started in 1600 when the monopoly to trade in the East Indies was given to the East India Company by Elizabeth I. The East India Company was the biggest and most successful financial enterprise in commercial history and gradually came to rule the entire country. The company was not immune to mishap though and, after the Indian Mutiny in 1857, the government of India was transferred to the Crown. In 1877, at her personal request, an Act of Parliament was passed declaring Victoria Empress of India.

Imperialism is generally seen as a bad thing and British rule in India was in the main oppressive and unfair, but there were some positive legacies. The British introduced Western-style democracy, education for the Indian elite, English as a lingua franca, a railroad network and a unified system of law. Most importantly, the British promoted the idea of India as a unified state. In its heyday, because of Indian cooperation, the Raj was able to rule India, a vast subcontinent of many peoples, languages and religions, with only 50,000 troops and a tiny number of administrators. When that cooperation started to break down after World War I it was the beginning of the end for British Rule. India became an independent nation on 15 August 1947.

AN EYE FOR AN EYE MAKES THE WHOLE WORLD BLIND: GANDHI

Mohandas Gandhi (1869–1948), known as 'Mahatma' or 'great soul', led India to independence, which was finally achieved in 1947. He preached the doctrine of *satyagraha* or soul force and his campaigns of passive resistance against British rule were remarkably effective. He bitterly opposed the partition of India but in 1948 was assassinated by a Hindu fanatic who blamed him for giving in to Muslim pressure for the separation of India into two states – Pakistan and India. India's independence was the signal for the gradual dismantling of the British Empire and decolonisation.

INDIAN INFLUENCE

The influence of the subcontinent on the British way of life has been immense. Chicken tikka masala (a fusion of British and Indian tastes) is now Britain's most popular dish and every high street in the land boasts a curry house. Thanks to lonely expats adding a slug of gin to their daily dose of quinine water, taken to prevent malaria, gin and tonic is our national drink. And every day we use Indian words that recall the legacy of the Raj, such as bungalow, calico, cashmere, chintz, cummerbund, cushy, dungaree, gymkhana, juggernaut, jungle, khaki, loot, pariah, pukka, pyjamas, shampoo, shawl and thug.

DÉJÀ VU?: THE GREAT DEPRESSION

The Great Depression was a severe worldwide economic downturn that began in 1929 and continued until the outbreak of World War II in 1939. It was triggered by the **Wall Street Crash** of 29 October 1929 when, after years of boom, the American stock market suddenly collapsed and $30 billion vanished into thin air on a single day known as Black Tuesday. Banks that had loaned investors money went bust, many businesses were bankrupted and around 15 million people lost their jobs. Agriculture was particularly hard hit due to a combination of falling prices and rising debt, and the fact that a vast swathe of America from the Great Plains of North Dakota to Texas and parts of the South had become a dust bowl through over-planting and the worst drought in US history. In these areas over 2 million destitute people abandoned their homes to migrate to the east and west coasts in search of work (their travails are described in John Steinbeck's masterpiece, *The Grapes of Wrath*). In 1933 President Franklin Roosevelt introduced the **New Deal**, spending millions of dollars of government money on public works, social benefits and subsidies to combat the worst effects of the crisis.

The effects of the Great Depression were felt throughout the world. The German Weimar Republic had been propped up by American banks who had loaned it money to pay the huge war reparations demanded by the 1919 Treaty of Versailles. Once these loans were called in, the German economy imploded. The consequent effects of mass unemployment played a huge part in the rise of the Nazi Party. Other countries had also been dependent on US banks for investment so world trade contracted and prices fell further. In Britain the Roaring Twenties gave way to the Hungry Thirties when thousands of unemployed people marched on London in a series of protests.

Ultimately the Great Depression only came to an end when countries all over the world began to rearm in the prelude to World War II. Let's hope that is one lesson from history we don't have to repeat.

UNITED WE STAND: THE GENERAL STRIKE

The General Strike of 1926 was the largest industrial dispute in British history. It started when the TUC (Trades Union Congress) called on trade union members to support the coal miners in their refusal to accept lower wages and worsening conditions. A trigger was the *Daily Mail's* Fleet Street printers' refusal to print an article criticising trade unions. Other print workers also downed tools in sympathy and on 3 May, some 2 million workers went on strike across Britain. In London, the main groups of striking workers were the dockers, printers, power-station workers, railwaymen and transport workers. The aim was to bring the capital to a halt and force the government to intervene on the side of the miners.

The government brought in the army to ensure that essential services continued and food supplies got through. Army barracks were set up in Hyde Park, which was also turned into a food depot. London's buses, trams, trains and delivery vans were kept running by a staff of non-unionised workers and university students. Ten days later the strike was officially ended but it was to prove a watershed in the British government's relationship with the trade unions.

THE JARROW MARCH

By 1933 almost a quarter of the British workforce was unemployed. In 1936 two hundred men from Jarrow in the north-east of England, where there was almost 70% unemployment, marched peacefully to London. Led by their local MP, Ellen Wilkinson, also known as 'Red Ellen', they wanted to explain their difficulties to Parliament and people in the south. They also demanded that a new steelworks be built to bring back jobs to their town, as Palmer's shipyard in Jarrow had been closed down in the previous year. This closure had compounded the problems of poverty, overcrowding, rotten housing and high mortality that already affected Jarrow.

POWER TO THE PEOPLE:
WHAT IS DEMOCRACY?

Democracy is defined as a system of government by the people ('*demos*' in ancient Greek) or in Abraham Lincoln's famous phrase 'of the people, by the people, for the people'.

In ancient Greece and Rome, where the main form of government was the city state, democracy was **primary** or direct: that is people governed themselves directly at an assembly attended by all citizens. In fact, since women and slaves were excluded it was not *that* democratic. Another form of democracy is **representative**, in which people vote for representatives of a political party to act for them in a parliament.

For centuries in Western Europe, monarchs ruled with absolute authority. The signing of Magna Carta at Runnymede in 1215 is often considered a key step on the path to democracy in the West, as it introduced the idea that the king's power could be subject to a constitution or law. The first elected parliament in England was Simon de Montfort's Parliament of 1265 but, because only the aristocracy were eligible to vote, it could not really have been described as democratic. Parliamentary democracy as we know it today took great leaps forward with the signing of the **Bill of Rights** in 1688, which codified individual rights and increased Parliament's influence, and the **Reform Act** of 1832 which broadened the right to vote.

In the eighteenth century the influence of thinkers like John Locke, Thomas Paine and David Hume and French '*philosophes*' such as Voltaire and Montesquieu brought about the **Age of Enlightenment**. Reason, not religion or the accident of birth, was now seen as the primary source of authority, and this was allied to faith in nature and belief in human progress through science and education. The philosophy of the Enlightenment became a major force for political and social reform, with Locke's belief that rulers derived their power from the consent of the people particularly significant in the French and American revolutions. Influenced by these thinkers, and the overseas revolutions, the nineteenth century saw Parliament gaining power and the monarchy taking on a more symbolic role.

BRITISH PRIME MINISTERS

Sir Robert Walpole (1721–42), Whig, perceived as a Norfolk parvenu who enriched himself by corruption

Spencer Compton, Earl of Wilmington (1742–3), Whig

Henry Pelham (1743–54), Whig

Thomas Pelham-Holles, Duke of Newcastle (1754–6 and 1757–62), Whig

William Cavendish, Duke of Devonshire (1756–7), Whig

John Stuart, Earl of Bute (1762–3), Tory

George Grenville (1763–5), Whig

Charles Wentworth, Marquess of Rockingham (1765–6 and 1782), Whig

William Pitt 'the Elder', Earl of Chatham (1766–8), Whig, a brilliant orator whose later life was dominated by bouts of insanity

Augustus Henry Fitzroy, Duke of Grafton (1768–70), Whig

Frederick North, Lord North (1770–82), Tory

William Petty, Earl of Shelburne (1782–3), Whig

William Bentinck, Duke of Portland (1783 and 1807–9), Whig

William Pitt 'the Younger' (1783–1801 and 1804–6), Tory, became prime minister at twenty-four, the youngest ever to take office, fought a duel with a political foe and was part of a famous father/son prime ministerial dynasty

Henry Addington, Viscount Sidmouth (1801–4), Tory

William Wyndham Grenville, Lord Grenville (1806–7), Whig

Spencer Perceval (1809–12), Tory, the only British prime minster to be assassinated – by a businessman from Liverpool who blamed him for his financial failure

Robert Banks Jenkinson, Earl of Liverpool (1812–27), Tory

George Canning (1827), Tory, a famous libertarian who supported Greece in its War for Independence from Turkey and backed the Latin American struggle against Spanish rule. Fought a duel with Lord Castlereagh on Putney Heath

Frederick Robinson, Viscount Goderich (1827–8), Tory

Arthur Wellesley, Duke of Wellington (1828–30 and 1834), Tory, defeated Napoleon at the Battle of Waterloo in 1815 and later fought a duel over Catholic Emancipation

Charles Grey, Earl Grey (1830–4), Whig, had the famous blend of tea created for him

William Lamb, Viscount Melbourne (1834 and 1835–41), Whig, a favourite of Queen Victoria despite the scandal of his first wife Lady Caroline having a notorious affair with Byron

Sir Robert Peel (1834–5 and 1841–6), Tory, established London's Metropolitan Police force and gave policemen their nicknames of 'peelers' and 'bobbies'

John Russell, Earl Russell (1846–52 and 1865–6), Liberal

Edward Stanley, Earl of Derby (1852, 1858–9 and 1866–8), Conservative

George Hamilton-Gordon, Earl of Aberdeen (1852–5), Conservative

Henry John Temple, Viscount Palmerston (1855–8 and 1859–65), Liberal

Benjamin Disraeli, Earl of Beaconsfield (1868 and 1874–80), Conservative, the only Jewish prime minister so far and a famous dandy

William Ewart Gladstone (1868–74, 1880–5, 1886 and 1892–94), Liberal, nicknamed the Grand Old Man. Split his party when he tried to establish Irish Home Rule and was famous for his attempts to rescue London prostitutes

Robert Gascoyne-Cecil, Marquess of Salisbury (1885–6, 1886–92 and 1895–1902), Conservative

Archibald Primrose, Earl of Rosebery (1894–5), Liberal, enjoyed horse racing as well as politics and owned three Derby winners

Arthur James Balfour, Earl Balfour (1902–5), Conservative

Henry Campbell-Bannerman (1905–8), Liberal

Herbert Henry Asquith, Earl of Oxford and Asquith (1908–16), Liberal

David Lloyd George (1916–22), Liberal, the last Liberal prime minister

Andrew Bonar Law (1922–3), Conservative, the only British prime minister to be born abroad – in Canada

Stanley Baldwin (1923, 1924–9 and 1935–7), Conservative, held the nation together during the crisis over Edward VIII's abdication

James Ramsay MacDonald (1924 and 1929–35), Labour, the first Labour prime minister

Arthur Neville Chamberlain (1937–40), Conservative, embarked on a disastrous policy of appeasement in the 1930s which failed to halt the rise of Hitler

Sir Winston Leonard Spencer Churchill (1940–5 and 1951–5), Conservative, Britain's most famous wartime leader who led the country to victory in 1945. The only British prime minister to win the Nobel Prize for Literature

Clement Richard Attlee (1945–51), Labour

Anthony Eden (1955–7), Conservative, resigned after the Suez Crisis

Harold Macmillan (1957–63), Conservative, presided over a time of prosperity and the thawing of the Cold War

Sir Alec Douglas-Home (1963–4), Conservative, the first person to resign a peerage (Earl of Home) to become prime minister

Harold Wilson (1964–70 and 1974–6), Labour, founded the Open University and famously refused to support the Americans in the Vietnam War

Edward Heath (1970–4), Conservative, one of the rare bachelor prime ministers

James Callaghan (1976–9), Labour

Margaret Thatcher (1979–90), Conservative, the first and, so far, only female prime minister

John Major (1990–7), Conservative

Tony Blair (1997–2007), Labour, creator of New Labour and invader of Iraq

Gordon Brown (2007–), Labour

FROM ANARCHISM TO TOTALITARIANISM: MODERN POLITICAL MOVEMENTS

Anarchism: The belief that society can and should function without organised government.

Key moment: Anarchist thought has influenced a wide range of political movements from the Communards of Paris in 1871 to the hippies of the 1960s to today's anti-globalisation movement.

Communism: Closely related to socialism, Communism is the theory set out by Karl Marx in *The Communist Manifesto* of 1848 which advocates a system in which all goods and property are held in common, everyone works for the community and each receives enough to satisfy his needs. This is to be achieved through the overthrow of established governments by the **proletariat** (the working classes).

Key moment: The Russian Revolution of 1917.

Conservatism: The notion that things should be preserved as they are in society and government. Conservatives are opposed to the concentration of power in the state and tend to follow a moderate, law-respecting and traditionalist right-wing approach, believing that government can only achieve a limited amount.

Liberalism: A catch-all term for a range of political philosophies that demand the greatest possible freedom for the individual and emphasise free trade, freedom of expression, the right to elect governments, limited state control, respect for the rights of minorities, etc.

Key moment: The signing of the American Declaration of Independence in 1776 which formally stated the right of the individual to 'life, liberty and the pursuit of happiness'.

Nationalism: The belief that a community that shares a history, language, culture and common territory should be free to govern itself without outside interference. One of the most potent forces in politics, it often disastrously ignores the reality that many countries are made up of different peoples.

Key moment: The high point of nationalism was the French Revolution when citizenship was first equated with nationality, but there have been many low points like the ethnic cleansing in the Balkans in the 1990s.

Neoconservatism: A movement that evolved in the US in the 1970s as a reaction to liberal and leftist thought. Usually characterised by an emphasis on individual liberties, the promotion of democracy and a hawkish attitude to other countries that do not share neocons' views.

Socialism: At its most basic Socialism is the belief that the ownership and management of wealth and the means of production should be in public hands (usually the state) and not controlled by private individuals. There are many forms of socialism from the hard-line Marxism of the former USSR to the social democratic principles of many of today's political parties.

Key moment: Foundation of the welfare state, including the world's first national health system, by Clement Attlee's government of 1945.

Syndicalism: The doctrine that trade unions should run a nation's industries.

Key moment: When workers' committees owned and administered major enterprises in the former Yugoslavia before the fall of Communism.

Totalitarianism: A form of one-party government which seeks to control every aspect of public and private life.

Key moments: Hitler's Germany, Mussolini's Italy and Stalin's USSR.

THE VIETNAM WAR (1954–75)

The conflict in Vietnam started with Vietnamese Communists rising up against French colonial rule in the 1940s. Communist forces based in the north, led by the Nationalist leader Ho Chi Minh, defeated the French in 1954. An agreement was then negotiated to temporarily split the country into the Communist north and pro-American south, divided by a demilitarised zone (DMZ). Elections to decide a permanent solution were promised but never happened, and the Communists launched a guerrilla war to gain control of the whole country.

In 1965, driven by Cold War concerns about the 'domino theory' – the idea that if one Asian nation fell to Communism, others would follow – the USA intervened to support South Vietnam. The ensuing war was protracted and vicious. It is estimated that in twenty-one years of fighting,

4 million civilians were killed across North and South Vietnam, 1.1 million Communist fighters died, over 200,000 South Vietnamese soldiers were killed and 58,200 US soldiers died or went missing in action. The war was very unpopular in the US and internationally and in 1973 US forces were withdrawn, a humiliating climbdown. Communist forces seized Saigon and control of the whole country in 1975.

WONDERFUL WASHINGTON DC: HOW THE US GOVERNMENT WORKS

Back at the early beginnings of the shiny new United States, the Constitutional Convention had to organise how their youthful country would be governed honestly and effectively. They came up with the idea of splitting central government into three branches in order to prevent political decisions from falling into the hands of just one faction – this is called the 'separation of powers'.

The **president** looks after the executive branch, **Congress** is the legislative branch and the **Supreme Court** is the judicial branch. These different elements all work independently but they also interact with each other through what is known as a system of 'checks and balances'.

The president lives in the White House in Washington DC and is in charge of putting the laws decided on by the government into effect. He or she is also commander-in-chief of the US military and head of state (which means they are responsible for international negotiations). The president is aided and advised in his or her duties by the **vice president** and members of the **Cabinet**. The president's power is limited by the Constitution and also by Congress and the Senate. Every four years the public get to vote for their choice of president during the congressional elections and no president can serve more than two terms.

Congress is responsible for debating and passing laws. The US Congress is bicameral which means it is divided into two chambers: the **Senate** and the **House of Representatives**. The House of Representatives has 435 members. Each state has one member per district (the number of districts corresponds to the size of the population), which means that larger states have more representatives than smaller ones. There are also five members who represent Puerto Rico, Guam, American Samoa, the

Virgin Islands and the District of Columbia. Representatives serve for two-year terms. The Senate has 100 members and all states have two senators who serve for six-year terms. Every two years the public get to vote for their representatives and also for one-third of the senators. Congress meets in the Capitol in Washington DC in January and stays in session through to the summer.

The Supreme Court checks that any laws that are passed by the government do not undermine the Constitution. It also acts as the highest court in the USA and has authority over all federal courts. The Supreme Court is run by nine judges, led by the **Chief Justice**, who are elected for life by the president with the approval of the Senate. The Supreme Court meets in the Supreme Court Building in Washington.

THE MOST POWERFUL MEN IN THE WORLD: US PRESIDENTS

George Washington (1789–97)
John Adams (1797–1801)
Thomas Jefferson (1801–9)
James Madison (1809–17)
James Monroe (1817–25)
John Quincy Adams (1825–9)
Andrew Jackson (1829–37)
Martin Van Buren (1837–41)
William Henry Harrison (1841)
John Tyler (1841–5)
James Polk (1845–9)
Zachary Taylor (1849–50)
Millard Fillmore (1850–3)
Franklin Pierce (1853–7)
James Buchanan (1857–61)
Abraham Lincoln (1861–5)
Andrew Johnson (1865–9)
Ulysses S. Grant (1869–77)
Rutherford B. Hayes (1877–81)
James Garfield (1881)
Chester Arthur (1881–5)
Grover Cleveland (1885–9)

Benjamin Harrison (1889–93)
Grover Cleveland (1893–9)
William McKinley (1897–1901)
Theodore Roosevelt (1901–9)
William H. Taft (1909–13)
Woodrow Wilson (1913–21)
Warren Harding (1921–3)
Calvin Coolidge (1923–9)
Herbert Hoover (1929–33)
Franklin D. Roosevelt (1933–45)
Harry S. Truman (1945–53)
Dwight D. Eisenhower (1953–61)
John F. Kennedy (1961–3)
Lyndon B. Johnson (1963–9)
Richard Nixon (1969–74)
Gerald Ford (1974–7)
Jimmy Carter (1977–81)
Ronald Reagan (1981–9)
George Bush (1989–93)
Bill Clinton (1993–2001)
George W. Bush (2001–9)
Barack Obama (2009–)

YEEEEEEEE HAW! HEROES AND VILLAINS OF THE WILD WEST

American expansion into the lands to the west in the nineteenth century was seen in part as a fulfilment of manifest destiny, the idea that America was destined by God to grow and increase its bound-aries over enor-mous areas, spreading liberty and ideals to new lands. Throughout the 1840s, 1850s and 1860s hundreds of thousands of Americans (white and black) settled in the far west in search of a new life, travelling routes of thousands of miles and facing great obstacles and danger. Those pioneers who survived the great migration were often extraordinary characters, and they – good and bad – have left their mark in American lore.

Buffalo Bill (1846–1917)
Despite rather sinister modern *Silence of the Lambs* connotations, Buffalo Bill (William Cody) was a charming, if rather delusional, man of great derring-do who became famous for his adventures on the western fron-tier and for his 'Wild West Show' which toured across the world for over twenty years, wowing audiences from London to New York with its mock battles with 'Injuns'. According to none other than himself, he earned his nickname through his legendary sharpshooting – he killed four thousand bison in less than eighteen months.

Annie Oakley (1860–1926)
Born Phoebe Ann Mosey in Ohio, Annie became famous for her incred-ible skill with a gun in Buffalo Bill's 'Wild West Show'. She got her break by beating Frank E. Butler at a vaudeville show and winning $100. Then, like all good heroines, reader, she married him. Her most impressive trick involved hitting a playing card hurled into the air a dozen times before it touched the ground. Marvellous.

Sitting Bull (c.1831–90)
Originally named Jumping Badger, Sitting Bull inherited his far weightier name on the death of his father. He was a charismatic and mystic leader of the Dakota Sioux, and, with Crazy House, led Sioux and Cheyenne into the battle of Little Bighorn against General George Cruster's cavalry in June 1876. Sitting Bull was shot by police in 1890

and the army's subsequent pursuit of his followers led to the massacre at Wounded Knee.

Wyatt Earp (1848–1929)

Born in Illinois, Earp became chief deputy marshal of Dodge City, Kansas, at the age of twenty-eight, and having established peace in a relatively lawless place, moved on to do the same in Deadwood, South Dakota, and Tombstone, Arizona, eventually becoming deputy marshal for the whole Arizona territory. In 1881 he fought alongside his friend Doc Holliday at the OK Corral gunfight at Tombstone. They defeated the outlawed Clanton family – though historians are divided to this day over who were the true villains.

Billy the Kid (1859–81)

Born Henry McCarty, outlaw Billy the Kid grew up in Wichita, Kansas. He went to Arizona at the age of fourteen to work on ranches, and even among the rough men of the frontier soon earned a reputation for robbery and theft. He claimed to have killed twenty-one men in his lifetime, and was eventually captured by Sheriff Pat Garrett in 1880. Sentenced to death by hanging, he escaped from county jail, killing two deputies along the way, but his crimes caught up with him in 1881 near Fort Sumner where he was mortally wounded by Garrett.

MAJOR BATTLES OF THE AMERICAN CIVIL WAR

The Battle Of Bull Run (also called The Battle of Manassas) (Virginia, 21 July 1861)

In the traditional way of men at war, both the Union and the Confederate forces were initially each convinced they would win the American Civil War, and quickly. The hard-fought Battle at Bull Run, at which 22,000 Confederate forces resoundingly beat 30,000 Union forces and 5,000 men died, was the first time both sides realised the war would be long and bloody.

The Battle of Antietam (Maryland, 17 September 1862)

This was the first major battle to take place on northern soil. Confederacy General Robert E. Lee led 50,000 troops in an attempt to invade the north, but they were met and overwhelmed at Antietam Creek in Maryland by General McClellan's Union force of 70,000. Again, there were huge casualties on both sides – over 20,000 soldiers were killed or injured.

The Battle of Gettysburg (Pennsylvania, 1–3 July 1863)

Many consider this battle to have been the turning point of the American Civil War. After a decisive victory at Chancellorsville the previous month, General Lee decided to again invade the north. They were met by Union forces led by General Meade at the town of Gettysburg and after three days of intense fighting, the Confederacy was forced into a humiliating retreat – from this point onwards they would fight a defensive war. More men died in those three days of fighting than in any other military conflict on American soil – between 46,000 and 51,000 were killed. In November the same year President Lincoln made his historic **Gettysburg Address** at a dedication to a cemetery there in which he redefined America's democratic spirit:

> Fourscore and seven years ago our fathers brought forth on this continent a new nation, conceived in liberty, and dedicated to the proposition that all men are created equal.

> Now we are engaged in a great civil war, testing whether that nation, or any nation so conceived and so dedicated, can long endure. We are met on a great battle-field of that war. We have come to dedicate a portion of that field as a final resting-place for those who here gave their lives that this nation might live. It is altogether fitting and proper that we should do this.

> But, in a larger sense, we cannot dedicate . . . we cannot conse-crate . . . we cannot hallow . . . this ground. The brave men, living and dead, who struggled here, have consecrated it, far above our poor power to add or detract. The world will little note nor long remember what we say here, but it can never forget what they did here. It is for us, the living, rather, to be dedicated here to the unfinished work which they who fought here have thus far so nobly advanced. It is rather for us to be here dedicated to the great task remaining before us . . . that from these honored dead we take increased devotion to that cause for which they gave the last full measure of devotion; that we here highly resolve that

these dead shall not have died in vain; that this nation, under God, shall have a new birth of freedom; and that government of the people, by the people, for the people, shall not perish from the earth.

The Battle of Chattanooga (23–5 November 1863)

A Union force of 60,000 men under Ulysses S. Grant (who, aside from being beautifully monikered, would also go on to become president of the United States) fought 40,000 men under the command of Braxton Bragg (also in possession of an impressive name). The defeat of the Confederacy and subsequent scattering of men made the way clear for General Sherman's march through Georgia.

⤛ HISTORY AND ⤜
POLITICS
TEST PAPER

1. **Who is Constantinople named after?**

2. **Which of the following plots is connected with Mary Queen of Scots?**

a) the Gunpowder Plot
b) the Babington Plot
c) the Perkin Warbeck Plot
d) the Lost Plot

3. **Which event led to US involvement in World War II?**

4. **Prime Minister Henry Campbell-Bannerman was affiliated to which political party?**

a) Labour
b) Whig
c) Tory
d) Liberal

5. **When was the American Civil War?**

a) 1892–5
b) 1861–5
c) 1802–22
d) 1833–4

6. **Which pope came up with the idea of the Inquisition?**

a) Formosus
b) John XII

c) Gregory IX
d) Leo X

7. **Who was the last emperor of Ethiopia?**

8. **The *São Gabriel* was the ship of which explorer?**

a) Christopher Columbus
b) Francis Drake
c) Amerigo Vespucci
d) Vasco da Gama

9. **In which state did the Pilgrim Fathers land?**

a) New York
b) Massachusetts
c) Florida
d) New Hampshire

10. **Who was the British monarch during Benjamin Disraeli's time as prime minister?**

a) Edward VII
b) Victoria
c) Elizabeth I
d) George V

11. **British rule in India before 1947 was referred to as the:**

a) Khaki
b) Chintz
c) Raj
d) Partition

12. **What triggered the Great Depression in 1929?**

a) the South Sea Bubble
b) the Suez Crisis
c) the East India Company
d) the Wall Street Crash

13. What was undemocratic about ancient Greek democracy?

a) only aristocrats could vote
b) only free men could vote
c) only priests could vote

14. Which British prime minister fought a duel on Putney Heath?

a) Andrew Bonar Law
b) William Lamb
c) William Pitt the Elder
d) George Canning

15. What was the name of the treaty that ended the Boer War (1899–1902)?

a) Treaty of Transvaal
b) Treaty of Pretoria
c) Treaty of Vereeniging
d) Treaty of Ladysmith

16. Who was the first Holy Roman Emperor?

a) Henry the Fowler
b) Louis the Pious
c) Charlemagne
d) Maximilian I

17. What is syndicalism?

a) the doctrine that trade unions should run a nation's industries
b) a form of one-party government which seeks to control every aspect of public life
c) a radical nineteenth-century working-class movement for democratic reform
d) the belief in public ownership and management of wealth and the means of production

18. In 404 CE the capital of the Roman Empire moved to:

a) Avignon
b) Venice

c) Ravenna
d) Milan

19. Which pope instituted the doctrine of papal infallibility?

a) Pius IX
b) John Paul I
c) Alexander VI
d) Adrian IV

20. Who was responsible for the death of Thomas à Becket?

a) Henry VIII
b) Henry V
c) Henry II
d) Henry IV

21. Who sacked Rome in 410 CE?

a) the Vandals
b) the Franks
c) the Visigoths
d) the Huns

22. When did the Council of Trent take place?

a) 1545–63
b) 1762–89
c) 1121–5
d) 1832–1900

23. What is the Book of Kells?

24. When was the British colony of Hong Kong returned to China?

a) 1921
b) 1987
c) 1997
d) 1965

25. What subjects constituted the trivium in medieval education?

a)   arithmetic, geometry, astronomy
b)   grammar, logic, rhetoric
c)   music, logic, rhetoric
d)   grammar, geometry, astronomy

26. In what language did Karl Marx write *The Communist Manifesto*?

a)   German
b)   Russian
c)   English
d)   French

27. Which English martyr, before his execution in 1556 in Oxford, placed his right hand into the flames in order to symbolise his rejection of the recantations he had made against his faith?

a)   Nicholas Ridley
b)   Thomas Cranmer
c)   Hugh Latimer
d)   Edmund Campion

28. Who was the author of the *Ninety-Five Theses*?

a)   John Calvin
b)   Martin Luther
c)   Ulrich Zwingli
d)   John Knox

29. Who of the following was NOT an Egyptian pharaoh?

a)   Khufu
b)   Cleopatra
c)   Bufu
d)   Snefru

30. Which British prime minister owned three Derby-winning horses?

a) Archibald Primrose, Earl of Rosebery
b) James Ramsay MacDonald
c) Arthur Balfour
d) Robert Gascoyne-Cecil, Marquess of Salisbury

∽ ECONOMICS ∽

'It's the economy, stupid.' Well, the truth is some of us are a little stupid about the economy. In fact, who among us hasn't been baffled by bankers' bonkers business of wheeling and dealing, and longed for a simple guide to the ins and outs of the great money machine that rules all our lives? If these credit-crunchy days have brought intellectual insecurities as well as financial fretting, then this is the chapter for you. Don't worry, we'll start with the basics, introducing you to the simplest economic problem and key economic concepts such as supply and demand, economies of scale and market failure, before moving on to the more complex but no less fascinating economic theories and theorists who have particular resonance today such as John Maynard Keynes, once the darling of Franklin Delano Roosevelt and now re-embraced by Brown and Obama alike. So don't delay, start learning: economics truly is a subject that it pays to know about.

NUMISMATASTIC!: A BRIEF HISTORY OF MONEY

We humans have been using money in various forms for over five thousand years. Numismatists (people who like to study this area) will tell you that over the centuries shells, feathers, animal pelts, stones and of course food have all been used as forms of currency. Generally speaking, barter systems naturally develop into monetary ones since a higher value is often placed on certain things that may very well have no greater intrinsic value than other things. In short, money systems develop because of demand for key items.

Coinage is thought to have originated in China around 1100 BCE, with early denominations made in the shape of prized tools. The first nationwide coinage was introduced in 210 BCE, also in China, by Emperor Qin Shi Huangdi, in the form of the more familiar round coins with square holes punched through their centres. This design enabled lots of low-denomination coins to be strung together in large quantities, a practice that ultimately helped lead to the first use of paper money in the ninth century, as coins became prohibitively heavy.

In the West, it was the Lydians in what is now Turkey who developed the first sophisticated money system. Herodotus claims they were the first to forge coins in silver and gold in the seventh century BCE, but in fact they used a substance called electrum. The coins were not uniform in size or shape but were regulated accurately by weight and bore an image on one side as a sign of authenticity.

Of course, ever since there's been money, there have been forgers. Early Greek forgers made coins in base metals, applying a thin veneer of electrum to pass the money off as genuine. In many countries, genuine coins were clipped by counterfeiters, and the offcuts then melted down to form the precious layer on fake coins, until the milled edges that are still common today were introduced as a deterrent. Given what's at stake, it's unsurprising that the rich and powerful have meted out some eye-watering punishments to forgers through the ages. In medieval Germany they were boiled alive in oil, and in Russia molten lead was poured down their throats. Nowadays it's extremely hard to forge banknotes but in case you want to check that your sterling is genuine, here are some hints and tips:

- All notes have raised areas you can feel on their surfaces – the words 'Bank of England' should be one such area.

- If you hold them up to the light your notes should reveal a metallic thread running through them and a watermark of her august majesty's face.

- £5, £10 and £20 notes have foil patches with a hologram of Britannia that changes into the numerical value of the note and also should show the value of the note in red and green if placed under UV light.

THE ECONOMIC PROBLEM

You may feel that you are fully aware of your own economic problems, as you stuff that credit card bill down the back of the radiator and try to teach yourself how to darn socks, but above and beyond personal financial issues, you'll be glad to know that there is a much bigger problem lurking out there which economists are tasked with investigating and solving.

We live in a world that contains a mixture of limited and unlimited resources (for example, oil reserves are a limited resource but human creativity is unlimited). Obviously the limited ones tend to be trickier to manage. Simultaneously human beings have both basic needs and inexhaustible desires and wants. Rich or poor, we all crave better security and quality of life – and our wants, charitable and responsible, or greedy and aspirational like that dream convertible or holiday home in France, are almost always greater than the limited means available to satisfy them. So there you have the fundamental economic problem: what, how and for whom to produce, how to finance this and how to intervene, manage and guide the whole political economy. How do you use what you've got to give people what they want?

ECONOMIC FACTORS

One enlightening way of looking at an economy is to break down the resources (**inputs**) we use to produce goods and services (**outputs**) into the three magic **factors of production**. If you decide to set up your own cake shop, then you'll find that you use all these factors in order to provide your customers with tasty cakes.

Land refers to raw materials drawn from the world's organic and inorganic resources – not just rolling fields but forests, deserts, jungles, arctic wastes, oceans, fossil fuels, minerals, the atmosphere, water, seeds, cows, goats, pigs, salmon, turkeys, etc – all of Mother Nature's bounty. The land your cake shop stands on obviously counts as land, but so do the natural materials you use in your baking, like wheat for your delicious muffins and the sugar cane for your fancy icing.

Capital is what we use to produce goods or services: money, factories, machinery and equipment that aid the work of humans in transforming inputs into outputs. Your financial investment in your cake shop and your oven, mixing bowls and spatulas are all capital.

Labour is the human effort (both brawn and brains) it takes to turn inputs into outputs via the production process. Thinking up ideas for delicious new recipes and your elbow grease mixing up the ingredients and baking them to perfection are examples of labour.

(You can also add **enterprise** as an extra 'fourth factor' on the inputs side of the model to cover the way resources require organisation, trade networks and systems in order for them to be transformed into outputs. Your nous in combining all the other factors in your cake business counts as enterprise.)

Outputs are the vast variety of goods or services produced, from fish fingers to computers, from transport to retailing, from DVDs and haircuts to doorbells and sleigh bells and schnitzel with noodles. In your cake shop, your brownies, cupcakes, Danish pastries and Bakewell tarts are all outputs.

The questions of what to produce, how to organise economic factors to produce it and for whom it should be produced, are answered in most societies by three sectors: **the private sector** (privately owned, and some-times publicly quoted, commercial organisations primarily motivated by gains in cash flow, profits or asset appreciation) whose output is measured by revenues and profits, but whose gains may also include the rise in price of property and other investments; **the public sector** (governments that tax, borrow and spend to provide infrastructure and services and to regulate society); and **the voluntary sector** (non-profit-making organisations like charities and NGOs) motivated by religious, social and cultural aims.

A **mixed economy** is one that involves a combination of these three sectors. A **command economy**, such as the former Soviet Union, only involves the public sector as the government makes all economic decisions and ultimately owns everything, supposedly on behalf of their people. A **free market economy**, in contrast, is one in which all economic decisions are taken by the private sector. In practice, all economies are subject to national and international laws, taxes and regulations, so free market economies exist only in theory.

GREAT SCOT! ADAM SMITH: FOUNDER OF MODERN ECONOMICS

Eminent Scot, philosopher and economist Adam Smith was born in Fife, in 1723. He went to Glasgow University at the grand old age of fourteen and then on to Oxford, returning to Scotland in 1748 to lecture at Edinburgh, where he formed a close friendship with fellow sage David Hume. In 1763 he left academia to work as a tutor, a position which took him on a tour through France and Switzerland, bringing him into contact with the works of French philosophers Voltaire, Rousseau, Quesnay and Turgot. On his return to Kirkcaldy he began his great theory of economics, *An Inquiry into the Nature and Causes of the Wealth of Nations*.

The central idea of *The Wealth of Nations* was the call for '**an open and free market**': Smith was writing at a time when trade was heavily taxed and licensed. He argued that if individuals were released from these constraints to strive to better themselves, the prosperity of the whole of society would follow; this is known as the principle of '**the invisible hand**'. Most people assume the invisible hand refers to the influence of the laws of supply and demand, but in fact it refers to the way individuals following their own ends are naturally guided towards the public good, which is achieved automatically by relying on the free market. This is central to 'liberal' economics and the case for unrestricted capitalism – questioned by many today in the wake of the recent recession.

The Wealth of Nations is the founding text of the school of classical economics, which emphasised economic freedom and had a profound and long-lasting effect on politics and economics, not least encouraging the nineteenth-century governmental attitude of laissez-faire (literally meaning 'allow to do') and free trade held by Britain for most of that century.

CONSUMER POWER: ECONOMIC AGENTS

Economists, jolly old fellows that they are, spend a lot of time tapping their pencils against their desks and thinking about economic agents, those people or institutions whose decisions are key in influencing economic performance. You might be pleased to learn that you are undoubtedly one of these agents yourself, and it's even possible that you're involved in all three of the major overlapping groups they belong to. It may not be quite as exciting as being a secret agent but it is a role with immense power and responsibility nonetheless.

Consumers: Unless you live in a cave eating grass and drinking rainwater it's highly likely you fall into this category. As consumers, we're motivated in our billions by a huge variety of incentives, but economists need to make simplifying assumptions about us in order to analyse our actions – women, for example, tend to buy more books than men, the middle classes tend to eat out more – it's not rocket science, but it's crucial when it comes to solving the economic problem.

Firms: Whether private, public or voluntary, firms can have different incentives, but they must all make enough revenue to pay the costs they incur, including the costs of borrowing money, while providing and selling **goods** and **services.**

Governments: Governments legislate, guide and instruct individuals and firms and their relationships. Developed economies have highly evolved laws and social and national security services such as health, education, welfare, police and army. Governments borrow, raise and spend taxes, which vary according to political priorities: left-wing or social-democratic governments tend to redistribute some income from the relatively rich to the poor, whereas right-wing or conservative governments will tend to pursue policies of less intervention: to lessen taxes and allow private firms to operate in a freer market.

HOW ECONOMIES WORK (OR NOT): SOME KEY ECONOMIC CONCEPTS

Supply and Demand

At its simplest, consumers and taxpayers demand – be it a new washing machine or an appendectomy – and producers and governments supply. But, in reality, everyone both supplies and demands. Demand is how much of a product (goods or services) we, as economic agents, pay for (directly or indirectly). **Unmet demand** is how much of a product we are prepared to buy, but cannot – this is vividly illustrated at toyshops every Christmas where queues of desperate parents line up to attempt to hand over their cash for the latest talking doll or furry alien teddy that happens to be de rigueur among their progeny. Usually the lucky toy company hasn't anticipated this surge in popularity and unmet demand results.

The Price Is Right

Our choices when it comes to buying are dictated by our personal priorities (you probably buy less bacon if you're a vegetarian) and also by our ability to pay, which is affected by our income and by pricing (if you loved bacon, you still might buy less of it if it suddenly started costing £50 a packet). **Price elasticity of demand** is the measure of how much a change in price affects demand – generally, the higher the price, the lower the demand. Prices adjust to demand and demand adjusts to prices, but other factors can also cause shifts in demand, such as fluctuating incomes, fashion tastes and the price, quality and service of competing goods. **Price elasticity of supply** is the measure of how responsive supply is, up or down, to changes in price. The price at which supply and demand are equal is the **equilibrium price**.

Economies and Diseconomies of Scale

You may have heard the impressive phrase 'economies of scale' being bandied about and felt slightly baffled, but this is a simple concept. Basically, quite often the more you make of something, the less each individual item costs to produce. For example, if you make five pairs of shoes to the same design, then the designer's fee is only split between five. If you make 50,000 shoes using the same design then this cost is split 50,000 ways. It's also likely that the raw materials will cost less per shoe if you buy them in large quantities. The cost of producing each shoe is called the **unit cost**. Economy of scale is a reduction in unit cost caused by division of labour, bulk buying, spreading overheads (the operating expenses of a business such as renting premises, photocopiers, electricity, etc.) or through a firm's market power increasing as it wins more market share, and so on. It's also possible that as a firm grows, unit costs can rise, causing a **diseconomy of scale**: a company that grows very large might become a more bureaucratic, soulless organisation that fails to motivate its employees to work as hard as they did before, possibly leading to them stealing more stationery in order to try to find some meagre job satisfaction and consequently increasing overheads.

Monopolies and other Menaces: Market Failure

The drastic-sounding event of market failure occurs when resources aren't allocated efficiently, which results in the economy not working in a way that is beneficial to society as a whole. Because of this, market failure often justifies government intervention. If left entirely to private firms who are solely interested in turning a profit, **public goods** – such as roads, lighthouses, parks or police services – and **merit goods** – such as education, healthcare and libraries – which are good for society in general, would be underproduced because they don't create profits, so governments tend to provide these.

Another form of market failure is **anti-competitive practice** by big, bad monopolies or market abuse by oligopoly suppliers, where a few large suppliers collude to unfairly dominate a market. Market-based economies rely on competition to keep costs down, and when a particular product is in the hands of a very small number of suppliers the result is often excessively high prices, which is detrimental to society as a whole.

Market failure also comes about because of the imperfect knowledge of economic agents. Consumers are often not equipped to know what the long-term costs or benefits of certain products are or if they will fulfil their precise needs, so they don't necessarily buy things that are good for society – hence the roaring trade in fizzy drinks, heroin and 4 x 4s. Other examples are estate agents price-fixing or applicants for mortgages 'self-certifying' their income (such irresponsible latitude caused much of the sub-prime mortgage crisis).

Recession or Depression?

Recession is a word that strikes fear into the heart – bringing with it anxiety over salary cuts, unemployment, house repossessions, an end to exotic holidays and general gloom. A recession is usually defined as negative economic growth over two successive quarters (six months) or longer. Since the Second World War, Britain has seen recessions in 1974, 1975, 1980, 1981, 1991 and 2008. Hearteningly, recessions are expected by many economists and seen as unavoidable low points at the beginning or end of an **economic cycle** (also called a **business** or **credit cycle**). The average peak to trough of these cycles, judging by the last ten, takes one year, and recovery to the next peak takes roughly six years. Each cycle appears to have unique triggers, which is why there is no precise agreement about what causes recessions. Cycles can be global, or regional, or specific to individual countries. However, even though stalwart economists see recessions as normal, prolonged economic downturns without the usual recovery are much scarier creatures, known as depressions, such as the Great Depression of the 1930s. A well-known and somewhat bleak economist's joke defines a recession as when your neighbour loses his job and a depression as when you lose yours.

'In this world nothing can be said to be certain, except death and taxes': Fiscal Policy

Fiscal policy is the government's plan to balance tax revenues and public spending. It can be altered to change the distribution of income and to influence income and spending in the economy. Raising revenue and allocating spending is what the **Budget** is all about – every November the British government sets out its pre-Budget plans and delivers its final plan in March. Just over 60% of government revenue is drawn from those unavoidable top taxes: National Insurance (which is a **proportional tax** as everyone pays the same percentage of their income), income tax (which is a **progressive tax** as those who earn more pay more: once you earn over a certain amount you jump from paying 20% of your income to the government to paying 40%) and **VAT** or **sales tax** (which are **regressive taxes**, as they cost proportionally more of the income of those who earn less). And where does your hard-earned spondulicks, handed over in this way, go? Currently, social services, health and education account for just over 60% of government spending. During a recession, government expenditure tends to increase as more demands are placed on the welfare system when employment falls. This effect is known as an **automatic stabiliser**. When a government raises more revenue than it will spend this is called a **budget surplus**; when government spending is equal to revenue this is called a **balanced budget**; and when spending exceeds revenue you end up with a **budget deficit**. Ideally, fiscal policy should be run according to the **golden rule**, which states that governments should use tax revenue to fund everyday spending and only borrow to invest in the future, meaning that over the course of an economic cycle the current budget should not end up in deficit.

Money, Money, Money: Monetary Policy

Along with fiscal policy, monetary policy is the key component of a government's control over its country's economy. It is able to change the central bank discount rate (in the UK this is the Bank of England base rate) in order to influence the commercial banks' interest rates, the money supply, inflation and exchange rates. Lower interest rates make debt cheaper but also lower the incentive to save money.

TO REGULATE OR NOT TO REGULATE: JOHN MAYNARD KEYNES

Born into an affluent family in Cambridge in 1883, John Maynard Keynes (pronounced 'Canes') studied at Eton and then at Cambridge University, where he read Mathematics before turning his hand to Economics. He joined the Treasury and, at the end of the First World War, attended the 1919 Paris Peace Conference, from which he resigned in protest. What he witnessed in Paris prompted him to write *The Economic Consequences of Peace*. It became an instant best-seller, in part because of the fruity prose with which he demolished the Allied leaders. In it he argued that the hefty reparations demanded of Germany in the Treaty of Versailles would result in terrible ill feeling and revenge, and history proved him chillingly prophetic.

Keynes was an economic optimist and an extraordinarily gifted chap. He was a shrewd investor and built his own fortune twice (the second time after the calamitous Wall Street Crash); was a lover of the painter Duncan Grant; married the ballerina Lydia Lopokova; was close to the Bloomsbury set of Virginia Woolf, Vanessa Bell and Lytton Strachey; was chums with Bertrand Russell and Ludwig Wittgenstein, as well as many economists and politicians including Franklin D. Roosevelt and Winston Churchill; and was a founder of the Arts Council and a collector of paintings by Cézanne, Degas, Picasso, Braque, Seurat and Modigliani.

In 1936 Keynes published his most famous work, *The General Theory of Employment, Interest and Money*. His basic idea contradicted the neo-classical **Say's Law**, the counter-intuitive idea that 'supply creates its own demand'. Keynes argued that in times of recession the government should run **fiscal deficits** (spending more than it receives in tax income) to stimulate the economy and keep unemployment down. When the private sector will not invest or consume enough and there is excessive saving in the economy, the government should take up the slack by investing more, by increasing spending on public works for example, even if it means sharply increasing the national debt. After initial resistance, President Roosevelt adopted this policy with considerable success in the 1930s with his New Deal, lifting America out of the Great Depression.

Keynes's ideas persisted long after his death in 1946 in the period of 'post-war consensus politics' up to the 1973 oil crisis when all major industrialised countries plunged into recession and stock markets crashed. As inflation and unemployment together both took off and stayed high for the next twenty years, **monetarism** (see below) displaced Keynesianism as the dominant economic orthodoxy. Keynesian theory lost the attention of governments, until 2008–9, when a global recession ensued and world leaders including the American president, Barack Obama, and British prime minister, Gordon Brown, embraced Keynes once more.

IT'S ALL ABOUT THE MONEY:
MONETARISM AND MILTON FRIEDMAN

Born in New York City in 1912, Milton Friedman studied Economics at Rutgers University and joined the Division of War Research at Columbia University where he got his PhD in 1945. He later took a position at the University of Chicago where he stayed for thirty years and also worked at the National Bureau of Economic Research on the role of money in the business cycle. There, in 1963, with Anna Schwartz, an economic historian, he published *A Monetary History of the United States, 1867–1960* which postulated that 'inflation is always and everywhere a monetary phenomenon'. Friedman opposed government regulation of all kinds, including wage and price controls, as is shown in his influential book, *Capitalism and Freedom*. But he is probably best known, alongside Friedrich Hayek, as the father of the Chicago School of Economics and of **monetarism,** which is a modern version of the **quantity theory of money**.

The original quantity theorists were Nicolaus Copernicus, Jean Bodin, John Locke, David Hume and John Stuart Mill who stated that the average price level is determined by the quantity of money in circulation, given a fixed quantity of both real output (capacity) and velocity of money (how often money changes hands). **Velocity of money** is a very old idea in classical economics but it isn't much studied because it is tough to measure. The idea is that if money changes hands more quickly than before this is the same as if there were more money. As people left farms and villages to live in cities, the economy grew simply because more and more of daily life had to be paid for using money (instead of chickens or pigs or daughters). To understand this you need to know that the economy is only what is measurable by money!

Monetarism advises taming the economic cycle by simply controlling a country's money supply, such as via central bank interest rates.

In contrast to Keynes and his disciples, Friedman and his followers offered a simple solution to economic problems that conservative politicians could eagerly embrace. These famously included Jimmy Carter, Margaret Thatcher, Ronald Reagan, both Presidents George Bush, and many of their contemporaries in monetarism's heyday, from the 1980s until the noughties. Reducing government management of the economy to just the control of the money supply supported the idea that smaller government is better government. Monetarism thus provided an economic reason for dealing with economic problems by cutting government spending and privatising public spending programmes, transferring as much of the economy as possible to the private sector.

MICRO- OR MACRO-: HOW DO WE KNOW IF AN ECONOMY IS SUCCESSFUL?

Success is easy to comprehend for a business but not for a whole economy. It is tempting to consider a national economy to be a business on a grand scale, but is it? **Micro-** is very different from **macro-economics**. The former can be about individual businesses or a specific geographic locality or economic sector, whereas macro-economics deals with the big picture, the whole country or continent or even the whole world. Fiscal and monetary actions by governments are both part of macro-economics. The difference between the micro- and macro- is vast in scale.

In macro-economics, there are various concepts that measure how an economy's output is doing in money terms, and whether it is successful or not.

GDP: Gross domestic product is the total value of goods and services produced in a year within a country.

GNP: Gross national product is GDP plus income earned by a country's citizens abroad, minus investment income earned in the country by foreigners.

Wealth: Wealth comprises the value of property, investment and savings less debts. Wealth can be divided between cash, near cash, marketable and unmarketable assets. This term is not used much by economists, but is important to accountants and bankers when measuring companies' and households' financial situations. The national wealth of the UK is not a precise figure but it is more than seven times **national income** (the total amount of money earned within the country in a year).

Economic growth: This looks at percentage changes of GDP over time, and can show whether a country's economy is expanding or shrinking. Rich countries measure success as 2.5% annual growth on top of a 2–2.5% inflation rate. The economic figures that are quoted most often are **real** or **inflation-adjusted**, as opposed to current price, values. It is important to know that GDP figures are measured by a common worldwide standard of national income accounts. These deal in **weighted average** (aggregate) figures, by which we mean that if an economy grows by 3%, for example, this represents the balance of growth in some parts and contraction in others.

Inflation: Inflation – or increase in prices – is bad for consumers if prices rise faster than incomes. If prices rise faster at home than abroad, such as when domestic inflation occurs or the currency rises against other currencies, export goods become less price-attractive and imports more price-competitive. There are several measures of prices: the **consumer price index** (CPI) is based on a mixture of basic goods and services but excludes owner-occupied housing costs; the **retail price index** (RPI) is similar but includes owner-occupied housing costs; **core inflation** excludes items that are especially volatile to price movements like food and energy; and **headline inflation** is a measure of the total inflation that occurs including price hikes such as local taxes or rail tickets.

Unemployment: This is a key measure of the success or failure of an economy. It constitutes the proportion of the potential workforce registered as unemployed, excluding those in education or who are unable to work for age or health reasons.

Balance of payments: This is the measure of all money spent and received between different countries, including the balance of trade and the balance of non-trade payments such as transfers, investment inflows and outflows, investment income, interest and tax payments across a country's borders, and grants-in-aid to poor countries and NGOs such as the UN and, in Europe, to and from the European Commission. The net total is a **current account surplus** or **deficit**.

∽ ECONOMICS ∽
TEST PAPER

1. Which of the following is NOT a factor of production?

a) capital
b) labour
c) land
d) services

2. If the velocity of money in an economy is high then:

a) a small money supply is required to allow a high number of purchases
b) a large money supply is required to allow a high number of purchases

3. What sector do the Samaritans belong to?

a) private
b) public
c) voluntary

4. Who wrote *An Inquiry into the Nature and Causes of the Wealth of Nations?*

a) Milton Friedman
b) Gordon Brown
c) Adam Smith
d) Aristotle

5. What caused the 1973 recession?

a) the OPEC oil crisis
b) the sub-prime mortgage crisis
c) the US savings and loans crisis

6. A command economy:

a) involves a combination of public, private and voluntary sectors
b) only involves the public sector
c) only involves the private sector
d) only involves the voluntary sector

7. If tickets for a rush-hour train from Waterloo to Guildford are always oversubscribed, how price-elastic do you think the tickets are?

a) very elastic
b) inelastic
c) bouncy

8. In 1867 Karl Marx published which key work of economics:

a) *The Communist Manifesto*
b) *Duck Soup*
c) *On Liberty*
d) *Das Kapital*

9. The invisible hand means that:

a) in following self-interested aims individuals achieve prosperity for society
b) in following self-interested aims individuals achieve negative growth for society
c) supply will always equal demand
d) demand will always equal supply

10. Unmet demand is:

a) overstocks from excessive supply
b) crucial for a healthy economy
c) how much of a product consumers are prepared to buy but cannot
d) disastrous for an economy

11. **The total value of goods and services produced by a country including income earned by its citizens abroad is known as:**

a) GNE
b) GNP
c) GDP

12. **If a product is perfectly inelastic, in terms of price, what does this mean?**

a) if the price changes, demand changes dramatically
b) if the price changes, demand does not change
c) if the price changes, demand ceases

13. *The Wealth of Nations* **is considered the founding text of:**

a) neoclassical economics
b) Keynesian economics
c) classical economics
d) home economics

14. **If it costs you £36 to make 40 cupcakes, what is your unit cost?**

a) 90p
b) £4
c) 40p
d) £1

15. **What is an oligopoly?**

a) a type of sea anemone
b) a board game featuring horse races
c) a market with very few sellers
d) a market with one seller

16. **Which of the following is NOT a merit good?**

a) education
b) libraries
c) cigarettes
d) health care

17. A recession is usually defined as:

a) negative economic growth over two successive quarters
b) positive economic growth over three successive quarters
c) negative economic growth over three successive quarters
d) negative economic growth over two different quarters

18. Who said 'In this world nothing can be said to be certain, except death and taxes'?

a) Abraham Lincoln
b) Milton Friedman
c) Thomas Malthus
d) Benjamin Franklin

19. An economic situation is Pareto-efficient when:

a) there is no way to rearrange things to make anyone better off without making someone else worse off
b) there are several ways to rearrange things to make someone better off without making anyone else worse off

20. National Insurance is a:

a) regressive tax
b) progressive tax
c) proportional tax

21. When a government raises more revenue than it will spend it is left with:

a) a balance budget
b) a budget surplus
c) a budget deficit

22. Lower interest rates:

a) make it more expensive to have debts
b) make goods and services more expensive
c) make it cheaper to have debts
d) make it more profitable to save money

23. Which economist lost his fortune in the Wall Street Crash?

a) John Maynard Keynes
b) Karl Marx
c) Jean-Baptiste Say
d) Alan Greenspan

24. Which US president was responsible for the New Deal of the 1930s?

a) Franklin D. Roosevelt
b) Harry S. Truman
c) George Washington
d) Woodrow Wilson

25. When was the International Monetary Fund set up?

a) 1939
b) 1944
c) 1956
d) 1960

26. In terms of factors of production, what are fish categorised as?

a) labour
b) land
c) capital
d) enterprise

27. Increasing the money supply in an economy generally leads to:

a) deflation
b) inflation

28. What is fiat money?

29. What is commodity money?

30. *The General Theory of Employment, Interest and Money* **was written by:**

a) Adam Smith
b) Karl Marx
c) John Stuart Mill
d) John Maynard Keynes

❧ ART ❧
AND
DESIGN

The art world can seem daunting, impenetrable and achingly pretentious to the uninitiated, but the truth is that we humans respond to shape, colour, contrast and light from our earliest days, and we should not allow these skills to desert us as we travel through the journey of life. Art is a mark of our civilisation and achievement, and the greatest of it can move us to tears, joy, laughter or terror. This chapter will take your hand and lead you through the maze of modern art, help you to get savvy with sculpture, peruse the *pièces de résistance* of pop art and show you once and for all that the *Angel of the North* is not your great-aunt Nora from Newcastle. It will also fuse the practical and the creative for all you budding Botticellis, showing you how to paint an oil painting, how to take the perfect photograph, as well as key art-restoration techniques. For the theorists and thinkers among you, we'll tackle the age-old debate between form and function, and examine the history of design movements from Le Corbusier to Memphis.

EASEL PEASY: HOW TO PAINT
AN OIL PAINTING

Since the sixteenth century, oil painting has generally been regarded as the most impressive and expert medium to paint in. Artists from Rembrandt to Rothko have displayed superb mastery of the form. Perhaps you too have an oleaginous illusionist lurking within? Before you can even think of classing yourself with Jan Van Eyck, it's essential to prepare yourself with a well-stretched canvas and get to grips with three slippery paint ingredients.

- **Fixed or drying oils** dry and bind pigments in a flexible and tough 'skin'. Cold-pressed linseed oil is well regarded as it dries reasonably fast and is clean and clear.

- **Essential oils** evaporate, and therefore are used as thinners to disperse paints that have already been applied. Turpentine and white spirit are the most common.

- **Resins and balsams** add a transparent protective layer in varnishes, improving clarity and making pictures glossy. Examples include the exotic-sounding Venice turpentine, dammar resin, mastic and copal.

There is no magic combination of pigments that will guarantee your genius; generally, though, the rule of 'fat over lean' should be followed: finer paint with more oil (fat) should be painted over coarser-ground paint with less oil (lean). Lean oil paint dries faster than fat oil paint, so a layer should never be leaner than the previous one or it will dry first, making it susceptible to cracking.

RESCUE MISSIONS: A BRIEF GUIDE TO PICTURE RESTORATION

Before we initiate you into the heroic mysteries of reviving damaged masterpieces, it's important to be clear that there are two distinct jobs involved here. **Picture conservators** are chemists with an interest in art and **picture restorers** are artists with an interest in a day job. Both are involved in preserving a work from the ravages of time, nature and human beings. Below you will find a short guide to the kinds of travail they undertake to safeguard our artistic heritage.

Relining: The application of a new canvas to the reverse of an oil painting, at one time using glue, but normally now using a mixture of beeswax and resin melted through the old canvas onto the back of the paint layer. This not only flattens out lumpy canvases and welds tears together but also re-adheres any bits of flaking paint. The process also strengthens old works of art and gives them some protection from damp. In extreme cases where the original canvas has to be removed, the painting is protected from the front with thick layers of wax and release paper and the canvas is physically dismantled from the back, thread by painstaking thread.

Cradling: The application of wooden or metal straps to the back of a panel to correct warping or hold split pieces together.

Surface cleaning: Basically dusting; removing any surface dirt but leaving the original varnish intact.

Cleaning: Removing discoloured varnish and any other grime using solvents such as acetone and alcohol in varying strengths of solution. In certain cases, pictures are cleaned using scalpels rather than chemicals. Frescoes, having no varnish layer, are cleaned using a wide variety of methods, including rubbing with breadcrumbs.

Filling: All restorers have their preferred material for filling in areas of missing paint (a mixture of rabbit-skin glue and chalk used to be popular). Once the filler has been applied and allowed to dry, it is scraped down with a scalpel and rubbed with champagne corks until it is precisely flush with the surrounding paint.

Retouching: There are two ways to retouch, either to paint in the missing bit so that the naked eye cannot tell the difference from the original or to stipple the area with dots of colour that blend together from a distance and give the impression that the picture is intact.

Revarnishing: Mouldy or yellowed old glazes often need to be removed when cleaning a painting. Because this process can damage the paint below, restorers try to leave a very thin layer of the original varnish if possible. Once cleaning and retouching have been completed, a new layer of varnish is applied, often using a spray gun to achieve an even coat.

**WHEN GOOD PAINTINGS GO BAD:
TYPES OF DAMAGE**

Crackelure: crazing of the varnish or paint layer.

Islanding: breaking up of the paint layer into pools or patches of colour leaving exposed **ground** (background).

Overpaint: areas of paint applied by a previous restorer (or prudish owner keen to hide naughty bits behind fig leaves).

Yellowing: varnish discolouring with age, becoming jaundiced or brownish and obscuring the original colours and details.

Bitumen: a nasty chemical used in dark paint, mostly in the nineteenth century, which turns lumpy and treacly with time and is extremely deleterious.

STEALING BEAUTY: ART CRIME

The theft of treasure is nothing new but stealing art has captured the public imagination in a way few other crimes can hope to. But despite its sexy, glamorous connotations, art crime is the third highest grossing criminal enterprise worldwide, behind only drugs and arms trafficking. It hauls in a healthy profit of £1–4 billion annually, most of which goes to fund international organised crime syndicates, even terrorists.

Missing *Mona Lisa*
In 1911 the story goes that the self-styled Marqués Eduardo de Valfierno allegedly paid for the *Mona Lisa* to be stolen from the Louvre in Paris to help him sell various forgeries of it he had commissioned. It was recovered in 1913, when the cheeky fellow who had pinched it directly off the wall and hidden it under his clothes, Louvre employee Vincenzo Peruggia, tried to sell it to a Florentine art dealer.

Mislaid Munch
On the eve of the Winter Olympics in 1994 a gang of thieves stole Edvard Munch's *The Scream* from Norway's National Gallery. They broke in and escaped with the painting in less than a minute, leaving behind a handwritten taunt reading 'Thanks for the poor security'. The Norwegian government received a ransom demand of $1 million, but because they never had proof that those demanding the ransom actually had the painting, they refused to pay it. *The Scream* was eventually found undamaged later that year in a hotel near Oslo. As if this wasn't enough, another version of the painting was stolen in 2004 before being recovered in 2006.

Very Nearly Vermeer

Art crime is not restricted to theft but also extends to the sensational world of fakes. Some of the world's best forgeries may still be lingering in private or even museum collections. Faking a great work of art is the easy bit; providing the authentication for each work is the genius of the con. Hans Van Meegeren was a master forger who managed to trick the Nazis. In 1937, he submitted his first forgery, a supposedly unknown Vermeer titled *The Supper at Emmaus*, to Abraham Bredius, a prominent art critic. With Bredius fooled, Van Meegeren painted six more masterpieces, netting him a cool $60 million. But his crimes caught up with him when he was accused of collaborating with the Nazis by selling a Vermeer to Hermann Goering. He was charged with treason and in his defence admitted his forgeries. Ironically, he had to paint his final 'Vermeer' at his trial in order to prove his innocence. In the end he was sentenced to a year's imprisonment for deception.

HOW TO SPOT A FAKE

These days, we can avoid embarrassing moments on the *Antiques Roadshow* by relying on technology to tell a fake from the genuine piece of art in granny's attic. Increasingly, the art world is starting to use Fourier Transform Infrared (FTIR) and Raman microscopes to authenticate art pieces. Both provide a nifty way of identifying ingredients in a surface coating, reducing the need to chip off a sample of the paint. FTIR microscopes shoot infrared light at an artwork and measure what parts of the infrared spectrum the paints absorb before matching them to known pieces.

Of course, all this fancy equipment comes at a price; the FTIR could set you back £70,000. Better instead to start by studying some genuine works of the painter whose daubs you want to acquire to see if you can identify common denominators. Before you part with your hard-earned cash, get some serious connoisseurs and art scholars to cast an expert eye over the works with which you're planning to brighten up your living-room wall – chances are, they will detect any funny business.

PROGRESSIVE PIONEERS:
HEROES OF MODERN ART

Many sniff at modern art, especially when exhibiting a urinal seems to bring fame and fortune, but only a philistine would dismiss it out of hand. Yes, maybe you could do it, but no, you didn't. Modern art generally refers to work created since the latter part of the nineteenth century. Think of all the 'isms' and you have some of the major movements, from Impressionism in the 1870s all the way through to symbolism and art nouveau, Fauvism and expressionism, cubism, Futurism and constructivism, Dada and surrealism and abstract expressionism.

Wassily Kandinsky (1866–1944)
Kandinsky was one of the founding fathers of abstract painting and was also at the centre of two important groups – *Der Blaue Reiter* (Blue Rider) and Bauhaus. During his Bauhaus period he enjoyed growing fame and had his first one-man show in New York. Kandinsky often attempted to translate the experience of music into painted form and he laid the foundations for non-representational art in his three important series, *Impressions*, *Improvisations* and *Compositions*.

Painting to know: *Impression III (Concert)*(1911).

Henri Matisse (1869–1954)
Born in north-eastern France in 1869, Matisse was given a box of paints by his mother while recovering from appendicitis, kick-starting his genius. He became one of the founders of the Salon d'Automne in 1903 and showed his work with that of a group of his friends in 1905 to great acclaim. The art critic Louis Vauxcelles dubbed the group the 'Fauves' or 'wild beasts' and, as their leader, Matisse became known as the 'king of the beasts'. (Louis Vauxcelles had a knack for labelling art trends; he also invented the term 'cubists'.) He liberated his paintings from convention, using bold dots of pure colour and distorted form to express his inner emotions.

Painting to know: *The Green Line* (1905).

Pablo Picasso (1881–1973)

Pablo Picasso is often considered the most important artist of the modernist period. Together with Georges Braque, he is acknowledged as one of the fathers of cubism. As a child, Picasso's artistic talents developed at a prodigious speed and he held his first exhibition in 1901 in Paris. Picasso was part of an exclusive group of artists who lived in Montmartre and he counted Gertrude Stein as one of his patrons. Before he embarked on cubism, he went through a **Blue Period**, inspired by his friend Casamegas' suicide and characterised by a predominantly blue palette (as you might expect), and a **Rose Period**. In 1906–7, he painted *Les Demoiselles d'Avignon*, a great canvas filled with five enormous women, naked and half naked in their glorified ugliness. *Demoiselles* shocked the art world with its distorted forms. In 1912, Picasso began using collage, sticking objects onto canvases instead of painting them, a style which later became known as **synthetic cubism**. In the period between the world wars, Picasso reverted to classicism briefly and also toyed with surrealism. In 1937 he painted *Guernica* for the Spanish Pavilion in the Paris Universalle as a severe condemnation of the German bombing of the town. Picasso was prolific even in his old age, producing no less than 347 works in the space of seven months in 1968.

Painting to know: *Guernica* (1937).

Georges Braque (1882–1963)

Georges Braque was born in Argenteuil in the northwestern suburbs of Paris. One of the founding fathers of cubism with Picasso, Braque changed his style of painting dramatically after seeing Picasso's seminal work *Les Demoiselles d'Avignon*, which inspired him to paint *Nude* in the same style, with bold strokes, reinventing the world and its objects as he saw them.

Painting to know: *Still Life with Herrings* (c. 1909–11).

Edward Hopper (1882–1967)

Born in New York City, Hopper enrolled in a school for illustrators in New York but later transferred to the New York School of Art. His first one-man show was held at the Whitney Club in New York and the first major retrospective of his work took place at the Museum of Modern Art in 1933. Hopper painted an America of unfulfilled dreams – the alienation, disillusionment and loneliness of people in modern life, deserted streets, people alone in rooms, halls, offices, or far from home in hotels and motels. He is considered a cult figure in American painting and his filmic work greatly influenced the photorealists and pop artists of the 1960s.

Painting to know: *Nighthawks* (1942).

Marcel Duchamp (1887–1968)

Marcel Duchamp rejected conventional notions and practices, instead focusing on the *concept* of art as opposed to the *making* of art. Duchamp was a champion of the **Dadaists**, who wanted to wreak havoc within the art world. He used his work to provoke and challenge, and introduced the concept of the 'ready-made' – everyday objects that became elevated to objects of art by the artist's touch. *Fountain* is the most famous of his ready-mades: the original, which is now lost, was a standard urinal, laid flat on its back and signed with a pseudonym, 'R. Mutt 1917'.

Sculpture to know: *Fountain 1917* (replica 1964).

Mark Rothko (Marcus Rothkowitz) (1903–70)

Mark Rothko was born in Lithuania and emigrated to the United States in 1910. He was a founder, with Adolph Gottlieb, of The Ten, an abstract-expressionist group that sought to express a view of the world that was free from convention; to paint objects and events as though they were being seen for the first time. Rothko was an intellectual painter, inspired by Nietzsche and Mozart. He was concerned with finding his way through the transcendental and the mythical, using gigantic colour blocks in much of his work.

Painting to know: *Untitled* (*c.* 1958) Seagram mural in maroon, black, red and brown.

Salvador Dalí (1904–89)

Salvador Dalí was named after an older brother, whose premature death cast a shadow over his entire existence. Born in Figueras, Catalonia, he became the most famous surrealist painter. In 1921, he enrolled in the Academy of Fine Arts, in Madrid, and made friends with two important creative figures, the poet Federico García Lorca and the future film director Luis Buñuel. It was with Buñuel that he created the seminal film *Un Chien Andalou*, which created uproar when it was first shown in early 1929: in the first seventeen minutes, the audience saw its most famous and terrifying moment – a razor blade slicing an eye.

Picture to know: *The Persistence of Memory* (1931).

Francis Bacon (1909–92)

Francis Bacon was born in Dublin and moved to London in 1925. In 1945, he exhibited the triptych *Three Studies for Figures at the Base of a Crucifixion* and became an overnight sensation. Bacon had a penchant for the perverse and his work sought to reflect the horror and violence of modern existence as he saw it. Following his second retrospective in the Tate Gallery in 1962, he cemented his reputation as a major force in the international art world. Some of his most acclaimed triptychs are devoted to the death of his lover, George Dyer, who committed suicide the night before Bacon's retrospective in Paris in 1971.

Painting to know: *Three Studies for Figures at the Base of a Crucifixion* (1944).

Jackson Pollock (1912–56)

Jackson Pollock was born on a sheep ranch in Wyoming and his family shuttled between California and Arizona throughout his childhood. In 1930, Pollock moved to New York and enrolled in the Art Students League. In the 1950s, he and a young group of New York artists came to be known as **abstract expressionists**. Pollock called himself an 'action painter': combining physical action with inner expression, laying out his canvas on the floor and painting direct from cans of commercial paint, dripping, splashing and flinging swirls of colour. Pollock was killed in a car accident in 1956.

Painting to know: *Number 1* (1950).

Joseph Beuys (1921–86)

Joseph Beuys was considered one of the most important German artists of the post-war period. Highly provocative, his work resists conventional categories. During the 1960s and 70s he was a major pioneer of performance art and was involved in launching a new art movement, Fluxus, which sought to blur the lines between art and life. In 1965, he performed one of his most important 'actions' or performances – *How to Explain Pictures to a Dead Hare*. In it, he carried a dead hare, talking to it and touching each item with its paw in an exhibition held at the Schmela Gallery in Düsseldorf. Sweet.

Work to know: *How to Explain Pictures to a Dead Hare* (1965).

Lucian Freud (1922–)
In May 2008, Russian billionaire Roman Abramovich bought Lucian Freud's *Benefits Supervisor Sleeping* for $33.6 million at a Christie's auction in New York, making it the most expensive work by a living painter. Freud is one of the leading figurative artists today, painting his sitters with unflinching honesty, lumps, bumps and all. Born in Berlin in 1922, the grandson of Sigmund, Freud came to England in 1933. In 1951, his painting *Interior at Paddington* won a prize at the Festival of Britain. He was shortlisted for the Turner Prize in 1988 and 1989 and awarded the Order of Merit in 1993. He lives and works in London.

Painting to know: *Large Interior W11* (*after Watteau*) (1981–3).

Dan Flavin (1933–96)
Dan Flavin was born in Queens, New York, and spent almost three decades exploring the artistic possibilities of fluorescent tubes. Sounds bonkers? Well, it's actually very beautiful. His work echoed the theoretical assumptions of Marcel Duchamp – he turned ordinary, utilitarian fluorescent tubes into works of art by isolating them and placing them within an environment of art. His significant large-scale projects include lighting the entire rotunda of the Guggenheim Museum in New York to commemorate its reopening in 1992; a permanent installation of nine works in a former firehouse and Baptist Church in Bridgehampton, New York; and the Kunstbau Lenbachhaus, Munich.

Light installation to know: *the nominal three (to William of Ockham)* (1963).

ART GOES POP!: ANDY WARHOL AND THE BIRTH OF POP ART

Born Andrew Warhola in Pittsburgh in 1928, Andy Warhol is considered by many to be the grandaddy of pop art. He was a sickly child, suffering from St Vitus's Dance which confined him to his bed, and isolated him from his peers. This sense of exclusion would be with him for his whole life, as would a morbid fear of illness and hospitals.

Warhol moved to New York City in 1949 and began his career as a commercial artist, producing elegant fashion drawings for *Vogue, Harper's Bazaar* and the *New Yorker*. But he found fame, fortune and notoriety in the 1960s when he headed the brand-new pop art movement. Pop art aimed to make the everyday part of the artist's vernacular: mass-produced and mass-media objects, from Campbell's soup cans to Coca-Cola bottles and iconic figures from the Queen and Chairman Mao to Marilyn Monroe and Elizabeth Taylor were Warhol's subjects.

Early work was painted, but later Warhol switched to silk screening – making mass production part of the process as well as the final artwork. The preoccupation with mass production shows in the name of his studio – the Factory – a huge space lined with silver foil and paint, populated by his 'superstars', women like Edie Sedgwick, who would become his muses. He courted celebrities, choosing as his subjects people like Mick Jagger, Brigitte Bardot and Liza Minnelli, but he was no sucker for stars' success; his wry comment that 'In the future everybody will be world famous for fifteen minutes' has proved spookily prescient – from *Big Brother* to *America's Next Top Model*, everyone's after their very own fifteen minutes. Warhol was also a prolific film-maker, and while many of his works took the everyday and mundane to what must surely be bone-crushingly boring extremes (see the eight-hour epic *Empire*, in which the idea is that by training the camera on the Empire State Building and barely touching it, the camera produces the art, without the artist's intervention), some, like *Chelsea Girls* and *Blow Job*, have become classics of the genre.

Warhol survived a shooting by radical feminist Valerie Solanas, founder and sole member of SCUM (Society for Cutting Up Men) in 1968. The story goes that Solanas, a playwright, gave Warhol a script for consideration, which he then lost. After admitting his carelessness, he offered her a part in his film *I, A Man*, and from this point onwards her behaviour became increasingly erratic and obsessive. She shot Warhol three times at the Factory on the afternoon of 3 June. He was badly injured and suffered side effects for the rest of his life. He died on 22 February 1987 from a heart attack after a gall bladder operation.

AN EXHIBITIONIST EXHIBITION: *SENSATION:*
Young British Artists from the Saatchi Collection, September
1997, Royal Academy of Arts

Many may scoff, but *Sensation* is one of the few art exhibitions that
really took modern art to the masses when it hit the headlines towards
the end of the twentieth century. It was a controversial exhibition,
mounted by the most influential contemporary art collector of the time,
Charles Saatchi, and it contained works by forty-six young British
conceptual artists, including Damien Hirst, Jake and Dinos Chapman,
Sarah Lucas, Tracey Emin, Marc Quinn, Gillian Wearing, Ron Mueck,
Rachel Whiteread, Chris Ofili and Marcus Harvey.

The most infamous works were Damien Hirst's preserved shark, *The
Physical Impossibility of Death in the Mind of Someone Living*; Tracey Emin's
tent, *Everyone I Have Ever Slept with 1963–1995*; Marcus Harvey's *Myra*,
a portrait of the child murderer Myra Hindley, comprised of hundreds
of children's handprints; Chris Ofili's *The Holy Virgin Mary*, a portrait
of a black Virgin Mary, made of elephant dung and pornographic maga-
zines; and Marc Quinn's *Self*, a sculpture of the artist's head made with
nine pints of his own blood. Critical and public response was intense:
the show was hugely popular but also attracted much condemnation.
Many art critics dismissed it as purely an exercise in shock tactics, and
members of the public were outraged by what they saw as obscene
and immoral works. The response to *Myra* was particularly vociferous, and
it was pelted with ink and eggs on the opening day. The Young British
Artists featured in the exhibition have gone on to be influential and
significant members of the British art world.

A DESIGN FOR LIFE:
TWENTIETH-CENTURY DESIGN

Modernism (c. 1914–39)

Modernism was more a way of thinking than a specific style. As North
America and Europe rapidly industrialised at the end of the nineteenth
century, the rise of mass production meant that many new inventions
– domestic appliances, gramophones, telephones – became increasingly

available to the general public. Modernists proposed that design should be purposeful, honest and free from fussy adornments, and, crucially, that 'form follows function'. This meant that design should work well as well as look good. After the horrors of the First World War, modernists imagined a better world and thought that technology was the key means to achieving social improvement.

Modernism flourished in Holland (**De Stijl**) and Germany (**Bauhaus**), as well as Moscow (**Constructivism**), Prague and Paris (**l'Esprit Nouveau**). Designers in America, Europe and Scandinavia explored the use of new materials like fibreglass, plastic and plywood, such as Charles Eames with his lounge chair and ottoman, made with plywood, leather and metal; Finnish designer Alvar Aalto and his 'X' stool; and Arne Jacobsen's Egg chair which was constructed of moulded fibreglass, upholstered with foam rubber and then covered in material and supported by a chromed steel pedestal.

CORB: A MODERNIST GIANT

Le Corbusier (1887–1965) was a prominent figure in modernist circles in France, remaining at the forefront of the movement until after the Second World War. He was actively engaged in the arts, urban planning, architecture and design, as well as writing several significant theoretical texts. His celebrated Pavilion de l'Esprit Nouveau was a purpose-built house that embraced fully modernist ideas of standardisation, mass production and new materials. Furnishings included bentwood chairs, tables, modular built-in cabinets and shelving which divided the open-plan space into living, dining and study areas. The idea behind this living unit was, simply, a 'machine for living in'.

Famous works: Villa Savoye, in Poissy, and the Le Corbusier chaise longue.

Bauhaus (1919–33)
Established by Walter Gropius, a pioneer of modernist architecture, the Bauhaus was a leading proponent of the modernist aesthetic. It was a revolutionary school, replacing the traditional teacher–student relationship with the idea of a community of artists working together. Famous teachers include Wassily Kandinsky, Paul Klee, László Moholy-Nagy and Anni Albers. Its influence was immense and is still reflected in many

areas of design today. Students of the Bauhaus designed purpose-built housing, using prefabricated materials such as steel and concrete, as well as the interior furnishings. This was intended for public housing that could be built cheaply and in a short period of time, a pressing need following the war. The Bauhaus was closed by the Nazis in 1933.

Molto Memphis

In 1980 Ettore Sottsass, one of Italy's great architects, met with a group of young architects and designers with plans to design and produce a line of furniture. This collective was named after the Bob Dylan song 'Stuck Inside of Mobile with the Memphis Blues Again' which stuck repeatedly at 'Memphis Blues Again' on Sottsass's record player. Memphis design was free from formula, set designs, colours or decorations, and it broke the rules by using unconventional materials, ground-breaking shapes, kitsch motifs and gaudy colours. Interestingly, it was Karl Lagerfeld's choice of furniture for his Monte Carlo apartment.

ASPIRATIONAL ARCHITECTURE: FIVE GREAT LIVING SPACES TO COVET

Isokon Building (1934)

Architect: Wells Coates

Style: Modernist

Where: London, UK

What to say: One of the first modernist apartments with built-in Isokon furniture and home to many high-profile refugees from Nazi Germany, including Marcel Breuer and Walter Gropius, as well as doyenne of crime writing, Agatha Christie.

Fallingwater (1939)

Architect: Frank Lloyd Wright

Style: Modernist

Where: Bear Run, Pennsylvania, USA

What to say: Wright's most famous work – you practically live inside the surrounding beautiful scenery.

Case Study House No. 8 (The Eames House) (1949)

Architects: Charles and Ray Eames

Style: International

Where: Pacific Palisades, California, USA

What to say: A semi-prefabricated house made of a steel frame and coloured panels.

Malin Residence ('Chemosphere') (1960)

Architect: John Lautner

Style: Modernist

Where: West Hollywood, California, USA

What to say: Commissioned by the original owner to perch high above his in-laws' residence. A space-age wonder on a steep hillside, accessed via a sky bridge.

Fire Island House (1977)

Architect: Arthur Erickson

Style: Modernist

Where: Fire Island, New York, USA

What to say: The perfect beach house with a well-balanced sense of indoor–outdoor living and a sliding roof.

FROM TOTEMS TO TUBES: A BRIEF HISTORY OF SCULPTURE

Ancient Sculpture

In ancient civilisations, the power of sculpture lay in its perceived ability to work magic as well as serve a decorative or practical function: totems were the equivalent of animal relatives, and tribesmen 'became' animals when they put on masks. For example, in ancient Mexico, the serpent symbolised lightning and so the Aztecs sculpted two serpents at the mouth of Tlaloc, their rain god, to invoke rain. In early Egyptian and Chinese cultures, life-sized statues of servants and soldiers were created to provide dead kings with help in the netherworlds. Sculpted reliefs

Tlaloc

also became a way of telling stories and commemorating events – the Greeks and Romans carved their battles on the walls of temples and palaces. The Indians and Chinese created their Buddhas in beautiful forms too – first seen in reliefs in the frontier region of Gandhara and the Buddhas of Bamiyan (sadly destroyed by the Taliban in 2001).

The Italian Renaissance

Donatello (c.1386–1466) is considered the greatest sculptor of the early Renaissance period: his work seems almost to live and breathe. He had a huge influence on Michelangelo (1475–1564), one of the pioneers of the High Renaissance. Michelangelo's *David* is the idealised human form, a sculpture carved with exquisite detail – even today his beauty is awe-inspiring.

Modern Sculpture

Auguste Rodin (1840–1917) is a central figure in modern sculpture. In his works, most famously *The Thinker* and *The Kiss*, he often drew upon myths and imagery depicting passion and heroism. As the modernist movement gained momentum, sculptors such as Constantin Brancusi, Henry Moore and Barbara Hepworth chose to use simpler, more abstract shapes. Alexander Calder also contributed to the development of the form with his mobiles, using wire and sheet metal to create kinetic pieces. Another master, Alberto Giacometti, part of the Maeght gallery, created unique long, lean figures, derived from cubist frameworks.

For a long time, marble, bronze and wood were the favoured media employed by sculptors. But the 1930s became known as the 'New Iron Age' as artists discovered the malleable and durable possibilities of iron and steel. Julio González was celebrated as the father of welded metal sculptures. The Dadaists and surrealists also experimented with different ingredients and, in the post-war period, Donald Judd broke new ground with his use of industrial materials – Plexiglas, sheet metal and plywood – changing the way we view traditional ideas of sculpture.

Contemporary sculpture is a celebration of new forms, new materials and freedom from rules. With the advent of new technologies such as video, computers and the Internet, sculptors have an increasing array of media to play with. Exciting, isn't it?

FIVE SCULPTURE PARKS IN WHICH TO HAVE THE PERFECT PICNIC

Yorkshire Sculpture Park, England
Renowned for its changing outdoor exhibitions, there are also a significant number of Henry Moores to look at while you munch away on your sandwiches. And if the art doesn't do it for you, there's plenty of other stuff to look at: it is set within 260 acres of eighteenth-century parkland.

Baltimore Museum of Art Sculpture Gardens, USA
Made up of two terraced gardens, spread across nearly three acres of land in the heart of the city, the gardens boast modern and contemporary sculptures from Auguste Rodin, Henry Moore, Alexander Calder and Isamu Noguchi.

Jardín y Terraza de Esculturas, Venezuela
Part of the Fundación Museo de Bellas Artes de Caracas – the oldest art museum in Venezuela – the works on display are sculpted by a mixture of South American and international artists, scattered over lush tropical grounds.

Hakone Open Air Museum, Japan
Located within the Fuji-Hakone-Izu National Park, Japan's first open-air museum has over a hundred works, featuring Calder, Moore and even a pavilion dedicated to Picasso.

Sculpture by the Sea, Australia
Sydney hosts the world's biggest temporary sculpture exhibition for three weeks annually along its Bondi–Tamarama coastal walk as it heats up to summer. Pack a cold picnic and don't forget the beers.

SNAP HAPPY: HOW TO TAKE THE PERFECT PHOTOGRAPH

A good photograph is the result of thoughtful composition as well as the clever use of light and colour. Follow our simple guide and for a real treat invite the neighbours round to look at your holiday snaps once you've completed your portfolio.

Composition
The rule of thirds is the golden rule at work in composition. Imagine two horizontal and two vertical lines dividing your shot, then place subjects on either one of the four intersecting points. You can add emphasis to the ground or to the sky by positioning the horizon on the bottom or top line respectively. You can also use naturally occurring lines to create direction. Using lines that converge suggests distance, scale and depth, giving a two-dimensional image three-dimensional depth.

Focus
Our eyes are drawn to elements that are in focus. Use your zoom lens to increase or reduce the 'depth of field', the areas in front and behind the focal point which remain in sharp focus, to emphasise elements of your choice. Zoom to capture more of the view and increase the feeling of depth in your shot, but be careful to keep your hands steady as tiny movements become magnified and can cause blurring.

Light
Consider your light source – it is generally best to shoot with light behind you unless you want a silhouette effect against an interesting background. It is also important to consider how the light is affecting your subject: is he or she squinting? If you like bold bright colours, the light source should be shining directly on the subject. Side lighting can add drama, producing interesting shapes and structures with shadow. The best times for side lighting are at the beginning and end of the day. Sometimes it is necessary to use the flash. A note on that: it is best to bounce the flash off a reflective or white surface to produce a softer light.

Colour

Different colours affect the way we feel, so use them creatively when taking pictures. Red colours are warmer, contrasting colours add tension or drama to a shot, while using shades of the same colour will give a sense of harmony. Using the natural light at the start and end of the day will give photographs a warmer tone because of the orangeness of the light. Due to the bluer quality of midday light, photos taken then will have a harsher feel.

MASTERS OF THE FORM: A TOP TEN OF PHOTOGRAPHERS

Man Ray (1890–1976)

Man Ray, born Emmanuel Radnitzky in Philadelphia, was a legendary photographer, painter and maker of objects and films. In 1921, he moved to Paris and was promptly accepted by some of the leading artists and thinkers, becoming their unofficial photographer. He invented the 'rayograph', where a three-dimensional object is placed on top of photographic paper and exposed to light.

Famous works: Any of the untitled works from the *Rayograph* series (1920s).

Ansel Adams (1902–84)

Ansel Adams was born in San Francisco. A photographer, writer and conservationist, his images are icons of the American wilderness. Adams championed and played a crucial role in establishing the first museum department of photography, at the Museum of Modern Art in New York. A prolific writer, he published ten volumes of technical manuals and contributed hundreds of articles and reviews from 1922 to 1984.

Famous work: *Moonrise, Hernandez, New Mexico* (1941).

Cecil Beaton (1904–80)

Cecil Beaton was born in Hampstead, London, and was one of Britain's most celebrated portrait photographers. He was also a costume designer for the stage version of *My Fair Lady* and won two Oscars for its film version. The portraits he took were renowned for their elegance, glamour and style. As the most fashionable young photographer of the day, Beaton won a contract with *Vogue,* with whom he was associated for over fifty years.

Famous work: *Marilyn Monroe* (1956).

Lee Miller (1907–77)

Lee Miller was admired as much for her creativity and intelligence as for her classical beauty. Born in Poughkeepsie, New York, Miller began her modelling career on the cover of American *Vogue* before meeting Man Ray in Paris in 1929. She became both his lover and muse and under his guidance started to produce her own photographs. She documented subjects as diverse as surrealist Paris, her travels in Egypt and the war in Europe – capturing stark images of Nazi death camps in Dachau and Buchenwald, even Hitler's apartment in Munich.

Famous work: *Portrait of Space* (1937).

Robert Capa (1914–54)

Robert Capa is probably the greatest of war photographers. His pictures from the Spanish Civil War made him famous and he also captured some of the most memorable images on D-Day at Omaha Beach in 1944. In 1947, he founded Magnum Photos with Henri Cartier-Bresson, David Seymour, George Rodger and William Vandivert.

Famous work: *American soldier landing on Omaha Beach, D-Day, Normandy, France, June 6, 1944.*

Diane Arbus (1923-1971)

Diane Arbus was born in New York City and found most of her subjects there. She took pictures of couples, children, carnival performers, nudists, middle-class families, transvestites, people on the street, eccentrics, reaks and celebrities. For many in post-war America, they became symbolic representations of America in the 1950s and 60s. Her images are honest and unsettling. In July 1971, in a bout of depression, she killed herself.

Famous works: *A young man in curlers at home on West 20th St, NYC, 1966; A young Brooklyn family going for a Sunday outing, NYC, 1966.*

Annie Leibovitz (1949–)

Born in 1949 in Connecticut, Leibovitz began her photographic career with *Rolling Stone* in 1971. Two years later, she was named *Rolling Stone* chief photographer. In 1980 she shot the iconic image of a naked Lennon curled round a fully clothed Yoko Ono. Lennon was killed several hours later. While working for *Vanity Fair*, she shot one of the most famous covers of the day – of a heavily pregnant and naked Demi Moore cradling her belly.

Famous work: John Lennon and Yoko Ono, cover of *Rolling Stone* magazine Lennon commemorative issue following his assassination, 1980.

Martin Parr (1952–)

Martin Parr was born in Epsom, Surrey, and studied photography at Manchester Polytechnic from 1970 to 1972. As a child, his interest in photography was encouraged by his father, himself a keen amateur photographer. Parr is well known for his unique take on social commentary and the use of inventive imagery; he makes us look at familiar things in a brand-new way.

Famous work: *Guardian* Cities Project: *Guardian* newspaper photos taken over the course of eight months and ten cities in 2008.

Mario Testino (1954–)

Mario Testino was born in Lima, Peru, and moved to London in 1976, selling portfolios at £25 a pop to wannabe models. He came to prominence after shooting Diana, Princess of Wales for the cover of *Vanity Fair* in 1997. Fashionistas and luxury brands love his highly polished and immaculately styled campaigns. He is also credited with bringing the reign of the supermodel to a close, championing instead quirkier young models such as Kate Moss, Stella Tennant, Sophie Dahl and Gisele Bündchen (when no one else cared for her Amazonian curves).

Famous work: Diana, Princess of Wales, cover of *Vanity Fair*, 1997.

David LaChapelle (1968–)

David LaChapelle was born in Connecticut. At the age of nineteen, he moved to New York and was offered his first professional job by Andy Warhol to shoot for *Interview* magazine. LaChapelle shoots a world that is larger than life, a strange combination of reportage and surrealism.

He is well known for his groundbreaking use of computer graphics and futuristic fashion shoots. In 1997, he was awarded the International Center of Photography's Infinity Award, and he was also Pamela Anderson's maid of honour at her wedding to Kid Rock.

Famous work: His trilogy of books, *LaChapelle Land, Hotel LaChapelle* and *LaChapelle Heaven to Hell*.

A FAMOUS PAINTING IN DOT-TO-DOT

What better way to get acquainted with one of the world's greatest works of art than by drawing it yourself. Here you can experience the thrill of being an artist without necessarily being a genius master of oils. For a completed version of this dot-to-dot masterpiece please see the 'answers' section at the end of this book.

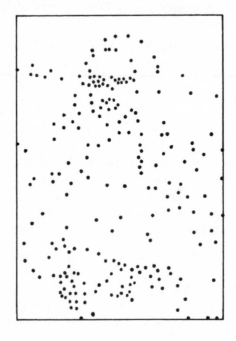

∽ ART AND DESIGN ∽ TEST PAPER

1. What are Venice turpentine, dammar resin, mastic and copal examples of?

a) essential oils
b) fixed or drying oils
c) cocktails at Harry's Bar in Venice
d) resins and balsams

2. Who sculpted *The Thinker?*

a) Barbara Hepworth
b) Henry Moore
c) Auguste Rodin
d) Constantin Brancusi

3. Which of the following is NOT a painting by the master Picasso?

a) *The Pipes of Pan*
b) *Three Dancers*
c) *Seated Bather*
d) *Fountain*

4. Whose film-like work, such as *Nighthawks*, greatly influenced photorealists and pop artists of the 1960s?

a) Juan Gris
b) Toulouse-Lautrec
c) Edward Hopper
d) J. S. Lowry

5. Modernists believe that design should be:

a) frivolous
b) fancy
c) functional
d) funny

6. In oil painting, what does the phrase 'fat over lean' mean?

a) the paint you put down first should have a lower oil content than subsequent layers
b) always favour buxom life models over skinny minnies
c) the paint you put down first should have a higher oil content than subsequent layers

7. Georges Braque is considered a founding father of cubism along with which other painter?

a) Lucian Freud
b) Vincent Van Gogh
c) Pablo Picasso
d) J. S. Lowry

8. In ancient Mexican sculpture, the serpent is a symbol for what?

a) rain
b) wind
c) sunshine
d) lightning

9. *The Green Line* (1905) is a key work of which painter?

a) Pablo Picasso
b) Georges Braque
c) Joseph Beuys
d) Henri Matisse

10. What does the term 'Fauves' mean?

11. Whose *Benefits Supervisor Sleeping* was bought by Roman Abramovich in 2008 for $33.6 million, making it the most expensive work by a living painter?

a) Cy Twombly
b) Lucian Freud
c) David Hockney
d) Gary Hume

12. Which technique is Jackson Pollock most famous for?

a) pouring paint on to canvas directly from the can
b) screen-printing
c) watercolours

13. In which European city was Lucian Freud born?

a) Vienna
b) Berlin
c) London
d) Paris

14. Marcel Duchamp was a champion of which surrealist art movement?

a) the Dididsts
b) the Dodoes
c) the Dadaists
d) the Duddus

15. In what year was Pablo Picasso born?

a) 1880
b) 1881
c) 1890
d) 1891

16. Which of the following series was NOT painted by Wassily Kandinsky?

a. *Impressions*
b. *Improvisations*
c. *Compositions*
d. *Transitions*

17. For which landmark New York restaurant did Mark Rothko paint his Seagram series?

a) the Waldorf
b) the Four Seasons
c) the Hard Rock Café
d) Le Cirque

18. Which of the following was a prominent figure of the modernist movement?

a) Salvador Dalí
b) Le Corbusier
c) Damien Hirst
d) Michelangelo Caravaggio

19. Donatello sculpted during which artistic period?

a) Rococo
b) Modernist
c) Renaissance
d) Impressionist

20. Who designed the Beijing National Stadium, the Bird's Nest?

a) Herzog & de Meuron
b) Nicholas Grimshaw
c) Zaha Hadid
d) Mica de Haas

21. Who designed *Fallingwater*?

a) Wells Coates
b) Charles and Ray Eames
c) Arthur Erickson
d) Frank Lloyd Wright

22. Which singer-songwriter's lyrics inspired the Memphis movement?

a) Paul Simon
b) Elvis Presley
c) Bob Dylan
d) Bob Marley

23. FTIR microscopes shoot what at a painting to spot a fake?

a) infrared light
b) ultraviolet light
c) white light
d) water

24. Which tormented painting was stolen on the eve of the Winter Olympics in Norway in 1994?

a) *Mona Lisa*
b) *Guernica*
c) *The Scream*
d) *Young Parisian*

25. Which decade of twentieth-century sculpture became known as the 'New Iron Age'?

a) 1920s
b) 1930s
c) 1940s

26. Which Flemish painter is considered the father of oil painting?

a) Jan Van Eyck
b) Gerard David
c) Hieronymus Bosch
d) Jan Vermeer

27. Which of the following movements would NOT be considered a school of modern art?

a) symbolism
b) expressionism
c) constructivism
d) neoclassicism

28. Which of the following is NOT a top tip for eager Van Eycks?

a) use stiff brushes for most oil painting
b) dry your oil paintings in a dark room
c) be adventurous
d) dry your oil paintings in a light room

29. *The Persistence of Memory* (1931) is a key work of which surrealist artist?

a) Marcel Duchamp
b) Salvador Dali
c) Frida Kahlo
d) Max Ernst

30. The sculptor Dan Flavin used primarily which material?

a) Plexiglass
b) neon light tubing
c) plywood
d) tissue paper

❧ BREAK TIME ❧

After all that sterling brain training it's important that you take a few minutes to get outside, run around and let off steam. Here are some vigorous games to help you get going.

STUCK-IN-THE-MUD
Players: 3+

Stuck-in-the-mud is a slightly more sophisticated form of that old favourite, tag, in which one player is chosen as 'It' and must chase the other players to try to tag them. In stuck-in-the-mud the player they touch becomes 'frozen' and must stay absolutely still at the point where they've been tagged. The only way they can be unfrozen to run free again is if another player crawls through their legs. The object of the game for 'It' is to freeze all the players they're chasing.

DODGEBALL
Players: 12–30

Dodgeball is a rough-and-tumble lark of a game invented by our American cousins and should be played in a large hall or outside in a field. The only equipment required is a ball – ideally a football or volleyball and nothing too small, hard and lethal – and two equal-sized teams.

Team A arranges itself in a large circle around Team B and begins throwing the ball at the trapped Bs in their midst. Only Team A players can catch the ball; all Team B players can do is scuttle around trying to avoid it. When a Team B member is hit by the ball they move into the Team A circle and join in trying to hit their erstwhile teammates, until only one persecuted player is left and hailed as the winner. It's sensible to agree a ground rule before beginning play that no blows to the head or face count.

Another version of this thrilling exercise is for the two teams to line up opposite each other on either side of an agreed dividing line and throw lots of balls at their opposition. In this game everyone who is hit by a ball is eliminated and has to go and sit on the sidelines and cheer their plucky teammates on.

MARBLES
[Players: 2+]

For the less athletic of you, marbles offers a diverting experience, involving both tactics and physical skill. You will need your own equipment – an array of different-coloured glass balls which are often handed down through families. To create the playing space, a circle is drawn in chalk or sand on the ground, inside which an agreed number of each player's precious marbles is placed. A line is then drawn some way away from the circle behind which all the players stand. One by one they pitch marbles from their remaining cache into the fray, aiming to knock their desired prize outside the circle. Any marbles they knock out become their property and gain them points and another go. Unless, to avoid tears, all the players agree beforehand that they will get their own marbles back at the end of the game.

CONKERS
[Players: 2]

September and October are the perfect times for conkering, when the horse-chestnut tree drops its seeds. Simply stand under a horse chestnut and fling a stick at it until the seeds fall down. You'll then have to break through the green knobbly outer casing. Once you have your conker, pierce a hole in it using a skewer. Thread a piece of string through and secure with a knot. You are ready to play. You can decide who goes first by tossing a coin, but you should also remember that a fiver – a conker that has been victorious five times – should take precedence over a mere twoer. Whoever goes first is then allowed to attempt, using an overarm throw, to hit the other player's conker, which is dangling on the end of the string between his knuckles, as hard as he can. If he succeeds, he gets another go; if not, the play switches. The winner is the conker (or knuckle!) that survives – by the end one will be completely mashed.

FOUR SQUARE
[Players: 4]

To play four square, all you need is a football and a large open space where you can draw a square about 5m x 5m onto the ground with chalk. This square is then divided into 4 inner squares which are each numbered.

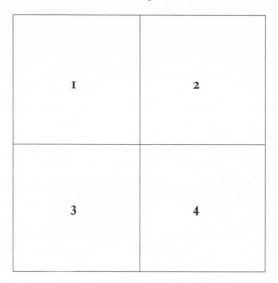

Each player picks a square and the player in square 4 begins the game by bouncing the ball on the ground and then bouncing it into another square. The receiving player must allow the ball to bounce once before punting it onto a different square but if it bounces twice in their square before they manage to hit it then they are penalised by moving into square 1 – the lowest position on the board. All the other players move up to make room for them. Players also get penalised for bouncing the ball outside the squares' boundaries and suffer the same punishment. The idea of the game is to get to square 4 by the time the bell for the end of break time rings.

∽ BREAK TIME ∽
TEST PAPER

1. A WAYWARD WORDSEARCH

How many types of beverage can you find in the following puzzle?

T	Y	E	K	S	I	H	W	R	B
S	E	P	T	C	E	C	E	S	Q
C	T	Q	U	S	I	T	S	A	P
H	A	O	U	B	T	D	F	I	E
N	R	C	U	I	P	E	E	G	R
A	E	W	B	T	L	L	E	R	R
P	T	Y	M	A	E	A	N	H	Y
P	R	E	E	B	H	G	I	N	R
S	O	U	Z	O	X	E	W	O	J
N	P	I	N	I	T	R	A	M	K

2. APPETISING ANAGRAMS

The following are all anagrams of dishes you might eat at a French restaurant. Work out what each one is.

case lotus
self grogs
ferried smut

puce tree zest
camel racer me
fake sitters
labial soubise
arise fog
pilferer soot
nattier tat

3. RASCALLY RIDDLES: SOME CONUNDRUMS

a) What goes round the world but stays in a corner?
b) What is full of holes but still holds water?
c) What gets wet as it dries?
d) What comes once in a minute, twice in a moment, but never in a thousand years?
e) What belongs to you but other people use more than you do?
f) What gets larger the more you take away?
g) What is the beginning of sorrow but the end of sadness, always in risk but never in danger?
h) What has been around longer than humankind but is less than a month old?
i) What should you keep after giving it to someone else?
j) How do you tell the difference between a tin of tomato soup and a tin of chicken soup?

☙ SCIENCE ❧

We are all scientists. Even if you spend your days wafting around in a velvet smoking jacket, garlanded in flowers and reading poetry to your delicate darling under willow trees, and shiver at the thought of a laboratory or a test tube, you will still find that you know something about science – even if it's just that you should cover your mouth when you cough in case you pass on your poetic consumption to some unwitting passer-by. The great triumvirate of Chemistry, Physics and Biology has a great deal to teach us about our environment – from how nuclear bombs work, to what happens to your body when someone stamps on your foot, to the future of space travel, the tricky nature of viruses, and how much we can blame on our genes. Science never gets dull as new discoveries are being made in all these areas all the time – once you have the basic principles mastered you can open the door to a whole new world of adventure that just gets more and more fascinating by the day. Onwards, brave explorer!

THE HUMAN GENOME PROJECT

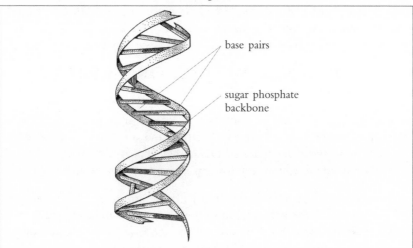

base pairs

sugar phosphate backbone

In olden times, adventurers keen to leave their mark on history mapped the uncharted territories of the world, but now the focus has shifted from the massive to the minute. In 1990, an international group of scientists began a groundbreaking project to map the human **genome**. 'Genome' is the word used to describe all the **DNA** in a particular organism, including both genes and non-coding material. DNA is made up of four different chemicals (adenine, thymine, guanine and cytosine), called **bases**, arranged in pairs, and the order of these base pairs, as they are arranged in unique sequences of **genes**, defines the different characteristics of an organism, from its hair colour to its susceptibility to certain diseases. The human genome has an impressive 3 billion pairs of bases.

The Human Genome Project aimed to identify every human gene and establish the sequence of the bases in order to unlock the secrets of the relationship between genes and traits and diseases. Blood and tissue samples from different people were used in the experiment because although we, and our genes, differ from each other (unless we're identical twins), these differences are much, much smaller than the similarities between all our genomes: only 0.1% of DNA is thought to vary from one person to the next. (This is why forensic scientists have to match between four and six specific DNA markers to establish DNA connections between suspects and crime scenes.) In 2003 the momentous task of the sequencing was successfully completed, but investigations into the discoveries that have been made continue.

GENE GENIE: NATURE OR NURTURE?

Deep in the nuclei of your cells, your DNA is stored in genes which are all packed up neatly in your 23 pairs of chromosomes (in each pair one chromosome comes from your father and one from your mother). A gene is a specific pattern of DNA that acts as a code to tell your body to produce certain proteins that cause growth or other functions.

Put simply, both chromosomes in a pair contain genes that look after the same job – for example, how your ear lobes look, whether you have dimples and what hair colour you end up with. The chromosome from your mother might have one version of a gene – say for ginger hair – and your father's might have another – say for brown hair: these different versions of genes are called **alleles**. Alleles are either dominant or recessive: dominant alleles show their influence in a person whatever happens, but recessive alleles only show up if both chromosomes carry the same kind of allele.

Ginger genes are recessive so this means that in order to have red hair a child must inherit ginger alleles from both parents; if one of them gives a brown-hair allele this will win out and the child will be saved from playground bullying. Cystic fibrosis is also caused by recessive alleles, so two perfectly healthy parents can both have cystic-fibrosis alleles (this is called being a 'carrier') and if they both happen to pass this allele on to their child then the child will have cystic fibrosis. However, they might also have perfectly healthy children if one parent passes on their non-cystic-fibrosis allele, even if the other passes on the cystic-fibrosis allele.

More and more, researchers are finding genetic codes that seem to influence many different elements of a person's life: certain genes are thought to predispose people to conditions as wide-ranging as breast cancer (mutated BRCA1 and BRCA2 genes lead to a three to seven times increased risk in women), osteoporosis (a certain allele of the LRP5 gene leads to a 30% increased risk and a particular allele of TNFRSF11B increases risk by 20%), obesity (people who inherit a certain allele of the gene FTO are 70% more likely to be obese than those who don't) and cocaine addiction (a study of coke addicts showed that they were 25% more likely to carry a particular version of the CAMK4 gene than non-addicts).

Antenatal testing to screen foetuses for serious genetic disorders such as Down's syndrome has been in place for many years, but adult predictive tests that promise to tell you if you are genetically predisposed to certain diseases are becoming more widely available. However, questions have been raised over the accuracy of these checks and the scientific establishment is not yet confident that enough studies have been carried out to make them properly useful.

It's important to remember that not everything is determined by our genes. As studies on identical twins show, environmental factors also influence all areas of our lives, from how we look and how we act to how susceptible we are to disease. If you took one twin and brought them up in a rainforest in Papua New Guinea and put the other in a city flat in Hammerfest you would find that differences in diet and culture would probably mean that the twins would grow up to be quite different from each other, and possibly look quite different too.

NERVOUS TENSION:
HOW THE NERVOUS SYSTEM WORKS

Everybody knows that our thoughts, feelings and actions are primarily generated and controlled by the brain. However, have you ever wondered how that lump of grey matter sitting behind your eyes actually takes in what's going on around it and transfers all that information to the rest of your body? For example, how your hands know to hold this book near enough to your eyes for them to see the words, and how those words are getting to the bit of your brain that's sorting them out and making sense of them? You might have heard on the biology grapevine that your central nervous system is pretty key in these activities, but what about the sensory nervous system or the somatic nervous system or the parasympathetic nervous system – what do they do? Never fear, all shall be revealed below.

The first thing to know is that we divide the human nervous system into two parts: the **central nervous system** (**CNS**) and the **peripheral nervous system** (**PNS**). The CNS is made up of the brain and the spinal cord, which are connected together. The brain interprets the signals that it receives from the rest of the nervous system and enacts responses, also using nerves.

The PNS is made up of all those nerves that connect from the other parts of your body into your CNS. The PNS can be broken down into three parts:

*   The **sensory nervous system** comprises nerves that transfer information from your sensory receptors – such as the skin, taste buds, ears, nose and eyes – that carry messages of touch, taste, sound, smell and sight to the central nervous system. Sometimes the brain doesn't get involved in deciding a response to information received by these receptors and instead the nervous system acts immediately in a process called a **reflex action**. If someone stamps on your foot at a cocktail party in their size six stilettos, it is likely you will instantly pull your foot away (and possibly yell out an obscenity) without this response being instructed by your brain.

- The **somatic nervous system** comprises nerves that send information from the central nervous system to your **effectors** (the parts of your body that actually perform actions, like muscles and glands), allowing you to carry out such activities as whistling, tap dancing and cracking your knuckles.

- The **autonomic nervous system** comprises nerves that send information from the central nervous system to stimulate effectors to carry out unconscious actions like breathing, digestion, hormone release and blood circulation. Most of the time we are unaware of the autonomic system slaving away constantly in its efforts to keep us alive and maintain our internal equilibrium (**homeostasis**), but in stressful situations, such as when you receive your gas bill, you might suddenly become aware of your heart beating faster, or feeling breathless. This is because your autonomic nervous system is preparing to deal with whatever is threatening you (be it your energy supplier, a toddler having a tantrum or a rampaging tiger). The division of your autonomic system that deals with this response is called the **sympathetic nervous system**; the part that kicks in when you are relaxing is called the **parasympathetic nervous system**; and the third division is the **enteric nervous system**, which looks after your guts and internal organs like the pancreas and gall bladder.

GETTING ON YOUR NEURONES: WHAT ARE NERVES?

The various nervous systems are all made up of networks of nerve cells that run around the organs throughout your body. Nerve cells are also called **neurones** and are divided into three different types: **sensory neurones**, which carry information from your sensory receptors to the central nervous system; **relay neurones**, which carry information around the central nervous system; and **motor neurones**, which carry information from the central nervous system to your effectors. The information neurones schlep about is made up of tiny electrical impulses that travel through the branches of the neurones (**dendrites**) and down their lovely tail (**axon**), where the cell releases chemicals that cross the gap between neurones (called a **synapse**) and stimulate an electrical signal in the next neurone's dendrites, and so on.

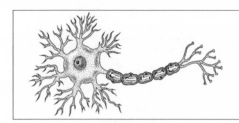

A MOTOR NEURONE

CATCH ME IF YOU CAN:
BACTERIA AND VIRUSES

Microorganisms that cause disease are often referred to as **germs** or **pathogens**. The two main types we can blame for our sniffles, sneezes and tummy upsets are **bacteria** and **viruses**.

Many different kinds of bacteria live merrily in and on our bodies all the time without causing us any trouble, however about 200 species are harmful to humans and once they have breached our body's defence system and begun to multiply their effects can cause discomfort, pain, irritation and sometimes permanent injury or death. Bacterial diseases come in many varied and gory hues, ranging from cholera, tuberculosis, tetanus and leprosy to salmonella and syphilis. Bacterial infections are often spread through the transfer of bad bacteria from human to human through food and water or touching, coughing and sneezing. Many bacterial diseases can be treated with antibiotic drugs but some strains, such as MRSA, have developed immunity against these medicines over time. It's not all bad news though – a certain amount of exposure to bacteria is thought to help develop and strengthen the immune system.

The word 'virus' comes from the Latin term for 'poison'. Viruses are ultramicroscopic and are spread in similar ways to bacteria. Hundreds of them are harmful to humans and other living beings. They carry out their sinister parasitical work by getting inside a living host cell and then using it to replicate themselves before spreading round the body. Rabies, polio, herpes, chickenpox, flu, measles, AIDS, and the common cold are all viral diseases. It is very difficult to treat viral diseases with drugs as it is difficult for the medicine to attack the virus without damaging the host cells. However it is possible to prepare the immune system to be more resistant to viral attack through vaccination. These days most children are immunised against polio, measles, mumps and rubella.

SPOTTERS' GUIDES:
IDENTIFYING NATURE

People these days don't get enough fresh air, so pull on your wellies and go for a health-giving walk whenever you can. If you're lucky enough to live in the country or near a park, you can also test your zoological and botanical identification skills while you're wandering about by looking out for animal tracks and using the information below to help you play Name that Tree!

COMMON BRITISH TREES

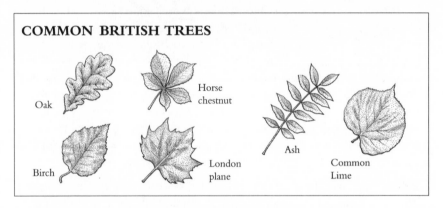

Oak

Horse chestnut

Birch

London plane

Ash

Common Lime

COMMON BRITISH ANIMAL TRACKS

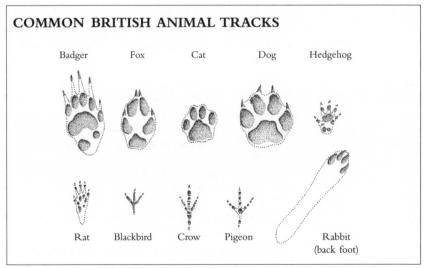

Badger   Fox   Cat   Dog   Hedgehog

Rat   Blackbird   Crow   Pigeon   Rabbit (back foot)

CHAMPION CHEMISTS: THE NOBEL PRIZE

The Nobel Foundation awards prizes every year in a variety of disciplines, one of which is Chemistry. The prize was made possible by the Swedish chemist Alfred Nobel (1833–96) whose own road to chemical success was a little rocky. His experiments with the explosive chemical nitroglycerine ($C_3H_5(NO_3)_3$) resulted in a terrible accident which killed his brother Emil and four other people in 1864. After this, the authorities banned Nobel from working in Stockholm and he was forced to move his laboratory to a boat on Lake Mälaren. However, in 1866 he discovered a way to make nitroglycerine safe to transport by packing it up in sticks with chalky earth called *kieselguhr*. This invention, which we know as dynamite, made his fortune. In his will, Nobel bequeathed much of his wealth to establish a set of prizes that rewarded leaders in the arts and sciences for achievements that benefited mankind.

Below, you will find an illustrious list of our twenty-first-century Nobel laureates in Chemistry with summaries of their prize-winning achievements in order to give you a snapshot of the areas of chemistry research that are changing our world right now. You may think that the process of ubiquitin-mediated protein degradation has nothing to do with you, but we hope to persuade you otherwise.

Year	Winner	Studies for which the Prize was awarded
2000	Alan J. Heeger Alan G. MacDiarmid Hideki Shirakawa	Discovery and development of conductive polymers. These scientists discovered that plastics (**polymers**) could be made to conduct electricity. Previously, plastics were thought to work only as insulators (which is why the metal wiring in your house is wrapped in plastic tubing). This means that cost-effective

		plastics can now be used in electronic products in place of metals. New flat-screen televisions and 'light-emitting wallpaper' are apparently possible applications of this discovery.
2001	William S. Knowles Ryoji Noyori K. Barry Sharpless	Work on catalytic asymmetric synthesis. Most molecules in nature occur in two mirror-image forms. However, one of these forms is more likely than the other to be produced: they are **asymmetrically synthesised**. The different forms can have very different effects on cells. For example, one form of limonene makes things smell of lemons but the other makes them smell of oranges. It's important for the drugs industry to be able to manufacture whichever form of a particular molecule they need. These scientists were given the prize for their work on developing methods for synthesising particular forms using **catalysts** (a catalyst is simply a substance that speeds up a chemical reaction without being involved in it itself).
2002	John B. Fenn Koichi Tanaka Kurt Wüthrich	Development of methods for identification and structure analyses of biological macromolecules. **Macromolecules** are very large molecules, such as the DNA and proteins which make our bodies function as they do. These scientists were awarded the prize for their work developing methods to measure and identify different macromolecules. This work has implications for the development of drugs and foods and the detection of diseases like cancer.
2003	Peter Agre Roderick MacKinnon	Discoveries concerning channels in cell membranes. All our cells work together to make our bodies function by transferring water and other molecules like ions back and forth

		through their membranes. These scientists discovered how the water and ion channels between the cells work. Various diseases are a result of malfunctions in these channels, so these discoveries are important for developing new drugs to help with problems such as diseases of the nervous system.
2004	Aaron Ciechanover Avram Hershko Irwin Rose	Discovery of the process of ubiquitin-mediated protein degradation. All of our cells contain thousands of different proteins, such as enzymes and hormones, which carry out the body's jobs. New proteins are being created all the time, so to keep a balance other proteins have to be destroyed, or '**degraded**', by the cell. These scientists discovered that the cell labels which proteins should be destroyed by binding them to the molecule called ubiquitin. This work is important for our understanding of how cells function and regulate themselves and has implications for research into diseases such as cervical cancer and cystic fibrosis.
2005	Yves Chauvin Robert H. Grubbs Richard R. Schrock	Development of the metathesis method of organic synthesis. **Metathesis** is the reaction of two parts of two substances that results in two new substances. These scientists have developed ways of using catalysts to produce metathesis in order to synthesise new molecules. This has implications for the production of new pharmaceuticals, plastics and other materials.
2006	Roger D. Kornberg	Studies of the molecular basis of eukaryotic transcription. In order for an organism to grow and function, the genetic information contained in cells' nuclei has to be copied in a process called 'transcription'. The copy of the

		information (called **messenger-RNA**) is carried outside the nucleus and used to instruct proteins to initiate growth or other functions. Problems with transcription lead to illnesses like cancer and heart disease. Kornberg was rewarded for his discovery of how transcription works at a molecular level in eukaryotes. A **eukaryote** is an organism, such as a human or a yeast, whose cells contain a distinct nucleus contained in a membrane. These studies are important for our understanding of diseases and stem cell research.
2007	Gerhard Ertl	Studies of chemical processes on solid surfaces. Surface chemistry is the branch of chemistry that studies what happens at the interface of two different **phases**. Phases are the different states that matter can exist in, e.g. solid, liquid, gas. Ertl was awarded the prize for his investigations into the molecular processes that occur when gas hits a solid surface. His work gives important insight into areas such as chemical fertilisers, corrosion protection, catalytic converters in cars and the destruction of the ozone layer.
2008	Osamu Shimomura Martin Chalfie Roger Y. Tsien	Discovery and development of the green fluorescent protein (GFP). We all have tens of thousands of proteins in our bodies which control all our body's actions. Scientists study the roles of these different proteins in order to understand diseases but many of them are impossible to see under normal conditions. These scientists' work on the **green fluorescent protein (GFP)**, which is naturally found in the jellyfish *Aequorea victoria*, has enabled researchers to tag individual cells and proteins with GFP so that they can be seen and studied.

CHEMISTRY AT HOME:
MAKE YOUR OWN FIZZ BOMB

WARNING: This procedure can be messy and is best performed outdoors or in the bath tub. Be sure to protect your eyes and soft furnishings.

APPARATUS
1 non-leaky zipper freezer bag
250ml vinegar
125ml warm water
2tbsp baking soda
1 paper towel
1 pair scissors

METHOD

Cut your paper towel into a square 10cm × 10cm and wrap the baking soda neatly up inside it. Pour the water and vinegar into the plastic bag. Zip the bag halfway shut. Take a deep breath and then in one deft movement drop the packet of baking soda into the bag and zip it up fully. Quickly shake the bag and then put it down and step back.

CONCLUSIONS

Baking soda is a base and vinegar is an acid. They are on opposite ends of the pH scale (neutral substances sit in the middle of the scale). When they meet they cause a chemical reaction that creates bubbles of carbon dioxide gas which fill the bag and ultimately burst it.

ASTRONOMICAL OUTER SPACE

Our solar system is stuffed with planets (Mercury, Venus, Earth, Mars, Jupiter, Saturn, Uranus and Neptune and the dwarf planets Ceres, Eris and Pluto) and their orbiting satellites (natural ones like moons and the ones we stick up there to keep a watch on our neighbours) and

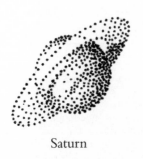

Saturn

thousands of comets and hundreds of thousands of asteroids all orbiting round the sun. Where planets orbit the sun in a roughly regular circular pattern, the balls of dust and ice we call **comets** orbit in long ellipses which explains why they suddenly turn up and then disappear for years (the most famous comet is probably Halley's Comet which stars in the Bayeux Tapestry and streams past us every seventy-six years or so). **Asteroids** are lumps of rock or metal that vary in size from a couple of metres in diameter to over 500km. (Asteroids under 10m diameter are usually called **meteoroids**, which become **meteors** – or shooting stars – when they flare through the earth's atmosphere and **meteorites** if they manage to reach the ground without burning up). There are lots of them sitting together comfortably in the asteroid belt between Mars and Jupiter but others ping around rather unpredictably – hence the worry that some day one will hit the Earth and cause mass devastation (many people think this is what killed the dinosaurs).

WHAT IS A LIGHT YEAR?

The speed of light is 300,000km per second. A light year is how far light would travel in one year: 9.46 trillion km. Our Galaxy, prettily named the Milky Way, is approximately 100,000 light years in diameter. Pretty whopping, we think you'll agree.

MOONING ABOUT

The names of the humble satellites orbiting our neighbouring planets are little-known and underused. They are often very beautiful and carefully decided upon these days by the snappily named International Astronomical Union's Working Group for Planetary System Nomenclature. You'll notice in the table below that each planet's moons tend to have a theme in their original naming strategies, even if the continuing discovery of new satellites has sometimes made this tricky to keep coherent.

PLANET	MOONS
Mercury	None
Venus	None
Earth	Moon
Mars	Phobos, Deimos. Named after the Roman god of war Mars's sons.
Jupiter	Io, Europa, Ganymede, Callisto (these big four are also referred to as the Galilean satellites because Galileo discovered them in 1610), Amalthea, Himalia, Elara, Pasiphae, Sinope, Lysithea, Carme, Ananke, Leda, Thebe, Adrastea, Metis, Callirrhoe, Themisto, Megaclite, Taygete, Chaldene, Harpalyke, Kalyke, Iocaste, Erinome, Isonoe, Praxidike, Autonoe, Thyone, Hermippe, Aitne, Eurydome, Euanthe, Euporie, Orthosie, Sponde, Kale, Pasithee, Hegemone, Mneme, Aoede, Thelxinoe, Arche, Kallichore, Helike, Carpo, Eukelade, Cyllene, Kore, S/2003 J2, S/2003 J3, S/2003 J4, S/2000 J11, S/2000 J5, S/2003 J9, S/2003 J10, S/2003 J12, S/2003 J15, S/2003 J16, S/2003 J17, S/2003 J18, S/2003 J19, S/2003 J23. Named for the Roman king god Jupiter's lovers, companions and children – apart from S/2003 J2 – S/2003 J23 obviously.
Saturn	Mimas, Enceladus, Tethys, Dione, Rhea, Titan, Hyperion, Iapetus, Erriapus, Phoebe, Janus, Epimetheus, Helene, Telesto, Calypso, Kiviuq, Atlas, Prometheus, Pandora, Pan, Ymir, Paaliaq, Tarvos, Ijiraq, Suttungr, Mundilfari, Albiorix, Skathi, Siarnaq, Thrymr, Narvi, Methone, Pallene, Polydeuces, Daphnis, Aegir, Bebhionn, Bergelmir, Bestla, Farbauti, Fenrir, Fornjot, Hati, Hyrokkin, Kari, Loge, Skoll,

	Surtur, S/2004 S7, S/2004 S12, S/2004 S13, S/2004 S17, S/2006 S1, S/2006 S3, Greip, Jarnsaxa, Tarqeq, S/2007 S2, S/2007 S3, Anthe. In the main, named for famous giants from Greco-Roman, Inuit, Gallic and Norse mythology, particularly the Roman God of time Saturn's siblings, the giant Titans, and their relatives.
Uranus	Cordelia, Ophelia, Bianca, Cressida, Desdemona, Juliet, Portia, Rosalind, Mab, Belinda, Perdita, Puck, Cupid, Miranda, Francisco, Ariel, Umbriel, Titania, Oberon, Caliban, Stephano, Trinculo, Sycorax, Margaret, Prospero, Setebox, Ferdinand. Named for characters in the plays of William Shakespeare and Alexander Pope's poem *The Rape of the Lock*.
Neptune	Triton, Nereid, Naiad, Thalassa, Despina, Galatea, Larissa, Proetus, Halimede, Psamathe, Sao, Laomedieia, Neso. Named for relatives and companions of the Roman sea god Neptune.

STAR STORY

The centre of the solar system, the big chap in the middle, is the sun, on which we rely for our lives. The sun's heat and light energy is responsible for all our food and fuel. The sun is an average-sized star and is over a hundred times bigger than the Earth and in a constant state of nuclear reaction which creates the heat and light emanating from it.

The sun is essentially a massive ball of hot hydrogen and helium gas that has condensed due to the force of gravity. This gravitational pull produces high temperatures and pressure in the centre of the sun which lead to the hydrogen atoms breaking up into separate protons and electrons. When the protons get packed very tightly together, the incredible heat (approximately 15.6 million °C) and density cause them to fuse together. When four hydrogen protons fuse together they produce the two protons and two neutrons that make up the nucleus of an atom of helium. The helium nucleus has less mass than the original four protons, so the leftover mass is converted into energy. This process is called **nuclear fusion**.

The sun is about 4.6 billion years old and scientists estimate it has about another 5 billion years left to run after which it will have used up all its internal fuel. First it will get much hotter and brighter (it will boil away the Earth's oceans in about 3 billion years' time) and then much bigger, becoming a **red giant**, before it collapses into a smaller, denser, cooler **white dwarf**. Astronomers estimate that there are over 10,000,000,000,000,000,000,000 stars out there in the universe; however, this average chap we watch rise in the morning and set in the evening will always be the most important one for us.

NUCLEAR FISSION

Don't confuse what the sun gets up to with **nuclear fission** which we humans use to create energy by splitting the nuclei of atoms of the radioactive elements plutonium or uranium (these materials are used because they are relatively easy to split). When creating energy in a nuclear power station, a neutron is bashed into the nucleus of an atom which then splits into two smaller radioactive nuclei, releasing energy and two or three more neutrons which in turn bump into other nuclei starting a **chain reaction** and releasing more energy. Nuclear power is useful as you only need a small amount of fuel to create energy; however, the waste from these reactions is extremely toxic for many years so the power stations are expensive, and many think dangerous, to run.

Atomic Bombs (A-bombs) release huge quantities of destructive energy through nuclear fission of plutonium or uranium atoms, which is triggered using conventional explosives. On 6th August 1945 the Allied forces dropped the first atomic bomb ever used in combat on the Japanese city of Hiroshima, destroying about 60% of the city and killing nearly 130,000 people. Three days later another atomic bomb was dropped on Nagasaki destroying a third of the city.

Hydrogen bombs (H-bombs) release even greater quantities of destructive energy than atomic bombs through nuclear fusion which is triggered by an atomic bomb. They are referred to as thermonuclear weapons because the atomic bomb trigger produces very high temperatures, which are necessary to produce fusion.

TO BOLDLY GO: SPACE TRAVEL

Using conventional rocket propulsion and spacecraft engines our exploration of the universe is severely limited by the amount of time it takes to cover the vast distances involved. Even the clever Voyager spacecraft, which used the orbits of the planets they passed to slingshot them along at high speeds, took thirty years to reach the edge of the solar system. Research is taking place to develop solar sails, nuclear power or even antimatter spacecraft (as appear in *Star Trek*) to get round this problem.

WHAT IS ANTIMATTER?

The astonishingly clever British physicist Paul Dirac (1902–84) came up with the idea of antimatter in the 1920s when he was only twenty-six. He postulated that every particle ever made was created from the energy of the Big Bang alongside a mirror-image antiparticle of the same mass but opposite electrical charge. An antimatter electron is called a **positron**, an antimatter proton is called an **antiproton** and an antimatter neutron is called an **antineutron**.

Matter and antimatter do not get along well. When a particle comes together with its antiparticle, they annihilate each other and their masses are converted back into huge amounts of energy. Unfortunately, at the moment it takes more energy to create antimatter than it produces so we won't be using it as fuel for a while. Despite the fact that equal amounts of matter and antimatter were created, there also doesn't seem to be a lot hanging around in the universe (although scientists have discovered a large cloud of it at the centre of our Galaxy). Obviously if there was it would have caused the annihilation of all the lovely matter that makes up the stars, the planets, your mother-in law and everything else. This puzzles scientists and so they have created particle accelerators to replicate the conditions of the Big Bang in order to see what might have happened to allow matter to win the battle.

The Large Hadron Collider, which was completed in 2008, is one of these huge machines (it is 27 km in circumference and buried underground on border of France and Switzerland and involves scientists from 100 countries). A **hadron** is a tiny particle which is made up of quarks, such as a neutron or proton, and the LHC will mainly be firing protons at each other during its experiments. As well as investigating the inequality in existing matter and antimatter, it is hoped that the LHC will uncover other important facts about our universe such as the existence of other dimensions, evidence in support of string theory, the elusive Higgs boson particle, dark matter and dark energy and in fact a whole new theory of physics to update the Standard model which is what we currently use to explain how sub-atomic particles interact.

THEY SEEK HIM HERE, THEY SEEK HIM THERE: THE ELUSIVE HIGGS BOSON

Once upon a time everyone thought that atoms were the smallest particles around, but then scientists discovered that they can be broken down into electrons, protons and neutrons. Things didn't end there – they later discovered that protons and neutrons can be broken down into quarks. According to the standard model theory, scientists now believe that everything is made up of four different types of fundamental particle that can't be broken down into anything smaller: **quarks** and **leptons** (the elementary **fermions**) and the **force-carrying bosons** and the **Higgs boson** (the elementary bosons). However, they also suspect that there may be more elementary bosons out there to discover.

Dealing with the fermions first, the quarks are divided into the **up-quark**, the **down-quark**, the **charm-quark**, the **strange-quark** (yes, this sounds made up but it's all true!), the **top-quark** and the **bottom-quark**. The leptons are the **electron**, the **electron–neutrino**, the **muon**, the **muon–neutrino**, the **tau** and the **tau–neutrino**. These particles make up all matter.

The elementary bosons are force-carrier particles that transfer energy between fermions.

There are four forces in the universe: the **strong force**, the **weak force**, the **electromagnetic force** and the **gravitational force** and none of them have anything to do with Darth Vader. The strong force holds quarks together, the weak force causes radioactive decay, the electromagnetic force controls the interactions of particles with electrical charges and the gravitational force controls the attraction between all objects with mass. In the standard model all of these forces affect fermions through the exchange of bosons. Strong force is carried by the **gluon**, electromagnetic force by the **photon** and weak force by the **W** and **Z bosons**. Gravity should theoretically be carried by the **graviton**, but no one has managed to actually find one of these yet or been able to fit how gravity works into the standard model.

Scientists have also been unable to find the Higgs boson, which is thought to be the boson which carries mass between particles, and therefore would explain why some particles have mass and some don't. This is a very important little fellow to identify (it is sometimes referred to as the 'God particle') and establishing its existence or non-existence would change the face of modern physics. This is one of the jobs the Large Hadron Collider is setting out to do. The physicist Stephen Hawking has a particular interest in the results of this experiment, as he has bet $100 that the Higgs boson will not be found.

STRUNG OUT: AN INTRODUCTION TO STRING THEORY

As you'll see from the section about the Higgs boson above, scientists are finding it tricky to fit gravity into the standard model which aims to explain the way the universe works on the most fundamental level. Because of this, a lot of research is being carried out to try to come up with a **quantum theory of gravity**. One of the theories put forward to fill the gap is **string theory**, which proposes that all the fundamental particles described in the standard model are actually the same thing: a string which moves in different ways to give us the impression of different types of particle. String theory is mathematically pretty complicated stuff, but the general hope scientists have for it is that one day it will be possible to unite the various different theories being worked on by physicists into one big **Theory of Everything** which will unlock the mysteries of our universe.

BERNOULLI'S PRINCIPLE: A HOME EXPERIMENT

Daniel Bernoulli (1700–1782) was a brainy Dutch-Swiss scientist who discovered that as the speed of a moving gas or liquid increases, the pressure it exerts decreases. This became known as Bernoulli's Principle and you can prove it using the following experiment.

APPARATUS
1 balloon
1 hairdryer

METHOD

Blow up your balloon and bounce it around a bit. You will see that it will gradually sink to the ground unless you keep punting it up into the air. Then turn on your hairdryer and point it up towards the ceiling before placing the balloon in its stream. Gradually tilt the hairdryer to the side a bit and then back again.

CONCLUSION

The balloon is slightly denser than air and this causes it to sink when left to its own devices. The stream of air from the hairdryer keeps the balloon up but it also keeps the balloon in its grip when tilted to the side. This is because the stream of air from the hairdryer has a lower pressure than the surrounding air so the surrounding air keeps the balloon pushed into the stream.

∞ SCIENCE ∞
TEST PAPER

1. **What do Hyrokkin, Iapetus and Skathi have in common?**

2. **Which of the following is NOT a type of quark?**

a) charm-quark
b) beta-quark
c) strange-quark
d) up-quark

3. **What is homeostasis?**

a) the tendency of a system to maintain equilibrium
b) the tendency of a system to maintain chaos
c) the tendency of a system to maintain heat

4. **Most comets' orbits are:**

a) circular
b) square
c) triangular
d) elliptical

5. **What did Alfred Nobel invent?**

a) peace
b) sulphur
c) the catflap
d) dynamite

6. **Identify this leaf:**

7. Which of the following is NOT true of limonene?

a) it makes pears smell of pears
b) it make lemons smell of lemon
c) it makes oranges smell of orange

8. Which is there more of in the universe?

a) matter
b) antimatter

9. Which organ is responsible for producing the insulin in your body?

10. How does the sun produce energy?

a) nuclear fusion
b) nuclear fission
c) by burning wax
d) through friction

11. What is a eukaryote?

a) a red blood cell
b) an organism whose cells contain a distinct nucleus contained in a membrane
c) a flowering plant
d) an organism with a backbone

12. Where is the green fluorescent protein (GFP) found in nature?

a) in the leaves of plants
b) in algae
c) in a certain type of jellyfish
d) in mouse brains

13. What does the Large Hadron Collider do?

a) fires protons at one another
b) magnifies leptons
c) makes bagels
d) makes fuel for space travel

14. Where would you find a dendrite?

a) in a nerve cell
b) in a haystack
c) in a forest
d) in a muon

15. Which of the following is NOT a nucleon?

a) proton
b) neutron
c) electron

16. Which of the following is a dwarf planet in our solar system?

a) Mars
b) Enterprise
c) Eris
d) the moon

17. A catalyst is:

a) a type of lepton
b) a substance that speeds up a chemical reaction without being involved in it itself
c) a substance that never decays
d) a feline burglar

18. Where is DNA stored?

19. What are isotopes?

a) types of aggressive cleaning fluid
b) foodstuffs manufactured from tree bark
c) different forms of atoms of the same element which have differing numbers of neutrons
d) the number of protons in the nucleus of an element's atom

20. Which of the following is a type of neurone?

a) javelin neurone
b) marathon neurone
c) relay neurone
d) pentathlon neurone

21. Is a lepton a fermion or a boson?

22. How many DNA bases does the human genome contain?

a) 3 billion pairs
b) 46 pairs
c) 8 million pairs
d) 24 pairs

23. Which has a bigger pawprint, a fox or a badger?

24. What are adenine, thymine, guanine and cytosine?

25. A hadron is:

a) a particle made up of electrons
b) a type of force
c) a particle made up of quarks
d) an electromagnetic wave

26. If someone has XY sex chromosomes, what are they more likely to be called?

a) Gregory
b) Dorothy

27. How often does Halley's Comet become visible on Earth?

28. What is the name of the process through which our cells release energy from food?

a) perspiration
b) insulation
c) parturition
d) respiration

29. Who came up with the theory of antimatter?

a) Enrico Fermi
b) Albert Einstein
c) Alfred Nobel
d) Paul Dirac

30. Your central nervous system is made up of:

a)   your muscles
b)   your brain
c)   your brain and spinal cord
d)   your hands and feet

❀ CLASSICS ❀

We think we are terribly clever and modern and yet so much of our culture can be traced back to the glories of ancient Greece and Rome: from the mythological stories that still influence literature and art being created today, to our philosophical and political systems (not to mention roads, cities, underfloor heating and wine). It's no wonder that generations have turned back to the works of these rich and sophisticated cultures for inspiration. In Britain we are lucky enough to have visible evidence of the Roman Empire that once ruled our homeland in the wonderfully preserved remains of buildings and beautiful mosaics that have been left behind in places like St Albans and Bath. Our mother tongue also carries echoes from both ancient Greek and Latin, and a knowledge of the latter has been shown to make learning the modern Romance languages of Europe far easier than it is for people with no background in this under-appreciated subject. In this chapter we will fill you in on the exploits of the naughty gods and feisty heroes of Greece and Rome, introduce you to the stratifications of Roman society, and teach you how to read Latin poetry and swear like a legionary. *Ave, curcubita!*

PERSEPHONE'S PRECARIOUS POMEGRANATE: MYTHS OF GREECE (AND ROME) I

The ancient Greeks had a fabulous collection of stories to explain the world around them. They worshipped a pantheon of eccentric gods, with different areas of speciality (ranging from war and love to wine and shepherds), who spent a large proportion of their time having family rows and raping innocent mortals. After conquering them, the Romans basically copied the Greeks' religion, changing the names but keeping the stories and mixing them with their own in a process called **syncretism**. Ancient Greek and Roman mythology pops up all over the place in art and literature and scattered throughout this chapter are some brief summaries of a few of the most popular tales. (Where the names of characters differ between the Greek and Roman traditions, the Latin names are in parentheses.)

While picking flowers, virginal young Persephone (Proserpine) was snatched by gloomy Hades (Pluto or Dis), god of the dead, and whisked away to his underworld lair. Her poor mother, Demeter (Ceres in Latin, from which we get 'cereal'), goddess of agriculture, was so upset by the kidnapping that all the crops failed, so top god Zeus (Jupiter) demanded the girl be sent home, so long as she hadn't settled in and eaten any underworld food. But Hades tricked poor Persephone into sucking some pomegranate seeds, which meant she was forced to return to him for one-third of every year. Demeter spent these months missing her daughter and ignoring the crops, so this myth works as an **aetiological** (*aitia* = cause, *logos* = study) story explaining the existence of the seasons.

IT'S ALL GREEK TO ME: SOME USEFUL ANCIENT GREEK WORDS

Ancient Greek was all the rage between the Renaissance and the start of the last century, but alas it has fallen by the wayside somewhat and is sparsely taught in schools. However, its influence lives on in the many English words that have Greek origins, particularly in the fields of medicine and science. The following few core pieces of vocabulary will reinvigorate your English as well as giving you that incomparable flush of clever-clogs pleasure that etymology inevitably provides.

ANCIENT GREEK WORDS and their meaning	RELATED ENGLISH WORDS
a or *an* = without	anaesthesia
aesthesis = sensation	aesthetics
tele = far away	telephone, teleport, telegraph
phone = sound	phonics, phonetics, phonograph
megas = large	megaphone, megalith, megaton
mikros = small	microphone, miscroscope
phil- = liking or loving	philosophy, zoophilia
anthropos = human	philanthropy, anthropomorphic
paedo = child	paedophile, pederast
iatros = doctor	paediatrician, iatrogenic
phobos = fear	phobia, hydrophobia,
arachne = spider	arachnid, arachnophobia
gyne = woman	polygyny, misogyny
logos = study	gynaecology, logic
psyche = soul	psychology, psychiatry, psychic
angelos = messenger	angel
amphi = on both sides	amphibrach, amphibious
bios = life	biology, antibiotic, bionic
grapho = write	biography, graphics, photograph
autos = self	autograph, automaton
oikos = house	ecology
nomia = law	economics, autonomy

AUDACIOUS ARACHNE ANGERS ATHENA:
MYTHS OF GREECE (AND ROME) II

Arachne was a young woman from Lydia (now part of Turkey) who was a celebrity in the weaving world because of her incredible skills. She became a bit of a show-off and decided to challenge Athena (the goddess of weaving as well as war and wisdom) to an *X-Factor*-style Weave-Off. Athena created an astonishingly beautiful tapestry showing the gods punishing mortals who challenged them and naughty Arachne wove a scene showing the gods' amorous adventures. Athena was enraged by this cheek and destroyed the girl's work, upsetting Arachne so much that she hanged herself. However, Athena forgave her in the end and changed her into a spider, and her noose into a cobweb, so she could weave away to her heart's content.

HIP, HIP, HOORAY FOR HIPPOCRATES:
ANCIENT MEDICINE

Different schools of medicine developed in ancient civilisations all over the world, but one of the most important figures in the history of Western medicine is the ancient Greek physician Hippocrates. Born $c.460$ BCE on the island of Cos, Hippocrates is considered responsible for developing an ethical and logical approach to medicine, sensibly separating the job of the doctor from that of the priest and bringing clinical observation to the forefront in determining treatment. In treatises such as his *On Regimen in Acute Diseases*, Hippocrates and his followers, instead of believing that diseases were punishments sent from the gods, posited the theory that illness is caused by environmental factors and can be influenced by diet and lifestyle. Several of the works attributed to him, such as *On Haemorrhoids*, even recommend treatments which are still used today ('cutting, excising, sewing, binding, applying putrefacient means . . .').

However, some of Hippocrates' ideas weren't quite so modern. He developed the theory of humours to explain how the body became vulnerable to disease. In his view, a healthy person would have the **four humours** – blood, yellow bile, black bile and phlegm – in balance, and illness occurred as a result of any imbalance between them. This theory was amazingly influential right up until the eighteenth century and led to the great popularity of bloodletting, sometimes using leeches, as an attempted medical cure for diseases that were thought to result from an excess of blood.

PARIS' PROBLEM:
MYTHS OF GREECE (AND ROME) III

Paris was a feckless fellow, one of the stars of the story of the Trojan War. His father, King Priam of Troy, was warned in a prophecy that he'd be trouble and so he was left on a hillside as a baby (a common ancient method of solving the problem of tricky children). Unfortunately, he survived and one day, while looking after his cattle, came across three gorgeous goddesses, Athena, Hera (Juno) and Aphrodite (Venus), bickering about who was the most attractive. (The naughty goddess of strife, Eris (Discordia), had thrown a golden apple inscribed with 'For the fairest' at them while they were at a party and they all thought it was meant for them.) They asked Paris to judge between them. Hera offered him wealth and power if he picked her, Athena offered him military glory and wisdom, and Aphrodite offered him the most beautiful woman in the world. Being an archetypal trouser-led man, Paris chose Aphrodite. The only complicating factor being that the most beautiful woman in the world, Helen, was married to the Greek king Menelaus. Paris' elopement with Helen led to the destruction of Troy by the vengeful Greeks and Paris' own demise: the old sex and death two-step.

NARCISSUS AND ECHO:
MYTHS OF GREECE (AND ROME) IV

To avoid the attention of his wife Hera, the incorrigible adulterer king god Zeus came up with a sneaky plan to distract her while he embarked on his amorous adventures. He employed the nymph Echo to keep her chatting while he slipped off to have his wicked way with whatever mortal woman or nymph was flavour of the month. When Hera discovered this, as was her wont, she preferred to punish the women involved rather than her errant spouse. She cursed Echo so that henceforth she would only be able to speak the last words of other people's sentences. This didn't help Echo in her passionate love for the gorgeous youth Narcissus, who was less than charmed by her fascinating conversation. In her distress at being dumped, Echo ran off to live in some caves until she wasted away leaving only echoes behind her. However, Narcissus didn't have the last laugh, as the goddess of vengeance, Nemesis, was irritated by his belief that he was too good for the lovely ladies who fell for him. She put a curse on him that led him to a humiliating end. While hunting in the woods one day he knelt down at a pool to drink some water, but catching sight of his own reflection mistook it for that of a beautiful water nymph living under the surface. He fell desperately in love with this mysterious creature but was unable to take her in his arms without splashing water everywhere and seeing her disappear. Gradually he starved to death by the pool, transfixed by the beauty in the water. Where he lay the narcissus flower grew in his memory.

THE *AENEID*

Influenced by Homer's great epics, the *Iliad* and the *Odyssey*, the Roman poet Virgil (70–19 BCE) wrote his masterwork the *Aeneid* in order to celebrate the rule of the Emperor Augustus and set down Rome's founding myth, which connected the city to the ancient Greek heroes of the Trojan War. It is a highly influential work of art and a fantastic read, full of daredevil adventures and terrible hardships as well as being an astute piece of political propaganda (look out for the amazing sucking up to Big Gus in Book VI).

Book I: The poem begins with the famous words '*Arma virumque cano*' which means 'I sing of arms and the man', stating Virgil's intention to tell a story about conflict and the hero Aeneas. Seven years after the sack of Troy, Aeneas and his fellow survivors get caught in a storm at sea sent by the staunchly anti-Trojan goddess Juno. After landing on the coast of Libya, Aeneas travels to the nearby city of Carthage to seek assistance and Venus, his mother, inspires the Carthaginian queen Dido to fall in love with him in order to help him. Dido asks Aeneas to tell her his adventures.

Book II: Aeneas tells the story of the Trojan Horse and how he left the city with his father, his wife Creusa, his son and some other Trojans. In the confusion Creusa goes missing and Aeneas only discovers she is dead when he goes back for her and meets her ghost, who kindly reassures him that he will find a new wife in his future homeland.

Book III: Aeneas then tells of the survivors' exploits on their travels to Libya. It becomes clear it's not been an easy trip. In Thrace they discover treachery; in Delos the oracle of Apollo tells them to go to the land of Aeneas' ancestors (which they think means Crete); in Crete they catch the plague and the gods tell Aeneas to head for Italy instead; in the Strophades they are attacked by Harpies (hostile birds with women's faces); in Buthrotum they have a brief rest; in Sicily they're chased by the Cyclops; and in Drepanum Aeneas' father pops his clogs.

Book IV: Impressed by all of this, Dido falls hopelessly in love with Aeneas. Their affair distracts both of them from their duties until Jupiter sends Mercury to remind Aeneas of his responsibilities and he immediately sets sail for Italy. Dido is so distraught by his unceremonious exit that she commits suicide.

Book V: A storm forces the Trojans to land in Sicily where Aeneas arranges athletic competitions to honour the memory of his father. While the games are taking place, Juno inspires the Trojan women, who are bored of travelling and want to stay in Sicily, to set fire to the boats, but Jupiter sends a rainstorm to save them. After speaking to his father in a dream, Aeneas decides to leave the less hardy members of his party behind. The rest continue with him to Italy.

Book VI: When the ships land in Italy, Aeneas visits the Sibyl (a prophetess) at Cumae. She helps him enter the underworld, where he sees an unfriendly Dido and warriors from the Trojan War and speaks to his father who tells him about the illustrious future of the home that he is destined to found in Italy. This amounts to a pretty positive write-up of Augustan Rome.

Book VII: The Trojans sail up the coast to Latium where Aeneas arranges with the king to share territory and marry his daughter Lavinia. However, a nearby ruler called Turnus also has his eye on Lavinia, and Juno, unflagging in her plans to rain on Aeneas' parade, encourages Turnus to attempt to kick out the Trojans.

Book VIII: Aeneas goes to visit the amiable King Evander to ask for help. Venus gets her husband Vulcan to make special armour for Aeneas, which prophetically depicts future events in Rome's history.

Book IX: While Aeneas is away, Turnus attacks the Trojan camp. Two Trojans, Nisus and Euryalus, carry out successful night-time raids against the Latins but are eventually killed. Turnus then gets inside the Trojan camp and causes havoc.

Book X: Aeneas returns and joins the battle. After Turnus kills Evander's young son Pallas, Aeneas pursues him in a frenzy, but Juno saves her boy by leading him onto a nearby ship and cutting it loose to drift away from the battle.

Book XI: The Latins discuss Turnus and Aeneas settling the battle themselves. Turnus leaves to set an ambush and the warrior Camilla leads the Latins in combat until she is killed, forcing Turnus to abandon his plot.

Book XII: Finally, Turnus challenges Aeneas to single combat, but interfering Juno starts a scrap between the Latin and Trojan troops. In the ensuing battle Juno gives up her efforts to save Turnus in return for a promise from Jupiter that Aeneas' new settlement will adopt the name and language of the Latin people. Aeneas beats Turnus and considers sparing his life but kills him when he recalls the death of young Pallas.

POLYPHEMUS, THE CYCLOPS: HOW TO TRANSLATE LATIN UNSEENS

Aeneid, Book III, Virgil

> *vix ea fatus erat, summo cum monte videmus*
> *ipsum inter pecudes vasta se mole moventem*
> *pastorem Polyphemum et litora nota petentem,*
> *monstrum horrendum, informe, ingens, cui lumen ademptum.*
> *trunca manu pinus regit et vestigia firmat;*
> *lanigerae comitantur oves – ea sola voluptas*
> *solamenque mali.*

VOCABULARY

vix − scarcely	for, fari, fat-us − to speak	Ipse, -a, -um − himself, herself itself	pecus, -udis f. − animal, esp. sheep	moles, -is f. − mass
litus, -oris n. − seashore	notus, -a, -um − known	peto -ere, -ivi and -ii- itum − to make for	ingens -entis − huge	Cui − from or to whom
adimo, -imere, -emi, -emptum − to take away	manus, -us f. − hand	vestigium, -i n. − footstep	laniger, -gera, -gerum − woolly	comito, -are − to accompany
ovis, -is f. − sheep	solamen, -inis n. − consolation	malum, -i − disaster	ea − they	et − and

1. The first thing to do when faced with a passage of unknown Latin is to check out any tips you can get from the title and vocabulary you are given and then read the piece through a couple of times and try to get a sense of what's going on. If you know anything about Greek and Latin mythology you'll know that Polyphemus the Cyclops was a one-eyed giant who lived in Sicily and chowed down on various companions of Odysseus in Homer's *Odyssey* before the wily warrior blinded him with a stake. You might also know that Virgil's Latin epic, the *Aeneid*, is heavily influenced by Homer and his hero Aeneas also runs into the big unfriendly giant while in Sicily.

2. Once you've tried to get the gist of the piece, you then need to break the passage down into manageable portions. The best way to do this is to separate it into sections and write the vocabulary you've been given over the relevant Latin words. (Ideally you would use your skills at declensions and conjugations to identify the correct person, gender and number of whatever verb or noun you're looking at, but don't worry if that's a bit too much of a brain-strain.) It's important to remember the basic Latin grammar principle that the verb comes at the end of the sentence.

3. Once you've allocated the vocab, the next useful thing to do is to see if you recognise any of the other vocabulary from English words or other modern languages you might know. Using just your knowledge of English you might be able to puzzle out the following hints:

				summit?		mountain?	see?
Vix	*ea*	*fatus*	*erat,*	*summo*	*cum*	*monte*	*videmus*

	between?		vast?			movement?
Ipsum	*inter*	*pecudes*	*vasta*	*se*	*mole*	*moventum*

pastoral?					
pastorem	*Polyphemum*	*et*	*litora*	*nota*	*petentem*

monster?	horrendous?				light?	
monstrum	*horrendum,*	*informe,*	*ingens,*	*cui*	*lumen*	*ademptum.*

trunk?	manual?	pine?	rule?			firm?
trunca	*manu*	*pinus*	*regit*	*et*	*vestigia*	*firmat;*

				sole?	voluptuous?
lanigerae	*comitantur*	*oves*	*– ea*	*sola*	*voluptas*

solamenque   mali.

4. With the detective work above and a bit of rearranging of word order and lateral thinking, you might find you're able to come up with something along the lines of:

> They had scarcely spoken, when on the top of the mountain they saw the shepherd Polyphemus himself, moving his vast mass amongst the sheep and making for the known shore. A horrendous monster, deformed and huge, from whom the light had been taken away, he guides and makes firm his footsteps with the trunk of a pine tree in his hand. The woolly sheep accompany him, the only pleasure and consolation to him in these disasters.

It's not perfect, or by any means elegant, but it does make sense of what's going on and if you managed to get this far you should give yourself a pat on the back. When polishing up your effort it's worth remembering that the best translations don't adhere rigidly to a literal version of the Latin – it's just as important to get a sense of the tone and flow of the original. Here's how seventeenth-century Poet Laureate John Dryden put it:

Scarce had he said, when on the mountain's brow
We saw the giant shepherd stalk before
His following flock, and leading to the shore:
A monstrous bulk, deform'd, depriv'd of sight;
His staff a trunk of pine, to guide his steps aright.
His pond'rous whistle from his neck descends;
His woolly care their pensive lord attends:
This only solace his hard fortune sends.

Who knows where his 'pond'rous whistle' came from but you can see
how he's captured the drama, and even the giant's-footsteps-style phrasing,
perfectly. Clever old Dryden.

UNLUCKY OEDIPUS:
MYTHS OF GREECE (AND ROME) V

The birth of Oedipus was not a happy day for his dad, King Laius of
Thebes, as he was warned in a prophecy that the child would kill him
if it grew up. Because of this, Oedipus was tied up by his feet on a
hillside and left to die. However, some passing peasants rescued him and
gave him his name, which means 'Swollen Foot' in Greek. Many years
later, Oedipus unknowingly bumped into his father and, in self-defence,
killed him a road-rage incident. His next adventure involved the Sphinx,
a half-woman half-lion monster, who was terrorising the neighbour-
hood around Thebes. This pesky creature murdered travellers if they
couldn't answer her riddles. She asked Oedipus: 'What animal goes about
on four feet in the morning, two in the afternoon and three in the
evening?' Smart Oedipus answered 'Man', because humans crawl on all
fours as babies, walk on two feet as adults and need the help of a stick
when they are old. The Sphinx took her defeat badly and killed herself
in frustration, while Oedipus was feted by the Thebans for saving them.
As they were short of a king (the previous incumbent having been
killed in a row about chariots out on the road to Delphi), they crowned
Oedipus and married him off to Jocasta, Laius' widow (and, of course,
Oedipus' mum!). Nobody realised what had happened until Thebes was
afflicted by famine and plague and the oracle was consulted for help.
When the truth was revealed, Jocasta topped herself and Oedipus gouged

out his eyes in horror and left Thebes to wander in misery for years with his daughter Antigone, until he finally died at Colonus near Athens. Not a happy ending in sight (particularly when you consider the fates of Oedipus' four children: Eteocles and Polynices killed each other and poor Antigone was sentenced to be buried alive and hanged herself. Only Ismene may have escaped, and her fate is unknown).

ROMAN BRITAIN

From the mid first century CE to the early fifth century our fair island was ruled by those conquest-hungry legions from *bella Roma*. As the army moved through the country it established forts, around which important urban centres developed, connected to one another by roads to aid in the administration of the surrounding countryside. Some of these towns have remained important today, albeit under different names: Noviomagus Regnorum (Chichester), Camulodunum (Colchester), Corinium Dobunnorum (Cirencester), Ratae Corieltavorum (Leicester), Venta Belgarum (Winchester), Durovernum Cantiacorum (Canterbury), Eboracum (York), Verulamium (St Albans), Lindum Colonia (Lincoln), Aquae Sulis (Bath) and Londinium (London).

Roman town planning followed a similar formula each time, laying the streets out on a grid pattern. The centre of the town was the market square or **forum** with its attached **basilica** or town hall. As well as villas, the towns usually had shops, a temple, public baths and sometimes sophisticated sewage and water systems. Roman buildings were built in stone or brick and many of them endured after the Roman withdrawal that happened as the empire lost its grip on its territories in the fifth century. New buildings were constructed over the abandoned ones, as can be seen at sites such as Bath and St Albans where excavations have taken place. Many more still lie underneath modern towns.

HADRIAN AND HIS WALL

Publius Aelius Hadrianus (76–138 CE) grew up as a ward of the Emperor Trajan and was proclaimed emperor by the army in 117 CE after his guardian's death. Previously he'd been a respected soldier and he was also a great enthusiast in the fields of literature and architecture. He inherited a huge empire that was beset on all sides by barbarians. In Britain he decided he particularly needed to defend Rome's territory from marauding Scottish tribes. In 122 CE he ordered his soldiers to build a fortified wall from Wallsend to Bowness, along the boundary of Roman control. It took six years to construct and stretched for seventy-three miles, remaining in action until 400 CE, despite being breached by attackers three times over the course of its history.

A SMATTERING OF LATIN: SOME USEFUL LATIN PHRASES

ad hominem (to the person) – associated with a particular person
corpus delicti (body of the offence) – the facts and circumstances constituting a breach of law
deus ex machina (god from the machinery) – an unexpected power or event saving a seemingly hopeless situation
in utero (in the womb) – in the womb, before birth
memento mori (remember you must die) – a warning or reminder of death
in medias res (into the midst of things) – into the middle of a story, without preamble
passim (scattered) – to be found at various places throughout the text
prima facie (first face) – at first sight or based on a first impression
status quo (the state in which) – the existing state of affairs
vox populi (the people's voice) – public opinion, popular belief or rumour

HOW TO SWEAR IN LATIN

As the graffiti-covered walls of Pompeii prove, the Romans didn't just spend their time expanding their empire and lounging around on their underfloor heating sipping goblets of wine. They also knew how to insult each other in style; even classical greats such as Catullus and Martial weren't beyond a bit of poetic obscenity every now and then. Below you'll find a list of enjoyable snubs, slanders and slights. These are particularly useful when you're slightly too scared of your insultee to confront them in plain English.

amove te, curcubita! – piss off, pumpkin!

stulte! – you idiot!

delphinum natare doces – you're teaching a dolphin to swim (the Roman equivalent of teaching a grandma to suck eggs)

tace! – shut up!

asine! – you donkey!

meretrix! – whore!

nugas garris – you're talking rubbish

spurcifer! – you bearer of filth!

FROM THE SENATE TO THE PLEBS: WHO'S WHO IN IMPERIAL ROMAN SOCIETY

Ancient Rome was a pretty hierarchical place. Starting from the bottom of the pile, the most basic legal division was between those who were free and slaves. A **slave** (*servus*) was the property of his or her master and was either the offspring of slaves or a captive from battles with Rome's enemies.

However, there was the possibility of improving your lot even if you were on this lowest echelon, since slaves could be freed by their masters through a process called **manumission** (*manumissio*). This sometimes happened as part of a master's will, or as a reward for good service, or if the slave saved up enough of their wages to buy their freedom. An ex-slave was called a **freedman** (*libertus*) and could go on to have a career as a merchant, tradesman or even an adviser to the emperor, although they were excluded from certain rights of citizenship. As in many other ancient societies women played a secondary and officially non-political role in Rome. Within the family the father (*paterfamilias*) had absolute authority over the rest of the household.

Even if you were free and living in the Roman Empire this didn't necessarily mean that you were a **citizen**, with all the career opportunities, legal and other rights (such as being able to serve in the legions) that status conferred. As the empire grew, citizenship was given as a favour by the emperors to individuals and groups from captured territories.

Among citizens there were different levels of status. When Rome was still a kingdom (753–509 BCE) its inhabitants were divided into landowning **patricians** (*patricii*) and peasant **plebeians** (*plebs*). The patricians originally held all government offices but from the beginning of the Roman Republic (509–44 BCE) the plebeians rebelled and eventually gained equal social and religious rights. After this point the word '*plebs*' changed to mean the common people in general, as opposed to members of the senatorial and equestrian class.

The **senatorial class** (*ordo senatorius*) was the upper crust of Roman society and, just below them, the **equestrian class** (*ordo equester*) was originally made up of those noble families who had enough money to serve in the cavalry of the Roman army. The **senate** was Rome's main governmental advisory body, established back in the early days of Rome when it was a monarchy and influential through its republican years when it advised the two **consuls**, who were the highest authorities in Rome before the emperors took over the show. The six hundred senators were members of Rome's top aristocratic families, who qualified to join through their ancestry, their property and their experience holding official posts as magistrates. Less privileged citizens exercised their authority in the various **assemblies**, up until the early days of the Empire when the assemblies' powers were transferred to the senate and, in real terms, all power passed to the emperor.

From the time of Augustus until the end of the empire, the **emperor** (*princeps* or *imperator*) was top of the heap. The death knell of the republic was sounded in 44 BCE with the appointment of Julius Caesar as dictator for life. Previously the consuls had appointed dictators with absolute control over the state in times of emergency, but they had only ruled for six months. Before his murder by factions keen to wrest this exceptional power from him, Caesar named his grand-nephew and adopted son Octavian as his heir. Over the following years Octavian dispatched his political rivals (including Mark Antony and Cleopatra) and consolidated his position until he was chief of the armed forces, head of state religion and controller of the senate. In 27 BCE he jacked in the boring old name of Octavian and assumed the title of Augustus (meaning 'royal'), officially beginning the glory days of the empire.

∽ CLASSICS ∽
TEST PAPER

1. **What is the Greek goddess Demeter's Roman name?**

2. **What does *anthropos* mean in ancient Greek?**

a) spider
b) ant
c) human
d) cake

3. **Hippocrates was born in the:**

a) first century BCE
b) first century CE
c) sixth century CE
d) fifth century BCE

4. **What is the Roman goddess Discordia's speciality?**

a) childbirth
b) music
c) strife
d) war

5. **Who lost the Battle of Actium?**

a) Julius Caesar
b) Octavian
c) Brutus
d) Mark Antony

6. **Using your knowledge of ancient Greek, what do you think a 'graphologist' does?**

7. **If you were out walking in the ancient Roman countryside and a farmer came running up to you with a look of horror**

on his face to warn you about a marauding '*ingens ovis*' on the loose – what should you be looking out for?

a) a Cyclops
b) a giant sheep
c) an enraged Carthaginian
d) a huge whirlpool

8. **In the Hippocratic oath doctors promise to:**

a) avoid harming their patients
b) burn incense to honour Aesculapius
c) use leeches to purge their patients of excess blood
d) wash their hands before beginning work

9. **Who is higher up the social pecking order in ancient Rome, a senator or a knight (*eques*)?**

10. **What is the ancient Greek word for 'messenger'?**

a) *rhodon*
b) *angelos*
c) *messangos*
d) *mailos*

11. **What is the emperor-formerly-known-as-Octavian more usually called?**

12. **If you translated rock band Status Quo's name into English, what would be printed onto their tour T-shirts?**

a) Rockin' All Over the World with the Existing State of Affairs!
b) Rockin' All Over the World with Dry Land!
c) Rockin' All Over the World with From the Beginning!
d) Rockin' All Over the World with a Reminder of Death!

13. **Who was Oedipus' mother?**

14. **What is the etymology of the word 'psychiatry'?**

15. In Virgil's _Aeneid_, Dido was queen of:

a) Carthage
b) Troy
c) Latium
d) Kensington

16. Before Hippocrates, how did the ancient Greek population generally think disease was caused?

17. What does οἰκος (_oikos_) mean?

18. What was the Cyclops Polyphemus' official job?

a) cattle-rustler
b) shepherd
c) monster
d) harpist

19. What does the Latin word '_lumen_' mean?

20. In what profession might the Latin phrase '_corpus delicti_' be used?

a) medicine
b) gymnastics
c) law
d) politics

21. Who was Paris' father?

a) Apollo
b) Priam
c) Achilles
d) Hector

22. If your Latin dating website comes up with a suitable match for you and she has written her profession down as '_meretrix_', what should you expect her job to be?

a) barmaid
b) nurse

c) prophetess
d) prostitute

23. What were Oedipus' daughters called?

a) Helen and Clytemnestra
b) Antigone and Ismene
c) Iphigenia and Cassandra
d) Susan and Alice

24. In the theory of humours followed by Hippocrates, all people were supposed to contain a balance of the four humours. Some individuals were thought to have a bit more of one than the others and this was supposed to lead to a certain personality type. Match up the humours below with the type they are supposed to produce.

blood	phlegmatic
yellow bile	choleric
black bile	melancholic
phlegm	sanguine

25. Julius Caesar was the Emperor Augustus' what?:

a) father
b) great-uncle
c) grandson
d) second cousin

26. Why did Christopher Marlowe call Helen of Troy 'the face that launched a thousand ships'?

27. When did the Roman Republic begin?

a) 27 BCE
b) 44 BCE
c) 509 BCE
d) 778 BCE

28. **The ancient Greek gods were very keen on turning mortals into plants and animals. Match up the poor nymphs and girls in the list below with the flora and fauna they became:**

Daphne	spider
Arachne	cow
Io	nightingale
Philomela	laurel tree

29. **Who was Ptolemy Caesarion?**

a) Julius Caesar and Cleopatra's son
b) Mark Antony and Cleopatra's son
c) Cleopatra's older brother
d) Octavian's son

30. **Which of the following heroes survived the Trojan War?**

a) Achilles
b) Hector
c) Paris
d) Aeneas

❦ DRAMA ❦
AND
FILM STUDIES

Why it is that we love to watch other people dress up and pretend to be different people? Television has usurped theatre and cinema as the most commonly enjoyed visual entertainment of the great British public, but these forms still have something important to say to us about our experiences of the world. The ancient Greeks argued about the moral purpose of theatre – whether or not it led people astray or acted as a positive cathartic ritual – and this debate, particularly around violent films, continues today. In order to partake in these kinds of discussions, and others that will make you sound incredibly clever and cultured, it's important to have a background in the development of theatrical forms and the works of the greatest practitioners throughout history. In this chapter we will take you gently by the hand through the garden of earthly delights that is Drama and Film Studies, and lead you from the public spectacle of the ancient Greek amphitheatre over centuries to the hushed and magical darkness of the cinema stalls. On with the show!

CURTAIN UP!:
DIFFERENT FORMS OF THEATRE

For generations creative types have been writing and performing dramatic works that reflect and give insight into our world. The earliest records of plays come from about four thousand years ago and they are thought to have developed from religious rituals. Many different elements such as music, dance, improvisation and mime can be involved in theatre, but the most important thing is that a theatrical piece is performed live, directly in front of an audience: the word 'drama' comes from the ancient

Greek word '*drao*' meaning 'to do', and the word 'theatre' comes from the ancient Greek word '*theatron*' meaning 'viewing place'. For all of you who think the thespian world begins and ends with Shakespeare, here's a whirlwind guide through space and time to investigate some important theatrical traditions.

Ancient Greek Theatre

Greek theatre began with ceremonies celebrating the frisky wine deity Dionysus where **dithyrambs** (wild hymns with dancing) were performed by a **chorus** of actors. The change from ritual to play officially occurred in the sixth century BCE when a bright spark called Thespis (from whose name we get the term 'thespian') introduced a solo actor into the mix. As time went on, theatrical pieces in three different genres became the formal components of the Dionysia festival – **tragedy**, **comedy** and **satyr plays** (short comic pieces involving satyrs, funnily enough, that stood as a genre of their own).

Singing and dancing continued to be performed by the chorus, who also participated in the action. Actors wore stylised masks which allowed them to play multiple roles and also helped circumnavigate the problem that women were often the subjects of Greek plays but could not perform. The plays we have today come predominantly from the fifth-century BCE tragedians Aeschylus (who added a second individual actor in his plays), Sophocles (who added a third) and Euripides, and the comic playwright Aristophanes.

Noh Theatre

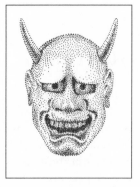

Noh is the most ancient and serious of Japanese dramatic genres. It evolved between the fourteenth and early seventeenth centuries in Japan and is still popular today. Noh (meaning 'accomplishment') developed from earlier rural entertainments involving acrobatics, music and dance called *sarugaku* and *dengaku*. These were transformed into elegant, refined plays for an elite audience by the playwright, actor and musician Kan'ami Kiyotsugu and his son Zeami Motokiyo. Noh dramas aim to achieve a sense of '*yugen*' ('grace') through carefully stylised performances based on mythological and literary subjects. The action focuses on one main actor, the *shite* (pronounced 'sh'tay'), who is beautifully costumed and often elaborately masked to allow him to appear as an old person, man, woman, god or monster. The performance also involves secondary characters, a chorus and musicians who accompany the dances and recitations.

Commedia dell'arte

In sixteenth-century northern Italy professional actors began to take folk stories, improvisation, masks, music, dance and acrobatics and develop them into a new theatrical medium. This became known as commedia dell'arte ('comedy of the artists') and remained a rambunctious popular entertainment for the next two centuries. This collaborative tradition concentrated on the actor as opposed to a written script and involved both male and female performers. Most commedia pieces involved stock characters which included the heroine Colombina, her grumpy father Pantalone, the blustering soldier Il Capitano and a bevy of comic servants including Arlecchino (also known as Harlequin), Pulcinella (who became our wife-beating Punch, of Punch and Judy fame) and Scaramuccia (Scaramouche).

Elizabethan Theatre

The arts flourished during the reign of Queen Elizabeth, and Bess was especially fond of performing players. Think of Elizabethan Theatre and of course William Shakespeare immediately comes to mind, but other greats were also writing at this time such as: Christopher Marlowe and Ben Jonson (like Shakespeare, Jonson was an actor as well as a playwright). Plays were performed at a variety of venues across London, but most famous is the Globe, which was built in 1599 and destroyed by fire in 1613.

Revenge Tragedy

Popular in Elizabethan and Jacobean times, revenge tragedy does what it says on the tin. The fashion for these shockingly violent stories of vengeance began with Thomas Kyd's *The Spanish Tragedy* (*c.*1590). Thomas Middleton was the master of the genre, as is illustrated by his *The Changeling* (*c.1652*), and John Webster's *The White Devil* (1612) and *The Duchess of Malfi* (*c.*1613) are also considered prime examples of this bloody, cathartic genre.

Restoration Comedy and Georgian Comedy of Manners

The restoration of King Charles II in 1660 heralded a joyous new dawn for British theatre, which had been suppressed during the killjoy Puritan Commonwealth. Charles issued a royal warrant decreeing that there would be no more boys in frocks onstage and that women should be allowed to act, and his patronage of the theatre led to the development of a particularly witty and bawdy kind of comedy written by playwrights such as the Williams Congreve and Wycherley. This genre was later developed into the more refined comedy of manners epitomised by the works of Richard Brinsley Sheridan and his chum Oliver Goldsmith.

Realism

The artistic movement known as realism influenced theatrical works from the nineteenth century onwards, and aimed to make plays as much like real life as possible by focusing on characters' psychological development, avoiding formal theatrical techniques such as soliloquies and paying particular attention to keeping the fourth wall unbroken. The Norwegian playwright Henrik Ibsen is often said to be the father of realism and Anton Chekhov, August Strindberg and Eugene O'Neill are also considered important proponents. The Russian actor and director Konstantin Stanislavsky brought realism to bear on actors' training with his system, which encouraged performers to recall their own experiences and emotions in their portrayal of their characters.

Theatre of the Absurd

The Theatre of the Absurd refers to the work of a number of playwrights mostly writing in the 1950s and 60s. The phrase was first used in an essay by French thinker Albert Camus, who believed that human beings inhabit a world that is alien, meaningless, and, of course, absurd. Samuel Beckett's *Waiting for Godot* is one of many plays that reflect this view of mankind as out of kilter, bewildered and alienated.

WHAT IS THE FOURTH WALL?

The fourth wall is the imaginary wall that separates the audience from the stage, through which they view the action of the play. In realist theatre the actors act as if the wall is really there, and there is no audience. If an actor addresses or acknowledges the audience directly, by yelling 'Hi, Mum!' or by speaking asides directed at them, they are 'breaking the fourth wall'.

Diagram of a Stage

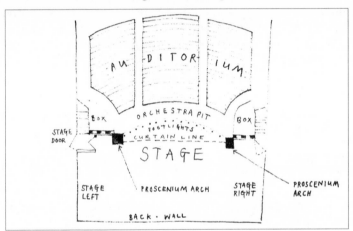

EIGHT OF THE BEST: CLASSICS OF THE THEATRE

It is tricky to summarise the crème de la crème of theatrical achievement: the ABC of illustrious and influential playwrights who fit the bill trips off the tongue in an embarrassment of riches . . . Aeschylus, Bond, Chekhov, Dumas *fils*, Euripides, Frayn, Genet, Hare, Ibsen, Jonson, Kyd, Lorca, Molière, Nestroy, Orton, Pinter, Qabbani, Racine, Shakespeare, Tendulkar, Udall, Vanbrugh, Wilde, Yeats, Zapolska . . . Where is *The Mousetrap*? you may cry. How could you have forgotten *We Will Rock You*? Of course you may compose your own list, but rest assured that all the curtain-raisers below are well worth your attention.

Antigone (c. 441 BCE)

Antigone is the last of Sophocles' Theban plays, following *Oedipus the King* and *Oedipus at Colonus*. It tells the rather sorry tale of Oedipus' daughter Antigone's efforts to bury her rebellious brother in accordance with religious rites. Her uncle Creon, the ruler of Thebes, forbids this and when she defies him he sentences her to be buried alive, resulting in her suicide. The gods then punish Creon by inspiring his wife and son to top themselves, leaving him a sad, lonely, but wiser, old man.

Doctor Faustus (c.1592)

Doctor Faustus is based on a famous German legend, transformed into beautiful and shocking poetry by Elizabethan *enfant terrible*, Christopher Marlowe. Bored of his studies, Faustus decides to learn the art of magic. He summons a charming devil called Mephistopheles, who agrees to serve him in return for him signing his soul away to Lucifer, which Faustus blithely does. Things don't go so well from this point and the play ends with one of Faustus' pals saying, 'See, here are Faustus' limbs, / All torn asunder by the hand of death.' The moral of the story being, always read the small print.

Hamlet (c.1601)

Shakespeare's tale of troubled Danish prince Hamlet comes from Norse legend. At the opening of the play Hamlet's father's ghost turns up demanding revenge on his brother Claudius for murdering him. In working himself up to this task, Hamlet commissions a play about the murder, accidentally kills the Lord Chamberlain, Polonius (leading to the insanity and suicide of his girlfriend Ophelia), casts aspersions on his mother Gertrude's honour (for marrying bad old Claudius), gets two of his friends bumped off in England for siding against him, and has a chat about a jester called Yorick to a gravedigger while man-handling the poor fellow's skull. Eventually Laertes (Polonius' son and Ophelia's brother) challenges him to a duel which leaves pretty much all of the remaining cast dead apart from Hamlet's stalwart pal Horatio, who is persuaded to live on to tell the prince's depressing story.

Le Misanthrope (1666)

Jean-Baptiste Poquelin (more commonly known as Molière) was an actor and playwright who wrote many comedies which are still popular today. *Le Misanthrope* (which was actually not a great success in its day) is regarded as his greatest glory. The hero of the play is uptight Alceste who eschews the common flattery, hypocrisy and etiquette that grease the wheels of social intercourse. Alceste believes in blunt honesty which gets him in all kinds of trouble and causes problems in his relationship with social butterfly Célimène, leading to his decision to retire entirely from human society and live in solitude. The play is celebrated for its multidimensional characterisation, which enriched the traditional genre of French comedy by developing straightforward farce and satire into something more thought-provoking and complex.

The Cherry Orchard (1904)

Anton Chekhov's *The Cherry Orchard* is a wonderful, beautifully paced play about the decline of the Russian aristocracy. Despite its melancholy feel, Chekhov originally intended it as a comedy. The plot concerns Mme Ranevsky's fruitless refusal to sell the cherry orchard on her estate in order to clear her debts. The piece ends poignantly when, after the estate's sale, Firs, the poorly family servant, gets locked in the house as everyone leaves. As he lies down on the sofa to die, 'the sound is heard, some way away in the orchard, of the axe falling on the trees'.

Mourning Becomes Electra (1931)

In this powerful work, Eugene O'Neill chose to retell Aeschylus' *Oresteia*, setting the tragedy within the family of a Northern general during the American Civil War. The action takes place over three plays – *Homecoming*, *The Hunted* and *The Haunted* – and deals with themes of incest, adultery, love, murder and revenge as the patriarch of a family returns home. Its genius lies in negotiating the space between the ancient and the modern: the setting of the Civil War allowed for a new sense of American mythology.

Waiting for Godot (1953)

In Samuel Beckett's *Waiting for Godot* (originally written in French as *En attendant Godot*) Estragon and Vladimir wait in vain for the appearance of someone called Godot. To occupy themselves, they muck about, chat, muse on the nature of human existence and think about suicide. In the first act a pair of characters called Pozzo and Lucky pass by. Later, a boy arrives, explaining that Godot will come the next day so the duo decide to leave, without actually doing so. The second act follows generally the same narrative. Beckett's pivotal modernist masterpiece explores the ennui and alienation of modern society and the play's openness to interpretation – from the political and historical to the psychological and religious – has made it hugely popular and much studied.

Look Back in Anger (1956)

Look Back in Anger by John Osborne dramatises a rather bleak love triangle between working-class 'Angry Young Man', Jimmy Porter, his wife Alison and her friend Helena. The play begins with Jimmy ranting against the complacency of middle-class society, particularly picking on poor pregnant Alison's family. Helena encourages Alison to leave Jimmy, then starts an affair with him herself. Months later, Alison returns having lost the baby. Helena leaves, feeling guilty, and the couple reconcile and end up playing their weird little love game of pretending to be a squirrel and a bear. The play pioneered a new genre called 'kitchen-sink drama' and heralded a wave of politically aware writers – such as Harold Pinter, Arnold Wesker and Shelagh Delaney – ending the dominance of 'Whoops – I've got a vicar in my closet' theatre visited only by the middle-class bourgeoisie.

THE MOST CHALLENGING STAGE DIRECTIONS EVER GIVEN

'Exit, pursued by a bear' from Shakespeare's *The Winter's Tale*. The perfect opportunity for a RADA graduate to dress up in a bear suit and run growling across the stage thinking 'What's my motivation?'

'Enter . . . Lavinia, her hands cut off, and her tongue cut out and ravished' from *Titus Andronicus*. Weaker-spirited performers tend to opt for some symbolic wafting of red chiffon tied to sleeves in response to this belter.

'As the castle burns, the bud on the roof bursts open into a giant chrysanthemum' from *A Dream Play* by Strindberg. A rousing challenge for the set designer.

'Hell is discovered' from Marlowe's *Doctor Faustus*. Just like that, easy-peasy.

'. . . the Stage is almost wholly dark: A symphony of Warlike Music is heard for some time; then from the Heavens (which are opened) fall the rebellious Angels wheeling in the Air, and

seeming transfix'd with Thunderbolts: The bottom of the Stage
being open'd, receives the Angels, who fall out of sight. Tunes
of Victory are play'd, and an Hymn sung; Angels discover'd
above, brandishing their Swords: The Music ceasing, and the
Heavens being closed, the Scene shifts, and on a sudden represents Hell: Part of the Scene is a Lake of Brimstone or rolling
Fire; the Earth of a burnt colour: The fall'n Angels appear on
the Lake, lying prostrate; a Tune of Horror and Lamentation
is heard' from Dryden's libretto *The State of Innocence and Fall of Man*.
A low-key curtain-raiser.

SHAKESPEARE'S SOLILOQUIES: MONOLOGUES WORTH MEMORISING

We are of the firm belief that people should memorise passages of great
writing more often. Not only does this keep your grey cells nimble but
it also means that your memory becomes a treasure trove of literary
gems which you can take out and turn over in your mouth whenever
you are lost for words. Who better to turn to for this kind of mnemonic
education than the greatest British playwright of all time, Mr William
Shakespeare?

A morsel of Macbeth for when you're feeling mournful:

> To-morrow, and to-morrow, and to-morrow,
> Creeps in this petty pace from day to day
> To the last syllable of recorded time,
> And all our yesterdays have lighted fools
> The way to dusty death. Out, out, brief candle!
> Life's but a walking shadow, a poor player
> That struts and frets his hour upon the stage
> And then is heard no more. It is a tale
> Told by an idiot, full of sound and fury,
> Signifying nothing.

Macbeth, Act V, Scene 5

A response of Romeo's for when you don't hear your partner ask you to take out the rubbish:

> O, speak again, bright angel! for thou art
> As glorious to this night, being o'er my head,
> As is a wingèd messenger of heaven
> Unto the white-upturnèd wond'ring eyes
> Of mortals that fall back to gaze on him
> When he bestrides the lazy-pacing clouds
> And sails upon the bosom of the air.

> *Romeo and Juliet*, Act II, Scene 2

A portion of Portia for when you've crashed the car:

> The quality of mercy is not strained;
> It droppeth as the gentle rain from heaven
> Upon the place beneath. It is twice blest:
> It blesseth him that gives and him that takes.
> 'Tis mightiest in the mightiest; it becomes
> The thronèd monarch better than his crown;
> His sceptre shows the force of temporal power,
> The attribute to awe and majesty,
> Wherein doth sit the dread and fear of kings;
> But mercy is above this sceptred sway,
> It is enthronèd in the hearts of kings,
> It is an attribute to God himself;
> And earthly power doth then show likest God's
> When mercy seasons justice.

> *The Merchant of Venice*, Act IV, Scene 1

DISTINGUISHED DRAMATURGE: BERTOLT BRECHT

Eugen Bertolt Friedrich Brecht (1898–1956) is one of the most important figures in modern theatre. A playwright, director, manager, theorist, critic and poet, he was also the founder of the influential Berliner Ensemble theatre company. Raised in Bavaria, he first came to public notice in Berlin with his 1928 musical work with the composer Kurt Weill *The Threepenny Opera*. Drawn to Marxism, Brecht's plays examined society and its problems and, specifically, protested against the rise of the Nazi Party, leading to his fourteen-year exile from Germany in 1933.

Brecht developed a style of writing and staging called '**epic theatre**', in which the audience is encouraged not to identify with the characters but to question the social and political issues being presented onstage. A mixture of *spass* (comedy), *gestus* (a stylised acting technique using gesture to sum up a character's attitude), song, placards, slides, loosely connected scenes and direct narrative is used to achieve a distancing effect called '*Verfremdungseffekt*' that keeps the audience on its toes. Brecht's influence on modern playwrights and film-makers all over the world has been enormous and his many plays – including *Mother Courage and her Children, The Life of Galileo, The Caucasian Chalk Circle, The Good Person of Szechwan* and *The Resistible Rise of Arturo Ui* – remain popular with audiences today.

A THEATRICAL GLOSSARY: WORDS TO HELP YOU CHATTER INTELLIGENTLY IN THE STALLS

Corpse: to break character by getting the giggles onstage.

Dramatic irony: when the audience knows something the characters don't.

Foil: a character in a play who acts as a parallel to the protagonist.

Proxemics: the use of space in the theatre, which gives us clues about the relationships between characters.

Rising action: the events that occur leading up to the play's climax.

Soliloquy: a speech where a character thinks aloud while alone on the stage.

Stage left: the actor's left.

Staging: the whole spectacle of a play including sets, costumes, choreography, props, lighting and sound.

Upstage/downstage (also referred to as **above/below**): towards the back of the stage/towards the front of the stage.

HOW TO ACT

The first tip for successful acting is to **be aware of your audience**. This doesn't mean standing downstage centre and barking your lines directly at the posh seats. Keeping the fourth wall in mind will help stop you getting nervous or corpsing.

Consider your character's objectives. Think about the effect you want to achieve in the scene you are playing. For example, delivering Hamlet's meditative 'To be or not to be . . .' skipping around the stage chortling may be unconvincing.

Project your voice. Don't yell but raise your voice so everybody can hear you. Keep your consonants and vowels clear and don't speak too fast or too slowly, or you'll end up boring everyone.

Listen to your fellow actors. Half of acting is reacting. Listening, rather than thinking about what you're about to do next, not only keeps you on top of your **cue lines** (the words another actor says before it's your turn to speak) but also results in a more natural response.

LIGHTS! CAMERA! ACTION!: THE BIRTH OF CINEMA

On 28 December 1895, Auguste and Louis Lumière showed the first projected film (a thrilling little number called *La Sortie des ouvriers de l'Usine Lumière*) to a public audience. However, as with most great innovations, this momentous occasion was the culmination of a series of breakthroughs by many scientists and inventors. For some time bright sparks had been experimenting with showing still images in quick succession to give the impression of movement. Few people these days enjoy Joseph Plateau's **phenakistioscope**, W.G. Horner's **zoetrope** or Eadweard Muybridge's **zoopraxiscope**, but they all contributed to the evolution of cinema. However, it was serial eureka merchant Thomas Edison and his British assistant William Dickson who made a great leap forward with their **kinetograph**. This mechanically fed a roll of film through a camera taking a sequence of photographs which could then be viewed through a **kinetoscope**. This inspired the Lumière brothers'

cinematograph which allowed the films to be projected onto a screen and viewed by large audiences. By the turn of the nineteenth century, cinematograph parlours and kinetoscope arcades were all the rage across both Europe and America.

BEING ISSUR DANIELOVITCH: FAMOUS FILM STARS' REAL NAMES

Archie Leach – Cary Grant
Frances Gumm – Judy Garland
Marion Morrison – John Wayne
Issur Danielovitch – Kirk Douglas
Doris von Kappelhoff – Doris Day
Betty Perske – Lauren Bacall
Diana Fluck – Diana Dors
Maurice Micklewhite – Michael Caine
Ramón Estévez – Martin Sheen

THE TALKIES: THE IMPORTANCE OF SOUND IN CINEMA

We take it for granted these days that movies have dialogue and sound effects but up until the 1920s all films were 'silent movies', accompanied by live music from a pianist or organist. Integrated sound allowing for characters' speech to be heard was hampered by two major obstacles – amplification and synchronisation. After experiments with phonographs and belts and pulleys, a strip of celluloid containing the soundtrack was developed that could run in sync with the visual film. Thus the 'talkies' were born, inspiring consternation in many members of the silent acting community who now had to learn new skills (some stars were even 'voiced' by different actors). Film genres were also transformed – alongside the staples of crime thriller, horror, western and melodrama, comedians like the Marx Brothers could now wow audiences with their verbal as well as physical gags. The musical also became a possibility: *The Jazz Singer* (1927), starring Al Jolson, was the first film to feature synchronised music and dialogue. The talkies also naturally required better scriptwriters, a need that led to the likes of William Faulkner, Raymond Chandler, Dorothy Parker and Ernest Hemingway writing for films.

A TRIP TO TINSELTOWN:
THE GOLDEN AGE OF HOLLYWOOD

Hollywood, Los Angeles, has long been the hub of the film industry in America. Its heyday stretched from the development of sound in the late 1920s up to the decline of the **studio system** in the late 1950s. This period, known as the **Golden Age of Hollywood** because of the quality and popularity of the work produced, was characterised by major studio heads such as Louis Mayer of MGM, Jack Warner of Warner Brothers and Harry Cohn of Columbia securing long-term contracts with actors, scriptwriters, directors and other film-making personnel, producing films on their own studio lots and exhibiting them in their own theatres. Studios heavily promoted their actors, establishing what became known as the **star system**, whereby leading performers became a major draw for audiences and celebrities in their own lives as well. The most dazzling stars of the time included Greta Garbo, Errol Flynn, Joan Crawford, James Cagney, Judy Garland, Humphrey Bogart and Marlene Dietrich.

BEYOND HOLLYWOOD: A WHISTLESTOP
TOUR OF GLOBAL CINEMA

Until 1914, the film industries in the USA, France, Italy, England, Scandinavia and Russia were evenly matched, but the First World War meant that the USA's peerless resources attracted a host of European émigré film talent of the likes of Charlie Chaplin, Greta Garbo and Victor Sjöström, cementing its position as the world leader in the industry. These days Hollywood no longer dominates as it once did – India (Bollywood), Nigeria (Nollywood) and China have all claimed to have outstripped the US in film production in recent years. Advances in communication mean that different cinematic traditions now intermingle happily and the treasures of world cinema, rich and various from the medium's very beginnings, are now more widely available than ever before. From the startling and enduring brilliance of the German new wave (Werner Herzog, Wim Wenders, Rainer Werner Fassbinder) to Korean revenge horror (Park Chan-wook);

from English kitchen-sink dramas of the sixties (*Saturday Night and Sunday Morning, Alfie, This Sporting Life*) to post-revolutionary Iranian cinema (Abbas Kiarostami, Jafar Panahi); from the great Senegalese director Ousmane Sembène to the New Zealand schlock-horror of Peter Jackson's early films; from *Los Olvidados* to *Les Parapluies de Cherbourg*; from *La Dolce Vita* to *Amélie*, from *Crouching Tiger, Hidden Dragon* to *City of God* . . . there is plenty to be discovered outside the American mainstream.

THE FILM FAMILY: HOW TO READ FILM CREDITS

Gaffer – electrician who lights the set

Best Boy – assistant to the gaffer

Foley Artist – creator of dubbed sound effects

Wrangler – animal handler

Dolly Grip – operates a wheeled platform (the dolly) on a track, to which the camera is fixed to film dolly (tracking) shots

Key Grip – in charge of all other grips, who are manual workers on set

Art Director – responsible for the design and construction of the film's sets

Director of Photography/DP/Cinematographer – works closely with the director to give the film the desired photographic quality

Editor – the person in charge of cutting the film together from the many hours of shot material

Producer – responsible for the administration of all aspects of the film, including the budget

Sound Designer – responsible for all sound recording on the film

Production Designer – decides the look of the film based on script, setting, period and the vision of the director

Casting Director – thinks of suitable actors for the film roles, conducts screen tests and auditions and selects the cast

Screenwriter – the writer responsible for the film script

Director – responsible for transforming the raw materials of story and script into the wonder of a full-length feature film

THE OLD MASTERS: TEN OF THE GREATEST AND MOST INFLUENTIAL DIRECTORS OF WORLD CINEMA

John Ford (1894–1973)

If one person can be said to have created the image of the American West in the popular imagination, it's John Ford. His great sweeping epics, photographed in Monument Valley on the Arizona/Utah border, have also shaped our view of what is cinematic. Ford learned his trade in the nascent Californian film industry, acting and contributing to many silent films (he played a Klansman in *The Birth of a Nation*) before his first directorial success, *The Iron Horse*, in 1924. His great strength was his ability to tell the stories of 'ordinary' people and he won plaudits and Oscars for a version of John Steinbeck's Depression epic *The Grapes of Wrath* and *How Green Was My Valley*, set in a Welsh mining village. But he will always be best known for his definitive westerns, frequently starring John Wayne or James Stewart, and many regard *The Searchers* as the finest of these, embodying as it does the great elements of the genre – a quest, an outsider, conflict and redemption – and delivering them with a conviction and visual poetry that is unsurpassed.

Jean Renoir (1894–1979)

The son of the great Impressionist painter, Renoir was drawn to the artistic possibilities of cinema early, making several silent features before embracing sound and making a string of masterworks through the 1930s, culminating in *La Grande Illusion* and *La Règle du jeu*, this last a top-to-bottom dissection of the foibles of French society played out against the backdrop of an evocatively photographed countryside. The film was considered so candid and barbed that it was banned in France for being 'demoralising' and a fully restored version wasn't released until 1956. Renoir was a great improviser and his films reveal the contradictions and weaknesses of his characters with a wry eye and great humanity. Most of all his films are a delight to watch, filled as they are with majestic light and beauty.

Sergei Eisenstein (1898–1948)

Eisenstein was a committed socialist and the people themselves were more often than not the heroes of his films. His great contribution lies in his perfection of innovative editing techniques that changed narrative cinema forever – images are juxtaposed in quick succession, in close-up and long-range, and using a variety of speeds and camera angles in order to control the rhythm, viewpoints and tension in the telling of the story. This can be seen in the battle scenes of his revolutionary film, *October: Ten Days That Shook the World*, which cuts back and forth from fleeing victims to pursuing assailants with ever increasing frenzy, thus heightening the drama and keeping the audience captivated. Eisenstein's montage style of film-making fell out of favour in the thirties as Stalin looked to less challenging types of film to promote the Soviet ideal.

Alfred Hitchcock (1899–1980)

Born in Leytonstone, the son of a grocer, Hitchcock was renowned as the Master of Suspense. His talents ranged from his technical expertise – as exemplified in *Rope*, an entire film that appears to be one extended shot – to his unparalleled gift for storytelling and his ability to transform the bizarre and macabre (as in *The Birds* and *Psycho*) into material for mainstream films. Hitchcock also had a healthy disregard for celebrity status and his subversive use of star actors like Janet Leigh, James Stewart, Ingrid Bergman and Cary Grant was extremely effective.

Akira Kurosawa (1910–98)

Kurosawa's films brought Japanese cinema to the attention of the world, although, ironically, he was deeply influenced by Western literature and cinema, making several films based on Shakespeare's plays including a pulsating version of *Macbeth*, *Throne of Blood*. His breakthrough film, *Rashomon*, is a perfectly executed exploration of the subjectivity of truth, retelling the story of a brutal crime from four different viewpoints. Hugely influential, two of his samurai films were remade as successful westerns – *Yojimbo* as *A Fistful of Dollars* and *The Seven Samurai* as *The Magnificent Seven*.

Orson Welles (1915–85)

A supremely talented polymath from an artistic family, Welles's films were incredibly ambitious, both technically and thematically, especially his masterpiece *Citizen Kane*. He created cinema of astonishing bravura and brilliance: the long, single tracking shot that opens *Touch of Evil*, the dazzling hall-of-mirrors chase sequence in *The Lady from Shanghai* and the all-pervading nostalgic melancholy of *The Magnificent Ambersons*, for example. Welles used a trusted cadre of actors in his work and was himself a performer of tremendous magnetism. However, his films were rarely commercially successful and his career is almost as much characterised by his financial struggles as by his achievements.

Ingmar Bergman (1918–2007)

Sweden's greatest director has become a byword for introspective, psychologically complex, often claustrophobic films, from the warm melancholy of *Wild Strawberries* to the avant-garde high drama of *Persona* and *A Passion*. His most famous film is *The Seventh Seal*, which opens with a game of chess on a beach between a knight and the hooded figure of Death. In the form of an allegorical medieval tale, it explores our attitude to mortality. Predictably, there aren't many laughs, but its powerful images and ideas are forever burned into the consciousness of all who see it.

Federico Fellini (1920–93)

Fellini left his birthplace in Rimini at eighteen to make his living as a journalist and cartoonist, when a chance meeting with Roberto Rossellini led him to co-write one of Italy's greatest post-war films, Rossellini's *Roma, Città Aperta*. He soon graduated to directing his own work and was at the forefront of a new generation of talented Italian film-makers. His films explore the margins of society – outsiders, circus clowns, prostitutes – frequently drawing on his own life for inspiration. He is most widely known for *La Dolce Vita* which follows a celebrity journalist around a spiritually bankrupt (but very beautiful) Rome, as he trawls the city's parties and nightspots. His later films were increasingly autobiographical, and in many ways bizarre, creating an almost burlesque world that is gloriously full of life and instantly recognisable as his own.

Satyajit Ray (1921–92)

The greatest of Indian directors, Ray's films are intimate depictions of Indian family life and society, imbued with warmth and insight. His background as an art director in an advertising company helped him to develop the pure, beautiful look and photography that shines through his films, reminiscent of Renoir, by whom he was greatly influenced.

His most famous achievement is the Apu trilogy of films, following the fortunes of a family in a rural village, using a non-professional cast. In *Days and Nights in the Forest*, Ray dissects the mores of the Indian middle classes, piercing the pretensions of the four protagonists as their short break in the country becomes a journey of self-discovery, bathed in luminous photography.

François Truffaut (1932–84)

As a critic, Truffaut came up with **auteur theory**, which posited the director as the single dynamic creative force at the centre of a film. His groundbreaking success was the strongly autobiographical *Les Quatre Cents Coups*, which embodied many of the ideals of emotional honesty and objectivity of the French **nouvelle vague** (or new wave) of the 1950s. Truffaut's most successful work, *Jules et Jim*, is the perfect synthesis of his philosophy of film: it is at once an engaging love triangle, a metaphor for the discord and damage of war, and a stunning piece of cinema employing faultless composition and inventive editing.

TEN TOP FILMS

Every ten years, since 1952, esteemed film magazine *Sight & Sound* has polled critics and directors for their choice of the greatest films of all time. Here is the most recent critics' list, from 2002. *Citizen Kane* has topped the poll every decade so far, except for the first list, where *The Bicycle Thieves* took the number-one slot.

1. *Citizen Kane*, 1941, Orson Welles, USA
2. *Vertigo*, 1958, Alfred Hitchcock, USA
3. *La Règle du jeu*, 1939, Jean Renoir, France
4. *The Godfather*, 1972, and *The Godfather Part II*, 1974, Francis Ford Coppola, USA
5. *Tokyo Story*, 1953, Yasujiro Ozu, Japan
6. *2001: A Space Odyssey*, 1968, Stanley Kubrick, GB
7. *Battleship Potemkin*, 1925, Sergei Eisenstein, USSR
8. *Sunrise*, 1927, F. W. Murnau, USA
9. *8½*, 1963, Federico Fellini, Italy
10. *Singin' in the Rain*, 1952, Stanley Donen & Gene Kelly, USA

AN INTRODUCTION TO FILM THEORY

Film theory seeks to examine cinema in the light of particular philosophical and intellectual systems of thought in order to interpret films on a fundamental level and discover what they reveal about the makers, viewers and societies that produced them. It also makes you sound very clever while you're buying popcorn.

Feminism
Feminist film theory examines the representation of women in film (particularly the widespread use of female stereotypes) as well as investigating the power structures that lie behind what is portrayed. Laura Mulvey's key essay 'Visual Pleasure and Narrative Cinema', identifies the pervasive phenomenon of the '**male gaze**' in cinema, whereby the audience watches the action from the default perspective of the heterosexual male. A feminist critique of *Pretty Woman*, in which we are presented with a sanitised view of prostitution that is the product of male wish-fulfilment, might conclude that the happy ending isn't quite so happy, as Vivian simply changes from one kind of male commodity to another.

Marxism
Marxist theory is the application of socialist thought to films. In particular, it is concerned with the social context of film, not only that portrayed but also that in which it is created. In this field, most Hollywood films can be seen as politically repressive products, promoting stereotypes and conformation to a socially conservative ideal. By contrast, truly Marxist film-making, such as that of the Russian director Sergei Eisenstein, relates the glory of the revolution in narrative form, but also expresses it in the montage editing style, which, with its sharp clashes, is representative of the conflict of class war.

Psychoanalytical
Pyschoanalytical interpretation of film explores the unconscious of the characters, makers and societies that produce cinema. Film lends itself well to such an approach – Freud came up with the notion of a 'dream screen' that the human mind creates, on which our fantasies

are played out. We as viewers use cinema as a form of wish-fulfilment, a literal 'dream screen'. Film-makers have frequently played with psychoanalytical ideas, notably in Spike Jonze's *Being John Malkovich*, which explores ideas of single/multiple consciousnesses and differing viewpoints.

∽ DRAMA AND ∽
FILM STUDIES
TEST PAPER

1. Who invented *Verfremdungseffekt*?

a) Jean Renoir
b) Bertolt Brecht
c) Charlie Sheen
d) Edward Albee

2. What is Orson Welles's most famous film?

3. Ancient Greek dramas were initially performed in honour of which god?

a) Dionysus
b) Artemis
c) Zeus
d) Hera

4. How many women have won the Academy Award for Best Director?

a) 0
b) 1
c) 4
d) 11

5. Noh drama involves:

a) music, dancing and masks
b) film and fireworks
c) female actors
d) elaborately decorated sets

6. Who directed *The Godfather*?

a) Albert R. Broccoli
b) Bernardo Bertolucci
c) Francis Ford Coppola
d) Federico Fellini

7. The imaginary wall that separates the audience from the stage is known as:

a) the fifth dimension
b) the first amendment
c) the fourth wall
d) the curtain

8. *Antigone* **is a play by the ancient Greek playwright:**

a) Euripides
b) Aristophanes
c) Aeschylus
d) Sophocles

9. What is a dolly shot?

a) the finale of a pornographic film
b) a tracking shot
c) a backlit shot
d) a scene involving animals

10. *Doctor Faustus* **is by which playwright?**

a) William Shakespeare
b) John Webster
c) Thomas Middleton
d) Christopher Marlowe

11. Which actor links these films?

Teacher's Pet
Mogambo
The Misfits

12. Who is the protagonist of John Osborne's *Look Back in Anger*?

a) Cliff Richard
b) Tommy Atkins
c) Jimmy Porter
d) Stanley Webber

13. Which famous film opens with a knight playing chess with Death on a beach?

a) *Mission Impossible*
b) *Wild Strawberries*
c) *Vertigo*
d) *The Seventh Seal*

14. 'Enter . . . Lavinia, her hands cut off, and her tongue cut out and ravished' is a stage direction from which play?

a) *Titus Andronicus*
b) *Coriolanus*
c) *Julius Caesar*
d) *Antony and Cleopatra*

15. What was the first musical film ever produced?

a) *The Birth of a Nation*
b) *The Jazz Singer*
c) *Singin' in the Rain*
d) *A Hard Day's Night*

16. W. G. Horner invented the:

a) phenakistioscope
b) cinematograph
c) zoetrope
d) zoopraxiscope

17. What was Judy Garland's real name?

18. **'Stage left' is:**

a)   the audience's left
b)   the director's left
c)   the actor's left
d)   the prompter's left

19. **What is the official term for the person who assists the electrician on a film set?**

a)   gaffer
b)   runner
c)   key grip
d)   best boy

20. **Film director Werner Herzog is particularly associated with which school of film-making?**

a)   avant-garde
b)   surrealism
c)   German new wave
d)   blockbuster

21. **In Samuel Beckett's play *Waiting for Godot*, when does Godot arrive?**

a)   on the second day
b)   in the afternoon
c)   on Tuesday
d)   never

22. **Which director is responsible for the films *Take the Money and Run*, *Love and Death*, *Radio Days* and *Hollywood Ending*?**

23. **Anton Chekhov's most famous play is called:**

a)   *The Cherry Orchard*
b)   *The Apple Orchard*
c)   *The Plum Orchard*
d)   *The Pear Orchard*

24. **Which film critic came up with 'auteur theory'?**

25. Which Japanese film is the famous western *A Fistful of Dollars* based on?

a)   *Yojimbo*
b)   *Woman in the Dunes*
c)   *The Seven Samurai*
d)   *Rashomon*

26. Scaramouche is a character from which theatrical tradition?

27. Which of the following is considered a Marxist film-maker?

a)   Aleksandr Drankov
b)   Sergei Eisenstein
c)   Frank Capra
d)   Leni Riefenstahl

28. Who is the most famous ancient Greek comic playwright?

29. Which famous film depicts the experiences of a creatively blocked Italian film director?

a)   *8½*
b)   *28 Days Later*
c)   *9½ weeks*
d)   *101 Dalmatians*

30. 'Put out the light, and then put out the light' is an ominous line from which Shakespeare play?

❧ MUSIC ❧

The official definition of music is that it is an art form involving 'the arrangement of sound in time'. Obviously, it's hard to express in words exactly what music is and how it works as it has its own language of melodies and rhythms, but ever since the first notes were transcribed scholars and experts have been analysing and interpreting musical compositions from Albinoni to Abba. Music is an incredibly expressive and versatile art that has beguiled and bewitched listeners for centuries and has also had a fascinating public role throughout history: be it buglers leading troops into battle, kings and noblemen showing off their cultivation and wealth by throwing elaborate concerts, choirs praising God in places of worship, or the classical music piped over the tannoy systems in Tube stations to keep angry commuters calm. Here we introduce you to some of the heroes of the classical era, teach you how to tell your sonata from your cantata, give you the heads up on what's going on in some of the most popular operas, and show you how to interpret those little tadpole notes that swim about on musical scores.

FROM PLAINCHANT TO PHILIP GLASS: A SHORT HISTORY OF MUSIC

Humans have probably been banging away on rocks and making their own unique attempts at harmony since the dawn of time, but over the last 1,500 years, written records have made it easier to define different developmental periods within this versatile art.

Medieval (c.500–c.1400)
Owing to the lack of literacy and the expense of writing manuscripts, not much music from medieval times was written down outside the monasteries. As a result, most of what has survived is religious, particularly **plainchant** (one line of melody, sung without accompaniment,

popular today in horror films). Harmonies in medieval music are very simple and sound quite unusual to modern ears. Secular music used delightfully named instruments such as the lute, dulcimer, hurdy-gurdy, sackbut (a predecessor of the trombone) and crumhorn.

THE INGREDIENTS OF MUSIC

Melody is a sequence of single tones.
Harmony is a simultaneous combination of tones.
Rhythm is the pattern of pulses and stresses in a piece of music.
Timbre is the characteristic quality individual tones are given by different instruments.

Renaissance (c.1430–c.1600)

During the bountiful Renaissance the cities of Italy were hotbeds of musical creativity, with figures such as Giovanni Pierluigi da Palestrina composing beautiful and enduring works. The majority of the music we know from this period is also sacred, though there were plenty of secular madrigals and instrumental works going around, and the lute was still one of the most popular instruments (showing that guys have always played the axe to get the girls).

The sacred music of the time was almost always unaccompanied, written for choirs, and characterised by smooth, homogeneous imitative lines, using what is known as a polyphonic style. **Polyphony** is a term derived from the Greek, meaning 'many sounds', and refers to when two or more strands of music sound at the same time. The key English figures of the Renaissance were Thomas Tallis and William Byrd, who is often regarded as the 'Father of British Music' and is also said to have inspired the name of the psychedelic sixties band, the Byrds.

The Baroque Era (c.1598–c.1750)

One of the main principles of baroque music was that it should move the listener's passions. Baroque composers emphasised contrasts and the use of **counterpoint** became a key feature (a combination of different melodies which work together harmonically). The bass became the controlling voice in compositions and the concept of an accompaniment, known as the '**continuo**', appeared, typically played on a harpsichord or organ.

Italy was the world leader in baroque music: the first operas were produced in Florence (c.1598), the first oratorio was peformed in Rome (1600), and the first public opera house opened in Venice (1637). Figures such as Alessandro Scarlatti, Giovanni Gabrieli, Tomaso Albinoni, Antonio Vivaldi and Claudio Monteverdi thrived at this time. Later on, Germany gained ascendancy, with music by composers such as Georg Philipp Telemann, George Frideric Handel and Johann Sebastian Bach flourishing at the courts of rich nobles.

The Classical Era (late 18th–early 19th centuries)

When people talk about 'classical' music, they are usually distinguishing it from pop. However, strictly speaking, classical music belongs to a specific period in the development of music in central Europe. The composers of this age aimed for beauty of melody and form, proportion, balance and control. Classical music is generally less complicated than baroque; it is usually **homophonic** (a single melodic line with accompaniment) with less reliance upon counterpoint. Purely orchestral music came into its own in this era, with symphonies, concertos and divertimentos being composed all over the place, and the harpsichord went out of fashion. The great names of this period were Wolfgang Amadeus Mozart, Ludwig van Beethoven and Franz Joseph Haydn.

The Romantic Era (c.1790–c.1900)

During the Romantic period, imagination became more important than the boring old restraint and good taste of the classical era. This led to freer musical forms like the **symphonic poem** (a symphony with a literary theme) and expressive songs and pieces for the piano. Operas, such as Richard Wagner's *The Ring of the Nibelung*, started dealing with more controversial issues, such as politics and nationalism.

Other key figures in this era were Franz Schubert, celebrated for writing dramatic and original song cycles; Johannes Brahms, famous for his orchestral works, piano compositions and his *German Requiem*; Pyotr Ilyich Tchaikovsky, a master of symphonies and ballets like *Swan Lake*; and Gustav Mahler, the composer of some of the most splendid symphonies ever written. During this era, performers also became superstars: Frédéric Chopin, Franz Liszt and Niccolò Paganini were the equivalents of Justin Timberlake in the Europe of their day.

The Modern Era (*c.*1900–today)

It is difficult to summarise all the different post-Romantic classical styles, but the uniting factor in modern classical music is the rejection of tradition. The twentieth-century Western musical scene included:

- *Impressionism*: music focusing on creating atmosphere, using both major and minor keys, **dissonance** (discords) and unusual scales. Key figures: Claude Debussy, Maurice Ravel.

- *Expressionism*: extremely emotional music, avoiding traditional forms to emphasise feelings. Key figure: Arnold Schoenberg.

- *Neoclassical*: music which revived classical forms in a new way, but also emphasised dissonance. Key figure: Sergei Prokofiev.

- *Minimalism*: music which limits the harmony, melody and other aspects dramatically. Key figures: Steve Reich, Philip Glass.

- *Serialism*: music where elements such as notes are ordered in a fixed series. Key figures: Alban Berg, Karlheinz Stockhausen, Pierre Boulez.

- *Aleatoric music*: music composed almost wholly by chance or at the whim of the performers. Key figure: John Cage.

FIVE CLASSICAL PIECES EVERYONE SHOULD HEAR

Miserere by Gregorio Allegri

This piece of choral music was composed in the 1630s for the papal choir in the Sistine Chapel and the Pope banned it from being performed anywhere else. A fourteen-year-old Mozart risked excommunication by transcribing it from memory. Look out for the amazing high notes the soprano has to sing.

Fifth Symphony by Ludwig van Beethoven

Written in 1808, this is the perfect symphony – everyone knows the 'duh, duh, duh, duuuuh' opening. During the Second World War, the BBC used these four notes to introduce radio broadcasts as 'dot dot dot dash' means 'V' for 'Victory' in Morse code.

Ouverture Solennelle, L'Année 1812 (1812 Overture) **by Pyotr Ilyich Tchaikovsky**
One of Tchaikovsky's best-loved pieces, this was commissioned during the reign of Tsar Nicholas II in 1880 to commemorate the 1812 defence of Moscow from Napoleon (it is famous for its use of bells and cannon fire). Tchaikovsky wasn't terribly fond of it, judging it noisy and lacking in artistic merit.

Variations on an Original Theme for orchestra ('Enigma') **by Sir Edward Elgar**
Elgar composed the *Enigma Variations* in 1898–9. The piece consists of a theme and fourteen variations, each variation depicting the character of one of his friends. The famous 'Nimrod' (Variation number 9) was written for Augustus Jaeger and is thought to depict a night-time walk, during which the chums discussed Beethoven. 'Nimrod' is played on Remembrance Sunday every year at the Cenotaph. The name 'Enigma' is commonly believed to refer to the puzzle of whom each variation represents and also to the idea, raised by some mysterious comments made by Elgar, that the theme is possibly a counterpoint to another well-known tune.

Rhapsody in Blue **by George Gershwin**
Written in 1924 for piano and orchestra, this piece is notable for merging jazz and classical music. It is instantly recognisable from its opening clarinet glissando (swoop). Gershwin played the piano at its first performance and the original score is blank for his improvised solos, merely stating 'wait for nod' to the conductor. We will never know exactly how that original version sounded.

UNTANGLE YOUR ARIA FROM YOUR ORATORIO: SOME CLASSICAL MUSIC FORMS

Form	Meaning
Aria	A self-contained song for a single voice, usually part of an opera, oratorio or other large vocal work.

Cantata	A piece of music to be sung. This term can be applied to various genres, but usually involves a chorus (and often soloists) with accompaniment.
Concerto	A piece of music for one or more soloists and an orchestra.
Fugue	A piece of music for three or more parts, in which each part enters at different times and imitates the others.
Lied	The German word for 'song'. Popular in nineteenth-century Germany, famous composers of lieder were Schubert, Schumann and Brahms.
Oratorio	A sacred work for soloists, chorus (or choir) and a large orchestra, intended for concert performance. Famous examples are Handel's *Messiah*, Haydn's *The Creation* and Bach's *St Matthew Passion*.
Overture	A piece of music, usually for an orchestra, which is used as an introduction to an opera, oratorio, ballet or dramatic work.
Rhapsody	An instrumental piece in one movement, often based on popular, national or folk melodies.
Sonata	An instrumental work typically for one or two instruments.
Symphony	A piece of music for orchestra, usually in four sections or 'movements'.

WUNDERKIND WOLFGANG:
WOLFGANG AMADEUS MOZART (1756–91)

The jazzily named Johannes Chrysostomos Wolfgangus Theophilus Mozart was born in Salzburg on 27 January 1756. A precociously talented youngster, he began composing at the tender age of five. His father, Leopold, was keen to exhibit his son's God-given (and profitable) talents so the young Mozart spent many of his early years touring the royal courts of Europe before working as a composer, teacher and performer in Salzburg and Vienna.

In 1782, he married Constanze Weber and his opera *Die Entführung aus dem Serail* was performed to great acclaim, even though its ambitious style was unappreciated by Emperor Joseph II ('Too many notes, my dear Mozart'). During the mid-1780s he composed six magnificent string quartets in honour of Haydn and also wrote around fifteen piano concertos, which some commentators see as his greatest achievements. The late 1780s and early 1790s saw Mozart composing his famous operas: *Le nozze di Figaro* (1786), *Don Giovanni* (1787), *Così fan tutte* (1790), *Die Zauberflöte* (1791) and *La clemenza di Tito* (1791). It is a testament to his phenomenal abilities that he was able to compose five such masterpieces in as many years, while composing other instrumental music at the same time.

In 1790 Mozart became ill, but before his death in 1791 he composed the famous *Clarinet Concerto in A major* and an unfinished but exquisite *Requiem*. Despite his fear that he had been poisoned, he died of natural causes and was buried in an unmarked grave leaving his wife with substantial debts. His legacy lives on in his technically brilliant, effortless, delightful melodies. It is this *joie de vivre*, combined with his revolutionary ideas, which makes Mozart's music so enduringly popular. A recent study by Harvard Medical School even discovered that listening to his work can reduce pain and stress levels.

FIGARO! FIGARO! FIGARO!:
AN INTRODUCTION TO TEN TOP OPERAS

Opera is a spectacular art form: a mixture of music, drama, poetry, visual arts and sometimes dance. However, for the uninitiated, the idea of hours of boredom listening to large-boned sopranos screeching melodramatically about bizarre subjects can seem unappetising. A good first step to enjoying opera is to have a vague idea of what is going on. Our brief guide below gives you the background to some of the most famous operas.

Dido and Aeneas (1680s) by **Henry Purcell**
The old work–life balance is brought to a tragic conclusion in this

great English opera. Trojan hero Aeneas and Queen of Carthage Dido are at the point of planning their wedding when a pesky sorceress rains on their parade by creating a fake god Mercury to remind Aeneas of his duty to leave Carthage and set up a new Troy. This causes a fiery row leading to Aeneas sailing off and Dido preparing herself for death.

Le nozze di Figaro (*The Marriage of Figaro*) (1786) by **Wolfgang Amadeus Mozart**

Lusty Count Almaviva is bored with his wife Rosiva and fancies his servant Figaro's fiancée Susanna. Figaro, Susanna and the Countess indulge in a melee of cross-dressing, disguises and misunderstandings in order to make the Count see the error of his ways. Eventually they succeed and the Count apologises to his missus.

Don Giovanni or *Il dissoluto punito* (*The Libertine Punished*) (1787) by **Wolfgang Amadeus Mozart**

The clue is in the title. Randy womaniser Don Giovanni tries to rape Donna Anna, the Commendatore's daughter, then kills the Commendatore when he tries to protect her. He then tries it on with Zerlina on her wedding day and his ex-girlfriend's maid before a statue of the late Commendatore tells him to repent or be damned. Don G picks the wrong option and sinks into a flaming abyss.

Il barbiere di Siviglia (*The Barber of Seville*) (1816) by **Gioacchino Rossini**

Count Almaviva has his eye on Rosina, creepy Dr Bartolo's ward. Figaro, the barber of Seville, is employed to aid the Count in his plans to get close to the carefully guarded girl, which include lots of disguises, misleading letters, deception and shaving. A happy ending is achieved with the marriage of the Count and his beloved.

La Traviata (*The Woman Who Strayed*) (1853) by **Giuseppe Verdi**

Violetta, a Paris courtesan, falls in love with Alfredo, gives up the day job and they live happily together until Alfredo's father persuades her to leave his son to save his family's honour. Not knowing this, dumped Alfredo publicly insults Violetta by throwing his gambling wins at her 'for services rendered'. When his father explains what's happened he rushes to Violetta's side just in time for her to die of consumption in his arms.

Der Ring des Nibelungen (*The Ring of the Nibelung* aka 'The Ring Cycle') (1869–1876) by Richard Wagner

Not strictly a single opera, Wagner's 'stage festival play' runs for over twenty hours and is made up of four works based on German and Scandinavian mythology (elements of which will probably be familiar to you from J. R. R. Tolkien's *The Lord of the Rings*.)

In *Das Rheingold* (*The Rhine Gold*) (1869), the water-nymph Rhine-maidens are surprised when Alberich the dwarf (*Nibelung* in German) steals their magic Rhinegold, which he makes into a ring with the power to rule the world. Meanwhile, chief god Wotan has got himself into a pickle with some giants who've been building his castle Valhalla and they kidnap his sister-in-law, the goddess Freia. Wotan steals the ring from Alberich to exchange for Freia – which makes the dwarf cross enough to put a curse on it.

Die Walküre (*The Valkyrie*) (1870) begins with Wotan's mortal son, Siegmund, running off with someone else's wife, Sieglinde, who also happens to be his twin sister. Initially Wotan sends his daughter, Brünnhilde the Valkyrie, to protect Siegmund against the angry husband, as he's keen to use Siegmund to get the ring back for him. However, his wife convinces him against this and, although the pregnant Sieglinde is saved, Siegmund is killed. Brünnhilde is punished for helping him by being sent to sleep on a rock surrounded by fire until someone rescues her.

Never fear, for in *Siegfried* (1876) Sieglinde and Siegmund's son, Siegfried, has grown up. He reforges the sword his dad got from Wotan and pops off to kill the giant who has the ring (who is now taking the form of a dragon), breaks Wotan's special spear, and then frees and falls in love with Brünnhilde.

In *Götterdämmerung* (*Twilight of the Gods*) (1876) Siegfried meets King Gunther, his sister Gutrune and the king's adviser Hagen (who is Alberich's son). Hagen wants the ring and gives Siegfried a magic potion to make him forget Brünnhilde and fall in love with Gutrune before stabbing him in the back on a hunting trip. Brünnhilde arrives in time to take the ring and return it to the Rhine maidens (in pursuit of whom Hagen drowns), before riding her horse into Siegfried's funeral pyre, as Valhalla also bursts into flame. Phew.

Aida (1871) **by Giuseppe Verdi**

Radames is the leader of the Egyptian army against the Ethiopians. Inconveniently, he is also the sweetheart of the Ethiopian slave (who is secretly a princess) Aida, which causes a great deal of agonising over loyalties for both of them. Their situation is not helped by the fact that the Egyptian princess Amneris has also taken a fancy to Radames. When the lovers are discovered together, Radames is condemned to be buried alive for treachery and Aida hides in his tomb in order to die with him.

Carmen (1875) **by Georges Bizet**

Feisty Carmen, a worker in a cigarette factory in Seville, stabs a colleague and then seduces a soldier, Don José, into letting her escape from custody. Don José is jailed for his pains and on his release elopes with Carmen and joins a band of smugglers. When he goes to visit his dying mother, Carmen runs off with a hunky bullfighter, riling Don José enough to stab her to death, wailing as she dies in his arms.

La Bohème (*Bohemia*) (1896) **by Giacomo Puccini**

La Bohème follows the high jinks of some arty types scraping together a living in a garret in Paris, where the poet Rodolfo falls in love with Mimi, a seamstress. However, Rodolfo breaks up with Mimi because he is too poor to look after her in her illness (the dreaded consumption again). In the end Mimi returns to Rodolfo to, you guessed it, die in his arms.

Madama Butterfly (*Madame Butterfly*) (1904) **by Giacomo Puccini**

A not-so-jolly tale of love, bigamy, betrayal, US-Japanese relations and suicide. While stationed in Nagasaki, Lieutenant Pinkerton enters into a sham marriage to get his leg over with teenage Cio-Cio-San, aka Madame Butterfly, before abandoning her, pregnant, for a nice American girl called Kate. When the Pinkertons return to Japan years later they decide that Butterfly's child would be better off with them and she gives her son up, before killing herself in grief.

BRILLIANT BEETHOVEN:
LUDWIG VAN BEETHOVEN (1770–1827)

Like Mozart, Beethoven was another young starter. He was born in Bonn, and by the age of eleven was deputising for his teacher as court organist and was on the cusp of having his first music published. In the 1790s he moved to Vienna and became a pupil of Joseph Haydn.

From 1795 to the early 1800s, Beethoven was popular with the Viennese aristocracy, and during this time he composed several important and influential works for the piano, including the 'Pathétique' sonata (1799) and the 'Moonlight' sonata (1801). However, 1802 was a bad year for Ludwig – it was at this point he realised that his hearing was slowly getting worse and there would be no cure. (By 1818 he was completely deaf and his visitors had to write their conversations down in notebooks in order to communicate with him.)

Beethoven's despair, however, seems to have sparked a new creative streak, in which he composed perhaps his most famous works. Many of his compositions from this period deal with heroic themes, in particular triumph in the face of adversity. For example, the 'Eroica' Symphony (his third), dedicated originally to Napoleon; the famous Fifth Symphony (with the dark and oppressive first movement in C minor giving way to a triumphant fourth movement in C major); and his only opera, *Fidelio*, in which a wife saves her prisoner husband from murder by a political enemy. Also during this period, Beethoven composed the beautiful Sixth 'Pastoral' Symphony and the superb 'Emperor' piano concerto.

After 1812, Beethoven's output diminished in quantity – he was depressed by his deafness, his dashed marital hopes and legal wrangles for custody of his nephew. However, from this background emerged some of his most profound pieces, including the *Hammerklavier* Sonata and his final, Ninth 'Choral' Symphony with the last movement incorporating the famous 'Ode to Joy'. Beethoven died in 1827 and his funeral was a grand affair, with around 10,000 mourners in attendance.

Beethoven's command of the basic elements of music is undoubted. What perhaps explains his incredible influence on future musicians is the intensity and emotion he brought to his compositions. He was an innovator – for example, introducing a chorus into a symphony; linking symphonic movements by theme; introducing new instruments to the orchestra. It has been said that Beethoven changed the purpose of music, from entertainment into something written for its own sake with its own power.

THE INSTRUMENTS OF THE ORCHESTRA

A full orchestra is a wondrous and mind-blowing thing to listen to, as the variety of instruments from the five different 'families' allows the ensemble to convey an array of multifarious different emotions, colours and dynamics.

Strings	Percussion
violin	xylophone
viola	*glockenspiel (similar to the xylophone, but made of metal)*
violoncello (or 'cello)	
double bass	*marimba (a larger version of the xylophone with wooden tubes rather than metal resonators)*
harp	
Woodwind	cymbals
flute	snare drum
piccolo (a higher version of the flute)	*bongos*
	tam-tam (a large cymbal, rather like a gong)
oboe	timpani (kettle drums)
cor anglais (a lower version of the oboe)	**Keyboards**
	piano
clarinet	*celeste*
saxophone	*harpsichord*
bassoon	*organ*
contrabassoon (or 'double bassoon')	
Brass	
trumpet	
French horn	
trombone	(The instruments in italics are not always
tuba	included.)

However, it's important to remember that the world of music is not just limited to the formal instruments of the orchestra. If you are planning your own avant-garde composition you might want to consider using the nose flute of South-East Asia, the sousaphone (a bass tuba that encircles the player), the hurdy-gurdy (a string instrument with a resin-coated wheel acting as a bow and a keyboard) or theremin (an electronic instrument which uses oscillators to produce notes when you wave your hands in front of it).

HOW TO BE HIP: JAZZ VOCAB

You might find that the clientele of jazz clubs often seem to be trying very hard to be effortlessly cool and a familiarity with the following insider terms could help you earn their respect.

Term	Meaning
Bebop	A style developed in 1940s New York with a rich rhythmic texture and emphasis on improvisation of melodies.
Boogie-woogie	Piano jazz popular in the 1930s based on blues chords with improvised melodies on top.
Cool	A style which developed in the late 1940s, based on bebop but quieter and more understated, and not using the faster tempos.
Free	A style which developed in the 1960s employing freer forms allowing musicians to break all the usual rules.
Fusion	A style developed in the late 1960s incorporating elements of rock into jazz.
Latin	A style based on Afro-Cuban, Brazilian or other Latin American music.
Mainstream	The style regarded as the norm. Based on bebop and incorporating the harmonic language of twentieth-century music.
Mouldy fig	A term used to describe and deride fans and players of trad jazz.
Standard	A tune universally known and played by jazz musicians.
Stride	A style of piano jazz from the 1930s, involving virtuoso right-hand playing and complex runs.
Swing	The dominant style from the 1930s, played by big bands.
Trad	The traditional style from the early 1900s, also known as Dixieland.

THE FIVE MOST SINISTER POP SONGS OF ALL TIME

Roy Orbison's 'I Drove All Night'
The Big O drives all night, creeps into his lover's room, wakes her from her sleep and makes love to her. He *then* asks if that's all right. Surely a bit late?

The Police's 'Don't Stand So Close to Me'
This Grammy Award-winning song was written by Sting, who used to be a teacher. It tells the tale of a pedagogue who is frustrated by the advances of a pupil half his age. Despite staff-room accusations, our hero is so overcome he starts to shake and cough. Sexy.

Gary Puckett and the Union Gap's 'Young Girl'
In this song, the narrator tells a girl that his love for her is way out of line as she's 'a baby in disguise'. He then tells her she'd better run . . .

Cliff Richard's 'Living Doll'
Sir Cliff shows off that he's got a 'Living Doll' who cries, talks, sleeps and walks (odd that crying is her main feature . . .). He invites us to touch her hair then plans to lock her in a trunk to stop the hunks getting to her. How romantic.

Doris Day's 'Teacher's Pet'
A perfect partner to 'Don't Stand So Close to Me', Doris tells us she wants to learn from the teacher's lips, and get a diploma in his lurve. She then says that she wants to bring him home to her ma. No doubt he'd get a very warm welcome.

HOW TO READ MUSIC:
A SIX-STEP GUIDE TO THE BASICS

1. The Stave
Music is represented on paper by a combination of symbols, all of which are arranged on a 'stave'. Each stave is made up of five lines, with each line and space representing a single note.

A stave:

2. The Clef

The first symbol you will see on a stave is a 'clef'. This is very important as it defines the register of the music. The clef shows which notes each line and space of the stave represents. The two most common clefs are the **treble clef** and the **bass clef**.

The two main clefs:

The treble clef is used for most voices and higher instruments, and generally for the right hand when playing the piano. The notes in music are named after the first seven letters of the alphabet: A, B, C, D, E, F, G.

The notes on the lines of the treble clef are:

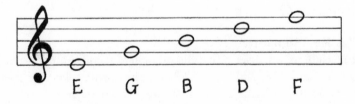

You can remember the order of these notes with the mnemonic 'Every Green Bus Drives Fast'.

The notes on the spaces are:

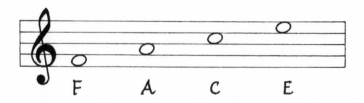

The bass clef is used for lower-pitched instruments (such as the trombone, bassoon and cello), for low voices and for the left hand when playing the piano.

The notes on the lines of the bass clef are:

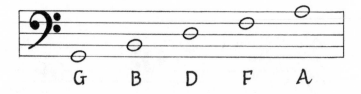

The notes on the spaces are:

3. The Key Signature

To the right of the clef you will often see a collection of symbols, known as 'sharps' (♯) and 'flats' (♭). These show which key the piece of music is written in (e.g. D major; F minor). If there is a sharp symbol on a line or a space, this means that in that particular piece of music, that note should be raised by a 'semitone' (half-tone). If there is a flat symbol, this means the note should drop by a semitone. These symbols may also pop up in the body of the music if a particular note needs to be sharp or flat on one occasion only.

An example of a treble clef showing that the piece is in the key of B major:

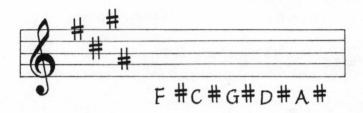

4. The Time Signature

To the right of the key signature there will be a time signature. This consists of two numbers one on top of the other. The top number determines how many beats are in a 'bar'. Written music is divided into bars, which are marked by vertical lines across the stave:

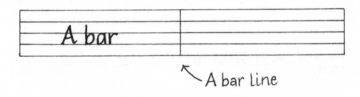

The bottom number determines the length of each beat, so 2 means a 'minim' (a half-note), 4 means a 'crotchet' (or quarter-note) and 8 means a 'quaver' (or eighth-note). Therefore, if a piece of music is in '4/4', there will be four crotchet beats to the bar. If a piece is in '6/8', there will be six quaver beats to the bar, and so on.

Some common time signatures:

5. Notes and their Values

The different notes are shown by different symbols indicating the length of the note. The note will be placed on the relevant space or line of the stave to show its pitch. The main note symbols are:

'Rests' are used to fill the gaps where notes are not played. These correspond in length to the various notes. Therefore, in a bar of 4/4, the value of the notes and rests will add up to 4 crotchets.

Notes and their corresponding rests:

6. Now you can read music!

Now you can read music and should be able to recognise the simple tune, 'Mary had a Little Lamb', set out below.

LA BELLA MUSICA: MUSICAL VOCABULARY

Helpfully, the descriptive words used on musical scores are always in Italian so here is a bit of basic vocabulary to help you work out whether you should be floating over the piano keys or slamming them Jerry Lee Lewis-style. Incidentally, the piano's full name is 'pianoforte' which means 'soft-loud' in celebration of its great versatility of volume.

Word	Meaning
adagio	leisurely
andante	at a walking pace
staccato	abruptly
legato	smoothly
forte	loud
piano	quiet or soft
mezzo-forte	moderately loud

presto	fast
rallentando/ritardando	becoming slower/holding back, slower
lento	slow
da capo	from the beginning
Fine	end
rubato	literally 'stolen'; flexible playing of the music stated, i.e. expanding or contracting what is actually written (used for emphasis and expression)
accelerando	getting faster
fortissimo	very loud
pianissimo	very quiet
sforzando	forcing; stressed
marcato	marked; stressed
acciaccatura	a 'crushed note'; a very short note played just before another

⬤ MUSIC ⬤
TEST PAPER

1. **What style of music is B. B. King most closely associated with?**

a) rock
b) soul
c) reggae
d) blues

2. **Identify the notes shown below:**

3. **When was Mozart born?**

a) 1756
b) 1975
c) 1821
d) 1730

4. **In *La Bohème*, what is the name of Rodolfo's girlfriend?**

a) Patty
b) Sue
c) Mimi
d) Titi

5. **What does it mean if you see the word '*andante*' written on a musical score?**

6. **What links the names Paul and Winston?**

7. **Which Tchaikovsky piece is famous for its use of cannons and bells?**

a) *1880 Overture*
b) *Spice Up Your Life*
c) *1812 Overture*
d) *1815 Overture*

8. **In which opera does a man have a baby with his sister before killing a dragon?**

a) Wagner's *Götterdämmerung*
b) Verdi's *La Traviata*
c) Verdi's *Rigoletto*
d) Wagner's *Siegfried*

9. **Which family in the orchestra does the saxophone belong to?**

a) brass
b) woodwind
c) percussion
d) strings

10. **In musical notation, what does this symbol mean?**

♭

11. **What is the name of the style of modern music which mixes hip hop and rock with traditional Indian instrumentation, melodies and harmonies?**

12. **What was the name of Elvis Presley's first number-one hit in the UK?**

a) 'Jailhouse Rock'
b) 'Always on My Mind'
c) 'All Shook Up'
d) 'Green Door'

13. How many quavers are there in a crotchet?

a) 5
b) 4
c) 8
d) 2

14. What is counterpoint?

a) a combination of different melodies which work together har-
    monically
b) two or more strands of music sounding at the same time
c) a type of needlecraft
d) one line of melody, sung without accompaniment

15. Which musical period is Alessandro Scarlatti associated with?

a) Romantic
b) baroque
c) modern
d) medieval

16. For what occasion did Handel write _Zadok the Priest_ in 1727?

a) Remembrance Sunday
b) the coronation of George II
c) the defeat of Napoleon at Waterloo
d) his brother's marriage

17. What is an oratorio?

a) a piece of music to be sung
b) a piece of music used as an introduction to an opera
c) a piece of music for one or more soloists and an orchestra
d) a sacred work for soloists, chorus and large orchestra

18. Which of the following is NOT an opera by Mozart?

a) _Le nozze di Figaro_
b) _Die Zauberflöte_
c) _Il barbiere di Siviglia_
d) _La clemenza di Tito_

19. What does the word 'pianoforte' literally mean?

20. Which of the following is NOT a real instrument?

a) sousaphone
b) crumhorn
c) tam–tam
d) dinger

21. If you were talking to a jazz aficionado and he mentioned 'stride', what would he be talking about?

22. What musical style is Beyoncé associated with?

a) punk
b) jazz
c) R & B
d) indie

23. If you were in Dollywood, visiting Ms Dolly Parton, the queen of country and western, and she offered you a fiddle, what would she be giving you?

a) a violin
b) a hurdy-gurdy
c) a flute
d) a drum

24. What is this pretty symbol?

25. What is aleatoric music?

a) lyric-based rock
b) music composed almost wholly by chance
c) extremely emotional music
d) dramatic and original song cycles

26. What was Louis Armstrong's biggest selling single?

a) 'Don't Smoke in Bed'
b) 'Heebie Jeebies'
c) 'Hello Dolly'
d) 'Babe'

27. Who wrote *Swan Lake*?

a) Johann Strauss
b) Gustav Mahler
c) Franz Liszt
d) Pyotr Ilyich Tchaikovsky

28. What is the name of Madonna's seminal album?

a) *Mean Green*
b) *Dead Red*
c) *Think Pink*
d) *True Blue*

29. Who composed the *St Matthew Passion* in 1727?

a) Wolfgang Amadeus Mozart
b) Johann Sebastian Bach
c) Ludwig van Beethoven
d) Edward Elgar

30. In Wagner's *Ring* cycle, who is Brünnhilde's father?

a) Wotan
b) Alberich
c) Hagen
d) Pete

∽ MODERN ∽
LANGUAGES

We live in an age in which society demands that everything must be bigger, better, faster, stronger; where speed is of the essence, where mobile phones and high-speed Internet connections link us from Timbuktu to Truro. You can flirt with a Vietnamese girl from the safety of your London bedroom, or send emails to your colleagues in Glasgow from a plane 30,000 feet above the Atlantic. On top of all of that, it seems as if the whole world speaks English (or more correctly American). So the learning of foreign languages may seem superfluous to our needs, but only the extremely myopic would adopt this stance: taking the time to learn another culture's mother tongue can be infinitely beneficial and intellectually satisfying.

Languages are the key to discovering the fascinations and faults, the intricacies and idiosyncrasies of our world. Languages articulate national stereotypes: the flamboyance of Italian, the logic of German, the sexiness of French. Of course, only a true polymath would be able to ensure that nothing is lost in translation, but even a rudimentary grasp of foreign tongues can open up new worlds to you. And, crucially, it can also ensure that you are always able to ask your way to the nearest railway station. So forget desperate homesick weekends with your penfriend in La Rochelle. Banish memories of Madame Dupont and *Tricolor* and the numbing terror that preceded your German oral exam. In these pages you will discover the secrets of the hieroglyph, how to communicate with an Italian without even moving your lips and, yes, even how to order frogs' legs in a French restaurant. *Bon appétit!*

HEAVENLY HIEROGLYPHS

Far from just being an ancient comic strip featuring disembodied hands, birds, feathers, lions and snakes, hieroglyphs are the individual symbolic images used to represent sounds and words in the ancient Egyptian written language. This may look like an odd kind of language to us but many early writing systems used pictograms and many scholars believe that our modern alphabets are almost all related to hieroglyphs in some way: our letter 'B' for example is derived from the hieroglyph representing 'shelter'.

Hieroglyphics were probably only understood and used by royalty, priests and state officials from around 3000 BCE and died out completely in the fourth century CE after simplified forms of the language were developed, leaving no one to pass on the knowledge of the mysterious images. For the next 1,400 years hieroglyphs were shrouded in darkness until the discovery of the Rosetta Stone. Part of the problem with unlocking the code was that people assumed that the pictograms represented concepts. In fact, the 700–800 symbols can be divided into two groups: those which represent ideas and those which represent sounds. Ancient Egyptian words were made up of a combination of the two types of glyph.

f (horned viper)

b (foot)

d (hand)

w (quail chick)

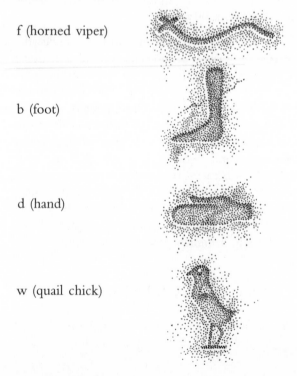

THE ROSETTA STONE

One of the most wonderfully fortuitous moments in the history of archaeology occurred in 1799 when a Napoleonic soldier in Egypt stumbled across a very special rock buried in the ground near the town of Rosetta (now el-Rashid). Inscribed on this mysterious tablet were three different sets of characters. Originally carved in 196 BCE, the text consists of a memorial to the good works of the ruling Pharaoh written in ancient Greek, demotic (a simplified form of hieroglyphs) and hieroglyphs. At the time of the discovery, hieroglyphs were frustratingly unintelligible to Egyptologists, but the enigma was unlocked in 1822 by the British and French scholars Thomas Young and Jean-François Champollion who matched them up against the translatable ancient Greek.

After Napoleon's defeat, the stone passed into British hands and has been exhibited in the British Museum since 1802 (apart from a two-year spell fifty feet underneath Holborn in an Underground station to protect it from bombing during the First World War).

FRANÇAIS SIMPLE: SIMPLE FRENCH

Pronunciation

French is one of the most sensual and sonorous languages around – master the art of speaking French and you will almost certainly find your confidence increasing in seductive situations. Get it wrong, however, and you will sound *très stupide*. Pronunciation is a tricky skill to acquire and some find it the hardest aspect of learning a language.

Les Accents

Acute accents only appear on the letter 'e', as in '*é*', which you'll find we use in our anglicised French word 'fiancé'.

Grave accents can be found on '*è*', '*à*', and '*ù*', but the only one you need to change the pronunciation for is '*è*' which should sound like the 'e' in 'there'.

The **cedilla,** which is found sinking gently beneath 'ç', softens the letter, as in '*garçon*', pronounced 'gar**ss**on'.

The **circumflex**, which looks like a little hat ('ê') – *un petit chapeau*, if you want to get into the spirit of things – sitting on top of a vowel doesn't affect the pronunciation significantly so don't worry about it.

The key to speaking good French is practice: very little in life comes easily without effort, and pronunciation and vocabulary are prime examples of this truism. A handy method to get to grips with many words as quickly as possible is to write them out (with their English translations) and stick them on notes around the house. It's best to make your vocabulary chime with its environment so that, for example, you see '*le lait*', '*le beurre*', '*le jus d'orange*' etc. every time you open the fridge door. Whenever you come across one of your notes you must recite the words out loud – even if this does perplex people about what you're up to in the bathroom.

Nouns
All French nouns are either masculine or feminine and there is no way of predicting which gender an object will be. Genders must be learned because articles, adjectives and some verbs have to agree with nouns (they change depending on the gender of the noun they follow or precede).

The gender of some nouns seems obvious: '*homme*', 'man', is masculine; '*femme*', 'woman', is feminine. But don't be complacent – others can be counter-intuitive: '*personne*', 'person', is always feminine, whether the person is male or female. It's also worth remembering that many nouns and adjectives that refer to people (and some animals) have both a masculine and a feminine form, such as '*un ami*' for a male friend and '*une amie*' for a female friend. Nouns ending in '*e*' don't change their ending – they remain the same whether they are masculine or feminine: a goat or '*chèvre*' doesn't change whether it's a billy goat or a lovely lady goat. Thankfully, objects have a fixed form that never changes: a book is always '*un livre*'.

Almost every French noun has a different form for singular and plural. The plural is often made, as in English, by adding an 's'. However, there are exceptions of course: nouns ending in '*s*', '*z*' or '*x*' stay the same in the plural forms, for example '*le fils*' ('the son') and '*les fils*' ('the sons'). Nouns ending in '*u*' take an '*x*' in their plural form: '*gâteau*' ('cake') becomes '*gâteaux*' ('cakes').

Articles

Articles in French change according to the gender of the noun and whether it is singular or plural. If the noun is masculine then the definite article ('the') is '*le*' and the indefinite article ('a') is '*un*'. If a noun is feminine then the definite article is '*la*' and the indefinite article is '*une*'. If either gender of the definite article precedes a vowel or '*h*' then it is written as '*l'*' (unless the 'h' is aspirate, as in 'le héros'), For plural nouns, the definite article is '*les*' and the indefinite is '*des*', irrespective of gender.

Verbs

Most French verbs are regular and end in '*-er*', '*-ir*' or '*-re*'. For these verbs, you simply remove the '*-er*' '*-ir*' or '*-re*' from the infinitive and follow the set pattern of endings that are added to the stem depending on the person attached to the verb. You can see these nice, well-behaved regular endings in the table below.

Regular Verbs

TO ASK: *Demander*

PRESENT	PAST	FUTURE
I ask: *je demande*	I asked: *j'ai demandé*	I will ask: *je demanderai*
you ask: *tu demandes*	you asked: *tu as demandé*	you will ask: *tu demanderas*
he/she/one asks: *il/elle/*	he/she/one asked: *il/elle/*	he/she/one will ask
on demande	*on a demandé*	*il/elle/on demandera*
we ask: *nous demandons*	we asked: *nous avons demandé*	we will ask: *nous demanderons*
you (plural) ask: *vous*	you (plural) asked: *vous*	you (plural) will ask
demandez	*avez demandé*	*vous demanderez*
they ask: *ils/elles demandent*	they asked: *ils/elles ont*	they will ask: *ils/elles*
	demandé	*demanderont*

Some essential -er verbs to acquaint yourself with are:

parler: to speak   *adorer*: to adore   *manger*: to eat
tomber: to fall   *marcher*: to walk   *espérer*: to hope
gratter: to scratch   *nager*: to swim   *habiter*: to live/reside

TO FINISH: *Finir*

PRESENT	PAST	FUTURE
I finish: *je finis*	I finished: *j'ai fini*	I will finish: *je finirai*
you finish: *tu finis*	you finished: *tu as fini*	you will finish : *tu finiras*
he/she/one finishes:	he/she/one finished:	he/she/one will finish:
il/elle/on finit	*il/elle/on a fini*	*il/elle/on finira*
we finish: *nous finissons*	we finished: *nous avons fini*	we will finish: *nous finirons*
you (plural) finish:	you (plural) finished:	you (plural) will finish:
vous finissez	*vous avez fini*	*vous finirez*
they finish:	they finished:	they will finish:
ils/elles finissent	*ils/elles ont fini*	*ils/elles finiront*

Other essential –ir verbs to acquaint yourself with are:

dormir: to sleep   *courir*: to run   *mourir*: to die
grossir: to get fat   *gemir*: to groan   *obéir*: to obey
rougir: to blush

TO WAIT FOR: *Attendre*

PRESENT	PAST	FUTURE
I wait: *j'attends*	I waited: *j'ai attendu*	I will wait: *je attendrai*
you wait: *tu attends*	you waited: *tu as attendu*	you will wait : *tu attendras*
he/she/one waits:	he/she/one waited:	he/she/one will wait:
il/elle/on attend	*il/elle/on a attendu*	*il/elle/on attendra*
we wait: *nous attendons*	we waited: *nous avons attendu*	we will wait: *nous attendrons*
you (plural) wait:	you (plural) waited:	you (plural) will wait:
vous attendez	*vous avez attendu*	*vous attendrez*
they wait: *ils/elles attendent*	they waited:	they will wait:
	ils/elles ont attendu	*ils/elles attendront*

Other –re verbs to learn are:

vivre: to live   *apprendre*: to learn   *surprendre*: to surprise
comprendre: to understand   *descendre*: to descend   *prendre*: to take
vendre: to sell   *mettre*: to put

Irregular Verbs

Lovely though the pleasingly predictable patterns of regular verbs may be, there are some rebel verbs that do not obey these rules. Irregular verbs have endings that don't follow a particular pattern. Three of the most important verbs in French – *'avoir'* ('to have'), *'être'* ('to be') and *'aller'* ('to go') – are irregular.

TO HAVE: *Avoir*

PRESENT	IMPERFECT	FUTURE
I have: *j'ai*	I had: *j'avais*	I will have: *j'aurai*
you have: *tu as*	you had: *tu avais*	you will have: *tu auras*
he/she/one has:	he/she/one had:	he/she/one will have:
il/elle/on a	*il/elle/on avait*	*il/elle/on aura*
we have: *nous avons*	we had: *nous avions*	we will have: *nous aurons*
you (plural) have: *vous avez*	you (plural) had: *vous aviez*	you (plural) will have:
		vous aurez
they have: *ils/elles ont*	they had: *ils/elles avaient*	they will have: *ils/elles auront*

TO BE: *Être*

PRESENT	IMPERFECT	FUTURE
I am: *je suis*	I was: *j'étais*	I will be: *je serai*
you are: *tu es*	you were: *tu étais*	you will be: *tu seras*
he/she/one is: *il/elle/*	he/she/one was:	he/she/one will be:
on est	*il/elle/on était*	*il/elle/on sera*
we are: *nous sommes*	we were: *nous étions*	we will be: *nous serons*
you (plural) are: *vous êtes*	you (plural) were: *vous étiez*	you (plural) will be:
		vous serez
they are: *ils/elles sont*	they were: *ils/elles étaient*	they will be: *ils/elles seront*

TO GO: *Aller*

PRESENT	PERFECT	FUTURE
I go: *je vais*	I went: *je suis allé*	I will go: *j'irai*
you go: *tu vas*	you went: *tu es allé*	you will go: *tu iras*
he/she/one goes: *il/elle/*	he/she/one went:	he/she/one will go:
on va	*il/on est allé/elle est allée*	*il/elle/on ira*
we go: *nous allons*	we went: *nous sommes allés*	we will go: *nous irons*
you (plural) go: *vous allez*	you (plural) went: *vous êtes*	you (plural) will go:
	allés	*vous irez*
they go: *ils/elles vont*	they went: *ils sont allés/*	they will go: *ils/elles iront*
	elles sont allées	

Once you have learned '*aller*' to your satisfaction, there is a legitimate way to cheat when you want to use the future tense of all other verbs. You can simply use '*aller*' plus the infinitive of the verb you want – for example, '*je vais demander*' means 'I am going to ask'.

FRENCH VERBS THAT TAKE ÊTRE

As you can see from the tables above, the past tense is constructed using the past participle of a verb with either '*avoir*' or '*être*'. Most verbs use '*avoir*' but there are sixteen tricky fellows that insist on using '*être*' instead. The easiest way to remember them is to think of the phrase '**Dr & Mrs Vandertramp**':

devenir – to become
revenir – to return
monter – to climb
rester – to stay
sortir – to exit
venir – to come
aller – to go
naître – to be born
descendre – to descend
entrer – to enter
rentrer – to come back
tomber – to fall
retourner – to return
arriver – to arrive
mourir – to die
partir – to leave

ÉCOUTEZ ET RÉPÉTEZ: USEFUL FRENCH PHRASES

It is important to attempt to communicate in the local lingo when you are visiting foreign climes. These few phrases should help you on your way, but be prepared to be met with some disdain in certain territories of *la belle France*. The French are understandably proud of their beautiful tongue, and many cannot bear to hear it being mangled in English mouths. This can be discomforting but *prends ton courage à deux mains*.

Hello: *Bonjour*
Good evening: *Bonsoir*
Goodbye: *Au revoir*
How are you?: *Ça va?*
I'm well, thank you: *Ça va bien, merci*
I'm called Sylvie: *Je m'appelle Sylvie*
Where is Jean-Claude?: *Où est Jean-Claude?*
He is with a woman: *Il est avec une femme*
She is not his wife: *Elle n'est pas sa femme*
I like cigarettes: *J'aime les cigarettes*
I am from Great Britain: *Je viens de Grande-Bretagne*
Where is the train station please? *Pour aller à la gare, s'il vous plaît?*

AU RESTAURANT

I'm hungry:	*J'ai faim*
I'm thirsty:	*J'ai soif*
I would like a big meal:	*Je voudrais un grand repas*
Please may I see the menu?:	*Est-ce que je peux voir le menu, s'il vous plaît?*
What would you like for a starter?:	*Qu'est-ce que vous voulez pour l'hors d'oeuvre?*
What would you like for your main course?:	*Qu'est-ce que vous voulez prendre pour le plat principal?*
I will have the steak and chips please:	*Je prends l'entrecôte et les pommes frites, s'il vous plaît.*
I am a vegetarian:	*Je suis végétarien (végétarienne if you are female)*
I don't want any pudding, just coffee please:	*Je ne veux pas de dessert, seulement un café, s'il vous plaît.*
I would like a beer:	*Je voudrais une bière.*
Please can I have the bill?:	*L'addition, s'il vous plaît.*

OTHER WORDS YOU MIGHT SEE ON A FRENCH MENU:

l'entrée – starter
l'eau – water
le pain – bread
le beurre – butter
les oeufs – eggs
les crêpes – pancakes (delightfully light and thin rather than squat, fat American pancakes – they can be filled with savoury or sweet ingredients)
le croque-monsieur – a grilled ham and cheese sandwich
le jambon – ham
le bifteck – steak (you can have this '*bleu*' meaning 'very, very rare', '*saignant*' meaning 'rare', '*à point*' meaning 'medium rare', '*bien cuit*' meaning 'medium well done' and, if you don't mind receiving looks of derision from the waiting staff, '*très bien cuit*' meaning 'well done')
l'agneau – lamb
le poulet – chicken
le boeuf bourguignon – scrumptious beef stew made with red wine, onions, garlic, mushrooms and herbs

le foie gras – goose liver
les escargots – snails
les cuisses de grenouille – frogs' legs
le cassoulet – meat and bean casserole typically including sausages, duck, haricot beans, tomatoes and herbs
les fruits de mer – seafood
les huîtres – oysters
la bouillabaisse – fish stew from the south of France made with fish, shellfish, vegetables and herbs
le fromage – cheese
les légumes – vegetables
le chou-fleur – cauliflower (literally '*chou-fleur*' means 'cabbage flower' which is an enchanting moniker for this rather dull vegetable)
les pommes de terre – potatoes
les champignons – mushrooms
la glace – ice cream
l'ananas – pineapple
la pomme – apple
le pamplemousse – grapefruit
la fraise – strawberry
le cassis – blackcurrant
le citron – lemon
le gâteau – cake

HOW MANY ESKIMO WORDS FOR SNOW ARE THERE?

The indigenous peoples of Greenland, Alaska, Canada and eastern Siberia are collectively known as Eskimos. However, in Canada the term Eskimo is considered derogatory and Inuit should be used instead, although not all Eskimos are Inuit. The Eskimos of the various regions speak different, but related, languages, referred to as the Eskimo-Aleut languages.

It's a myth that there are hundreds of words in Eskimo for snow; in fact, there are probably no more than four. In English we too have many words for types and forms of snow including 'hail', 'ice', 'sleet', 'slush', 'powder snow', 'snowflake', 'frost', 'snowdrift', 'icicle', 'snowball' . . .

ITALIANO ESSENZIALE:
HOW TO PRONOUNCE ITALIAN WORDS

Italian always sounds better if you really get into the spirit of the language. Speak with passion, wave your arms around, shout a little and over-enunciate wherever possible. Abandon all of your British reserve, lose your clipped and monotonous register and really go for it.

In Italian, letters that have an accent are stressed. Most Italian words are naturally stressed on the penultimate syllable.

a – is always pronounced as the 'a' in 'father'. e – **e**ight or g**e**t i – l**i**tre o – b**o**at or **o**ffice u – sp**oo**n	c – when a 'c' comes before an 'i' or 'e' in an Italian word it is pronounced 'ch' as in '**ch**urch'. When it is followed by 'a', 'o' or 'u' it is is pronounced as in '**c**at'. g – when a 'g' is followed by 'i' or 'e' it is pronounced as in '**g**entle'. When it is followed by 'a', 'o' or 'u' it is pronounced as in '**g**ate'. h – at the start of words is silent. z – lot**s** ch – luc**k** gh – **g**arden gl – mi**ll**ion gn – o**ni**on sc – when 'sc' is followed by 'i' or 'e' it is pronounced 'sh' as in '**sh**oot'. When it is followed by 'a', 'o' or 'u' it is pronounced as in '**sk**ate'.

LA PASSIONE!: ITALIAN HAND GESTURES

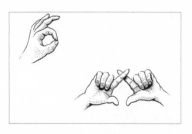

Giuro: I swear it

Devo andare al bagno:
I need the loo

Che barba: How annoying

È un po'toccato:
He's a little bonkers

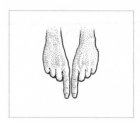

Se l'intendono:
Those two are thick as
thieves

COUNTING IN JAPANESE

Japanese can seem like a daunting and impregnable language to those of us who are unfamiliar with its alphabets. Its characters, however, are things of harmoniously proportioned beauty and a little knowledge may just save your life in a restaurant when you manage to avoid the *Special No.* 五 *Fugu* (the highly toxic blowfish, which can cause instantaneous death if incorrectly cooked).

Number	Character	Pronunciation
1	一	*ichi*
2	二	*ni*
3	三	*san*
4	四	*shi* or *yon*
5	五	*go*
6	六	*roku*
7	七	*shichi* or *nana*
8	八	*hachi*
9	九	*kyu*
10	十	*ju*

DEUTSCH HEUTE: GERMAN TODAY

Pronunciation

People often and mistakenly think of German as a guttural, unattractive-
-sounding language, especially when compared to the Romance
languages (those that are derived from Latin) of French, Spanish or
Italian. It's true that German lacks the sing-song qualities of its sultry
cousins, but there's a hidden beauty in its unerring logic and it is closely
related to our own mother tongue, so richly rewards closer inspection.

German words are usually stressed on the first syllable.

a – **ha**t or f**a**ther	b (when last letter in word or followed by a consonant) – ta**p**
e – b**e**t or h**ai**r	
i – h**i**t or s**ee**	ch (after 'a', 'o', 'u' or 'au') – as in Scottish lo**ch**
o – h**o**t or t**o**rn	
u – p**u**t or p**oo**l	ch (after 'ä', 'e', 'i', 'ö', 'ü', 'ie', 'äu', 'eu', 'y', 'l', 'r' or 'n') – somewhere between **h**uge and **sh**eep
au – h**ou**se	
eu or äu – b**oy**	
ei – m**i**le	d (when last letter in word or followed by a consonant) – ha**t**
ie – k**ee**n	
ä – p**e**t or **ai**r	g (when last letter in word or followed by a consonant) – bar**k**
ü – somewhere between br**oo**d and br**ee**d	
	h – sometimes silent
ö – **ear**n	j – **y**es
y – same as ü	qu – like '**kv**' in English
	ß – ki**ss**
	s (when first letter of word or followed by a vowel) – **z**ebra
	s (before 'p' or 't' and usually before 'ch') – **sh**op
	th – **t**op
	v – **f**ather
	w – **v**an
	z – bi**ts**

Nouns

In German, nouns are masculine, feminine or neuter and, helpfully, they always start with a capital letter.

Nouns ending in '-*ant*', '-*ast*', '-*ich*', '-*ig*', '-*ismus*', '-*ling*', '-*or*' and '-*us*' tend to be masculine.

Nouns ending in '-*a*', '-*anz*', '-*ei*', '-*enz*', '-*heit*', '-*ie*', '-*ik*', '-*in*', '-*keit*', '-*schaft*', '-*sion*', '-*sis*', '-*tät*', '-*tion*', '-*ung*' and '-*ur*' tend to be feminine.

Nouns ending in '-*chen*', '-*icht*', '-*il*', '-*it*', '-*lein*', '-*ma*', '-*ment*', '-*tel*', '-*tum*' and '-*um*' tend to be neuter.

Articles

As in the other languages we've peeked at so far, in German the definite and indefinite article match the gender of the noun they refer to – however German has three genders, to French, Italian and Spanish's paltry two. 'The' is '*der*' with masculine singular nouns, '*die*' with feminine singular nouns and '*das*' with neuter singular nouns. For plural nouns the definite article is always written as '*die*'. The indefinite is '*ein*' for masculine and neuter singular nouns and '*eine*' for feminine singular nouns.

Nouns in German are categorised by their gender and number like many other languages, but also by their role in the sentence: these categories are the **cases** of a noun. The article or adjective attached to a noun, or the noun itself, may change its ending depending on its case. The subject of a sentence (just in case you've forgotten, the subject is whatever performs the verb) is in the nominative case. In the sentence 'The dog eats the cake' the subject of the sentence is 'the dog'. In German this sentence is written as '***Der Hund*** ißt den Kuchen'. 'Der Hund' is in the nominative case.

The object of a sentence (whatever the verb acts upon) is in the accusative case. In the previous sentence, 'the cake' is the object. '*Der Hund ißt **den Kuchen**'*. This is why it is written as '*den Kuchen*'. In the nominative case (which is how nouns appear in the dictionary) it would be '*der Kuchen*'. '*Den*' is the accusative form of the article.

The indirect object of a sentence is written in the dative case. In the sentence 'The girl gives the cake to the dog' the indirect object is 'to the dog'. In German this sentence is written as: '*Das Mädchen gibt **dem Hund** den Kuchen.*'

A noun that owns something in a sentence is written in the genitive case. In the sentence 'The girl gives the man's cake to the dog' the part of the sentence involving something possessing something else is 'the man's'. In German this sentence is written as '*Das Mädchen gibt dem Hund den Kuchen **des Mannes**'*. 'The man' in the nominative case would be '*der Mann*' and '*des Mannes*' is the genitive form.

THE DEFINITE ARTICLE: The

	Masculine	Feminine	Neuter	Plural
Nominative	*der*	*die*	*das*	*die*
Accusative	*den*	*die*	*das*	*die*
Dative	*dem*	*der*	*dem*	*den*
Genitive	*des*	*der*	*des*	*der*

THE INDEFINITE ARTICLE: A or An

	Masculine	Feminine	Neuter
Nominative	*ein*	*eine*	*ein*
Accusative	*einen*	*eine*	*ein*
Dative	*einem*	*einer*	*einem*
Genitive	*eines*	*einer*	*eines*

Adjectives

Adjectives also have to match the gender, case and number of the noun they describe. 'Dog' in German ('*Hund*') is masculine but the word for 'girl' ('*Mädchen*') is neuter: '*der **schlechter** Hund*' means 'the bad dog' and '*das **schlechtes** Mädchen*' means the bad girl.

Verbs

The form of the verb in a German sentence changes according to the subject and tense of the verb. Regular verbs all neatly change their endings in the same way. The verb '*spielen*' ('to play') is an example of a regular verb ('*haben*' meaning 'to have' and '*sein*' meaning 'to be' are two of the most common irregular verbs to look out for). Most other verbs will change their endings like this:

TO PLAY: *Spielen*

PRESENT	PAST	FUTURE

I play: *ich spiele*
you play: *du spielst*
he/she/it plays:
  er/sie/es spielt
we play: *wir spielen*
you (plural) play: *ihr spielt*
 	
they play: *sie spielen*
	I played: *ich habe gespielt*
	you played: *du hast gespielt*
	he/she/it played:
	  er/sie/es hat gespielt
	we played: *wir haben gespielt*
	you (plural) played:
	  ihr habt gespielt
	they played: *sie haben gespielt*
		I will play: *ich werde spielen*
		you will play: *du wirst spielen*
		he/she/it will play:
		  er/sie/es wird spielen
		we will play: *wir werden spielen*
		you (plural) will play:
		  ihr werdet spielen
		they will play:
		  sie werden spielen

WIE KOMME ICH AM BESTEN ZUM BAHNHOF BITTE?: USEFUL GERMAN PHRASES

Good morning: *Guten Morgen*
Good afternoon: *Guten Tag*
Thank you: *Danke*
You're welcome: *Bitte schön*
Goodbye: *Auf Wiedersehen*
I'm called Harry: *Ich heiße Harry*
How's it going?: *Wie geht's?*
Good, thanks: *Gut, danke*
I come from Great Britain: *Ich komme aus Großbritannien*
I don't like chocolate: *Ich mag nicht Schokolade*
Where is Ron?: *Wo ist Ron?*
He is drunk: *Er ist betrunken*
I have two brothers: *Ich habe zwei Brüder*
How do I get to the train station please?: *Wie komme Ich am besten zum Bahnhof bitte?*

¡BUENÍSSIMO!: SPECTACULAR SPANISH

Castilian Spanish is one of four languages spoken in Spain, along with Galician, Basque and Catalan. Spanish is also the official language of most Latin American countries and is spoken by between 300 and 400 million native speakers, making it the second most-spoken language in the world. Spain is also one of us Brits' most-visited holiday destinations: you would be seriously misguided not to try to learn the basics. Think how it will aid you when you are haggling for that straw donkey or pair of ornamental castanets.

Pronunciation

Spanish vowels are always pronounced clearly. Letters that have an accent are stressed. '*V*' is pronounced like a very soft 'b', and '*j*' is a gutteral sound, rather like the one you would make if you were rude enough to be about to spit. '*G*' is pronounced 'he', except for when it's followed by the letters '*ue*' when it becomes a hard 'g', as in English. The letter '*c*' has two types of pronunciation depending on the vowel that follows it: before '*e*' and '*i*' it is pronounced 'th' and before '*a*', '*o*' and '*u*' it is pronounced as a 'k'.

Nouns

Like French, in Spanish all nouns are either masculine or feminine: Feminine nouns usually end in '-*a*', '-*dad*', '-*tad*', '-*tud*', '-*itis*', '-*sis*', '-*ion*', '*ed*' and '*umbre*'. Masculine nouns usually end in '-*o*', '-*l*', '-*r*', '-*y*'.

To make plural forms of Spanish nouns you usually add an '-*s*' to the singular if the noun ends in a vowel. If a nouns ends in a consonant then add '-*es*' instead, for example peseta: pesetas; español: españoles.

Articles

The gender and number of the noun determine what form the article takes. With masculine nouns, 'the' is '*el*' in the singular, and '*los*' in the plural. With feminine nouns, 'the' is '*la*' in the singular and '*las*' in the plural.

Verbs

The verb in a Spanish sentence changes according to the subject, the tense and sometimes the gender of the subject as well. If you are reading this chapter through from start to finish, you will probably have realised that this is a bit of a recurring theme in our study of modern languages.

Regular verbs

There are three different types of regular verbs: those ending in '*-ar*', such as '*hablar*' ('to speak'); those ending in '*-er*' as in '*comer*' ('to eat'); and those ending in '*-ir*', such as '*vivir*' ('to live'). Any verb that is a member of one of these groups will change its endings in the same way as all the other verbs in that group, much in the same way that any teenager who is a member of a particular clique will dress identically to their friends.

TO SPEAK: *Hablar*

PRESENT	PAST	FUTURE
I speak: *yo hablo*	I spoke: *yo hablé*	I will speak: *yo hablaré*
you speak: *tú hablas*	you spoke: *tú hablaste*	you will speak: *tú hablarás*
he/she/you (formal singular) speaks: *él/ ella/usted habla*	he/she/you (formal singular) spoke: *él/ ella/usted habló*	he/she/you (formal singular) will speak: *él/ ella/usted hablará*
we speak: *nosotros/nosotras/ hablamos*	we spoke: *nosotros/nosotras/ hablamos*	we will speak: *nosotros/nostras hablaremos*
you (familiar plural) speak: *vosotros/vosotras áis hablaís*	you (familiar plural) spoke: *vosotros/vosotras hablasteis*	you (familiar plural) will speak: *vosotras/vosotras hablaréis*
they/you (formal) speak: *ellos/ellas/ustedes hablan*	they/you (formal) spoke: *ellos/ellas/ustedes hablaron*	they/you (formal) will speak: *ellos/ellas/ustedes hablarán*

TO EAT: *Comer*

PRESENT	PAST	FUTURE
I eat: *yo como*	I ate: *yo comí*	I will eat: *yo comeré*
you eat: *tú comes*	you ate: *tú comiste*	you will eat: *tú comerás*
he/she/you (formal singular) eat: *él/ ella/usted come*	he/she/you (formal singular) ate: *él/ ella/usted comió*	he/she/you (formal singular) will eat: *él/ ella/usted comerá*
we eat: *nosotros/nosotras comemos*	we ate: *nosotros/nosotras comimos*	we will eat: *nosotras/nostras comeremos*
you (familiar plural) eat: *vosotros/vosotras coméis*	you (familiar plural) ate: *vosotros/vosotras comisteis*	you (familiar plural) will eat: *vosotros/vosotras comeréis*
they/you (formal plural) eat: *ellos/ellas/ustedes comen*	they/you (formal plural) ate: *ellos/ellas/ustedes comieron*	they/you (formal plural) will eat: *ellos/ellas/ustedes comerán*

TO LIVE: *Vivir*

PRESENT	PAST	FUTURE
I live: *yo vivo* you live: *tú vives* he/she/you (formal singular) live: *él/ ella/usted vive* we live: *nosotros/nosotras vivimos* you (plural familiar) live: *vosotros/vosotras vivís* they/you (formal plural) live: *ellos/ellas/ustedes viven*	I lived: *yo viví* you lived: *tú viviste* he/she/you (formal singular) lived: *él/ ella/usted vivió* We lived: *nosotros/nosotras vivimos* you (plural familiar) lived: *vosotros/vosotras vivisteis* they/you (formal plural) lived: *ellos/ellas/ustedes vivieron*	I will live: *yo viviré* you will live: *tú vivirás* he/she/you (formal singular) will live: *él/ ella/usted vivirá* we will live: *nosotros/nosotras viviremos* you (plural familiar) will live: *vosotros/vosotras viviréis* they/you (formal plural) will live: *ellos/ellas/ustedes vivirán*

Irregular Verbs

Some verbs are irregular. Can you guess what the three most popular and sought-after irregular verbs are? Yes indeed, they are '*estar*' meaning 'to be' and '*tener*' and '*haber*' meaning 'to have'.

TO BE: *Estar*

PRESENT	PAST	FUTURE
I am: *yo estoy* you are: *tú estás* he/she/you (formal singular) are: *él/ella/usted está* we are: *nosotros estamos* you (familiar plural) are: *vosotros estáis* they/you (formal plural) are: *ellos/ustedes están*	I was: *yo estuve* you were: *tú estuviste* he/she/you (formal singular) were: *él/ella/usted estuvo* we were: *nosotros estuvimos* you (familiar plural) were: *vosotros estuvisteis* they/you (formal plural) were: *ellos/ustedes estuvieron*	I will be: *yo estaré* you will be: *tú estarás* he/she/you (formal singular) will be: *él/ella/usted estará* we will be: *nosotros estaremos* you (familiar plural) will be: *vosotros estaréis* they/you (formal pural) will be: *ellos/ustedes estaran*

TO HAVE: *Tener*

PRESENT	PAST	FUTURE
I have: *yo tengo* you have: *tú tienes* he/she/you (formal singular) have: *él/ella/usted tiene* we have: *nosotros tenemos* you (plural familiar) have: *vosotros tenéis* they/you (formal plural) have: *ellos/ustedes tienen*	I had: *yo tuve* you had: *tú tuviste* he/she/you (formal singular) had: *él/ella/usted tuvo* we had: *nosotros tuvimos* you (plural familiar) had: *vosotros tuvisteis* they/you (formal plural) had: *ellos/ustedes tuvieron*	I will have: *yo tendré* you will have: *tú tendrás* he/she/you (formal singular) will have: *él/ella/usted tendrá* we will have: *nosotros tendremos* you (plural familiar) will have: *vosotros tendréis* they/you (formal plural) will have: *ellos/ustedes tendrán*

TO HAVE: *Haber*
This verb is used as an auxiliary verb meaning 'I **have** eaten the cake', rather than 'I **ate** the cake'.

PRESENT	PAST	FUTURE
I have: *yo he* you have: *tú has* he/she/you (formal singular) have: *él/ella/usted ha* we have: *nosotros hemos* you (familiar plural) have: *vosotros habéis* they/you (formal plural) have: *ellos han*	I had: *yo hube* you had: *tú hubiste* he/she/you (formal singular) had: *él/ella/usted hubo* we had: *nosotros hubismos* you (familiar plural) had: *vosotros hubisteis* they/you (formal plural) had: *ellos hubieron*	I will have: *yo habré* you will have: *tú habrás* he/she/you (formal singular) will have: *él/ella/usted habrá* we will have: *nosotros habremos* you (familiar plural) will have: *vosotros habréis* they/you (formal plural) will have: *ellos habrán*

THE FINGER-SPELLING SIGN-LANGUAGE ALPHABET

Even if you don't know any other sign-language gestures you can use this alphabet to spell out words – admittedly this makes for rather slow and awkward conversation but, in most circumstances, it is better than no communication at all.

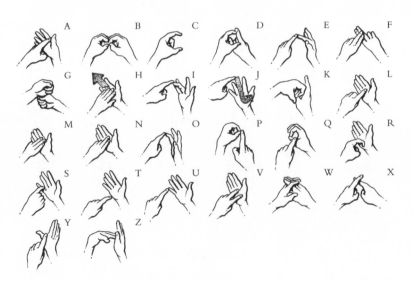

HOW DO I LOVE YOU? LET ME COUNT THE WAYS: 'I LOVE YOU' IN ELEVEN DIFFERENT LANGUAGES

Obicham te – Bulgarian

Jeg elsker dig – Danish

Je t'aime – French

我愛你　(*Wo ai ni*) – Mandarin

Kocham cif – Polish

Te amo – Spanish

Ti amo – Italian

Ich liebe dich – German

Σ αγαπώ (*s'agapo*) – Greek

Eu te amo – Portuguese

Ya liubliu tebyon – Russian

⤜ MODERN ⤚
LANGUAGES
TEST PAPER

1. **ORAL EXAMINATION**

   You meet your French skiing instructor for lunch in a Chamonix restaurant

   a) Ask for a table for two
   b) Request the menu
   c) Order a bottle of champagne
   d) Say you would like the oysters to start
   e) Order a rare steak with chips for your main course

2. **Name the films these famous quotes in translation come from:**

   a) *'J'adore l'odeur du napalm le matin'*
   b) *'Ho mangiato il suo fegato con alcuni fagioli di fava e un chianti piacevole'*
   c) *'Niemand legt Baby in die Ecke'*
   d) *'Necesitaremos un barco màs grande'*
   e) *'Demain c'est un autre jour'*
   f) *'Mi chiamo Bond, Giacomo Bond'*
   g) *'Gli darò un'offerta che non può rifiutare'*
   h) *'Yippie-kay-yay'*
   i) *'Die Kraft sei mit Ihnen'*
   j) *'Hasta la vista, baby'*

3. **In Italian, nouns are divided into:**

   a) gender, case and number
   b) gender and number
   c) case and number

4. **Identify the subject in the following German sentence:**

   Ein Mann geht in eine Bar

5. **Explain that you are from Great Britain to your German friend Hans and your French friend Jean-Claude.**

6. **Turn the following French words into their plural form:**

a) *le livre*
b) *un chapeau*

7. **How do you say 'How annoying' in Italian without saying a word?**

8. **How many Spanish languages are spoken in Spain?**

9. **How do you say 'I love you' in Portuguese?**

10. **Identify the following items on a French menu:**

a) *les huîtres*
b) *le pamplemousse*
c) *les cuisses de grenouille*

11. **Turn the following Italian words into their plural form:**

a) *il libro*
b) *L'uccello*
c) *la bicicletta*

12. **How do you say 'Cheers!' in Irish Gaelic?**

13. **What is 'Sunday' in Welsh?**

14. **When were scholars finally able to decipher ancient Egyptian hieroglyphs?**

15. **Who is credited with composing the Russian alphabet?**

16. What is the singular form of the following French words?

a) *fils*
b) *bateaux*
c) *livres*

17. Translate the following French sentences into English:

a) *J'ai fini le livre*
b) *Elle demandera le collier*
c) *Ils attendent l'autobus*

18. Name six French verbs which use '*être*' rather than '*avoir*' in the past tense.

19. What is the German word for Mr?

20. Give the French terms for the following:

a)

b)

c)

d)

21. If Peter is applying for a job with a French company, what is the polite way for him to sign off his letter of application?

22. How many Eskimo words for snow are there?

23. Identify whether the following Italian words are masculine or feminine:

a) *uccello*
b) *montagna*
c) *zia*
d) *bambino*

24. Underline the nouns in this German sentence:

Banken brechen zusammen, an den Börsen herrscht Panik.

25. If your German friend Heidi tells you that your home-made soup is '*schrecklich*', does she like it or dislike it?

26. If Pedro approaches you waving wildly and shouting '*Tù comiste mi torta!*', what is he accusing you of?

27. How do you pronounce the number 3 in Japanese?

28. In German, nouns ending in '*-chen*', '*-icht*', '*-il*', '*-it*', '*-lein*', '*-ma*', '*-ment*', '*-tel*', '*-tum*' and '*-um*' tend to be:

a) neuter
b) feminine
c) masculine
d) feminine plural

29. '*¡Esto es el colmo!*' is Spanish for:

a) That is the robber!
b) That is the cauliflower!
c) That is the last straw!
d) That is the ticket!

30. *Arrivederci* means goodbye in which language?

a) French
b) German
c) Italian
d) Spanish

⌀ HOME ⌀
ECONOMICS

In difficult financial times having a happy, healthy home becomes more important than ever. Good household management, thrift, making do and mending are all skills to be applauded and also make for an environmentally kinder lifestyle. Nothing is quite so satisfying as surveying your kingdom and basking in the warm glow of a well-run household, so take this opportunity to learn how to look after you and yours efficiently and enjoyably. In this chapter we will seek to take you several steps closer to the good life, so you can look forward to a sparkling future where you can knit all your own clothes, grow your own vegetables, cook your own banquets, sort out your own electrics, make your own cleaning products and even deliver your own babies. Self-sufficiency, here we come!

SHIPSHAPE AND BRISTOL FASHION: PANTRY MANAGEMENT

As Mrs Beeton said, the kitchen is 'the great laboratory of every household' and 'much of the "weal or woe"', as far as regards bodily health, depends upon the nature of the preparations concocted within its walls'. To help keep your laboratory in good health, there are certain foodstuffs that every home should have so that you can make a variety of nutritious and delicious meals at the drop of a hat.

Spices: black pepper, salt, mustard, chilli powder, bay leaves, mixed herbs, curry powder, cinnamon, vanilla extract

Tins: tomatoes, baked beans, chickpeas, tuna fish, anchovies, olives, soup

Dried goods: pasta, rice, noodles, sugar, plain flour, self-raising flour, baking powder, bicarbonate of soda, yeast, chocolate

Miscellaneous: stock cubes, honey, ketchup, soy sauce, Worcestershire sauce, olive oil, white wine vinegar, coffee, tea

Fresh foods: lemons, garlic, onion, potatoes, butter, cheese, milk

CLEANLINESS WITHOUT CHEMISTRY: HOW TO CLEAN YOUR HOUSE CHEAPLY AND SIMPLY

If you read the back of any manufactured household cleaning product, you're likely to feel you need a degree in Chemistry just to understand exactly what you're bringing into your home. Luckily, for those of us not terribly keen on polyacrylates, paradichlorobenzene, polyethylene glycol or phthalates, or those who might be put off by the friendly skull-and-crossbones warning signs on many detergent bottles, there are alternatives that you can make yourself using less complicated and unnatural substances.

Here are some effective cleaning methods that only involve four ingredients: white vinegar, bicarbonate of soda, lemon juice and elbow grease.

To remove limescale from a shower head: Fill a plastic bag with vinegar and tie it over the shower head so that it's fully submerged. Leave overnight then scrub off any remaining limescale.

To remove brown marks from glass oven doors: Mix bicarbonate of soda and lemon juice and scrub energetically.

For blocked and stinky sinks: Pour some bicarbonate of soda down the drain followed by vinegar and leave for a few hours.

To descale a washing machine: With the machine empty, run a hot wash with vinegar in the conditioner drawer.

To descale a kettle: Boil some vinegar in the kettle then leave to soak overnight. Remember to rinse well before making yourself a brew.

To deodorise whiffy fridges: Keep an egg cup of bicarbonate of soda in the back of the fridge to absorb odours.

To clean windows: Wipe windows with vinegar and then buff dry with scrunched newspaper.

BAKING BEAUTY: A BEWITCHING BAKEWELL TART

The history of the Bakewell tart is shrouded in mystery and there are different schools of thought as to what constitutes the authentic formula for its construction. According to one of the recognised authorities, the Bakewell Tart Shop in the eponymous town in Derbyshire, the recipe was invented by the slightly flustered cook of a Mrs Greaves in 1820 who misunderstood her mistress's instructions while preparing for a dinner party and mistakenly put the jam and pudding mix into the dish in the wrong order.

500g shortcrust pastry
8 tbsp raspberry or cherry jam
100g unsalted butter
125g caster sugar
3 eggs, beaten
½ tsp almond essence
150g ground almonds
25g flaked almonds

1. Grease a 20cm tart or baking tin with butter. Roll out the pastry on a floured surface until it's about 3mm thick and big enough to line the whole tin, including the sides. Prick the pastry all over with a fork.
2. Spread the jam thickly and smoothly over the pastry and then put the tin into the fridge to chill. Preheat the oven to 180°C (gas mark 4).
3. In a large bowl, cream the butter and sugar together (you'll need some elbow grease for this job and it's easiest if the butter is soft to begin with). Then add the eggs in gradual sploshes before mixing in the almond essence and ground almonds. Take the tin out of the fridge and spread this mixture over the top of the jam.
4. Sprinkle the top of the tart with the flaked almonds and bake for 30–35 minutes. Leave to cool and then serve dusted with icing sugar and perhaps with a splodge of cream. (Or you could do the kitsch thing and make it a Cherry Bakewell by icing it and sticking a glacé cherry on the top. Exceedingly good.)

A STITCH IN TIME:
HOW TO KNIT A SCARF

Surely it is everyone's dream to see a friend's face light up with joy as you hand over a delightful hand-knitted jumper featuring a daring design of prancing ponies. However, this is a complicated project involving some expertise and it is wiser to begin your knitting adventures with a more modest item of clothing such as a scarf, perhaps even a scarf for a doll. All you need are some satisfyingly clackety knitting needles and as bright and bold a colour yarn as you dare. We would recommend some No. 8 needles and acrylic wool if you are a beginner as they are the easiest to use.

1.	Make a slip knot on the shaft of one needle.	
2.	Hold this needle in your left hand (if you are right-handed). Hold the other needle in your right hand. Push the point of the right needle, from front to back, into the slip knot and under the left needle.	
3.	Keep holding the left needle in your left hand, but move your left fingers over to steady the right needle.	
4.	With your right index finger, pick up the strand of wool.	
5.	Let the right hand's grip on the needle go, and use your index finger to bring the strand of wool under and over the point of the right needle.	

6. Return your right fingers to the right needle, and draw the wool through the stitch on the left needle with the point of the right needle.	
7. Slide the point of the left needle into the back of the new stitch you've made and then remove the right needle.	
8. Pull the strand of wool gently to make the stitch snug on the needle.	
9. Push the point of the right needle, from front to back, into the stitch you have just made, and under the left needle. Repeat from step 5 onwards until you have the number of stitches on the left needle that you want. (This will be the width of your scarf.)	
10. Hold the needle with the stitches in your left hand and push the point of the right needle into the first stitch, from front to back, as before.	
11. With your right index finger, bring the strand of wool under and then over the point of the right needle.	
12. Draw the wool through the stitch with the point of the right needle.	

13. Slip the loop you have made on the left needle off, so that the new stitch is transferred to the right needle. Now begin the next stitch on the left needle and repeat steps 10–13 until you have completed a full row. Begin again at the top and repeat until your scarf is as long as you would like.	
14. When you want to finish, knit the first 2 stitches; then insert the left needle into the stitch you knitted first, and pull it over the second stitch and completely off the needle.	
15. Knit one more stitch, insert the left needle into the first stitch on the right needle, and pull it over the new stitch and completely off the needle.	
Repeat step 15 until one stitch remains; now cut the strand of wool from the ball, leaving roughly 5cm dangling. With your free needle draw the end up and through the last stitch to secure it and tie a knot.	

WHAT NOT TO FEED A PREGNANT PERSON

It is a sad fact that pregnant women not only have to put up with nine months of swollen feet, nausea and being banned from booze and fags, but on top of these hardships they are advised to avoid certain foods because they contain elements that can adversely affect the unborn baby. The worst possible menu to face a mother-to-be would be Stilton soufflé followed by shark's liver and espresso chocolate mousse for pudding.

Experts differ on exactly what is safe or desirable for a gravid gourmande, but if you are cooking for a pregnant partner or friend it is safest to steer clear of the following: caffeine; liver; soft cheeses; shark, swordfish or marlin; and raw or partially cooked eggs. You must also remember to wash salad and vegetables carefully so that no soil remains on them.

All terribly dull, but once the little one is out of the hatch, we recommend that you treat yourself to a slap-up dinner with lashings of wine while someone else takes care of babysitting duties.

A VARIETY OF VEGGIES: TYPES OF VEGETARIANS

A vegetarian is a person who abstains from animal food, especially meat, and is as a result often unwelcome at dinner parties. There are many different types of vegetarian. In this confusing modern world it is useful to know who eats what. This handy guide should help you prepare your menu.

Lacto-ovo-vegetarian: eats both dairy products and eggs.
Lacto-vegetarian: eats dairy products but not eggs.
Vegan: does not eat dairy products, eggs, or any other animal product.
Macrobiotic: mainly vegetarian, but sometimes eats seafood. No other meat, eggs or dairy products are consumed, and neither are white sugar, tropical fruits, potatoes, peppers and aubergines. Yawn.
Fruitarian: only eats fruits – including fruits that masquerade as vegetables: avocados and tomatoes.
Pescatarian: eats fish.
Pollotarian: eats poultry.

GREEN FINGERS:
BASIC GARDENING TIPS

In the wartime austerity years pretty much everyone with a garden made practical use of it to grow their own fruit and vegetables. Nowadays a garden is a luxury that you can use either to grow food or simply to fill with fragrant flowers for your visual and olfactory enjoyment. Gardening can be therapeutic and is a good way to get some fresh air, but there a few basics you need to know in order to make it a successful experience, rather than one where you end up staring wistfully at a patch of barren soil.

The basic principle of growing plants is that they need four things in order to thrive: **heat**, **light**, **moisture** and **food**.

- As a general rule it is important to know what kind of soil your garden has and how shady it is and to choose plants that flourish in this environment.
- You can improve your soil by digging in compost or soil enrichers from your local garden centre.
- You can make your own compost by putting all your uncooked vegetable food and garden waste (including tea bags, paper and crushed eggshells) into a composting bin. Composting bins are simple to make: cut the bottom out of a plastic dustbin and place the bin directly onto a patch of soil in your garden. Cover with a lid and then put all your waste into the bin where it will break down into compost after 6–9 months. It may seem strange, but it is a good idea to pee on your compost every so often, as the nitrogen in your urine helps activate it. Just bear your neighbours in mind when you are involved in this particular compost-enrichment practice.
- Once you have decided what to grow, you need to sow your seeds or plant your cuttings at the right time of year – you will find instructions on your seed packets.
- Remember to leave plenty of space between plants to allow them room to grow.

A FAMILY BASIC: STUPENDOUS SPAG BOL

Back in the 1970s, long before everyone was chowing down on buffalo mozzarella and rocket salads and gnocchi with sage butter, the influence of the grand cuisine of Italy on British home cooking was predominantly felt in the form of those two wonderful staples, spaghetti Bolognese and lasagne. Opinions can get heated over the best recipe to use to create these Anglo-Italian masterpieces (the inclusion of liver can lead to fisticuffs in some quarters), but the recipe below gives you the basic starting point for Bolognese sauce, from which to develop your own unique signature version.

Serves 4
1 tbsp olive oil
1 medium onion, finely chopped
250g finely minced lean beef
1–2 cloves of garlic, crushed
400g can of chopped tomatoes
½ tsp dried oregano or marjoram
Salt and black pepper to taste
400g spaghetti
grated Parmesan cheese to garnish

1. Take a roomy heavy-bottomed pan or casserole. Warm the oil over a medium heat, add the onion and gently sweat it until it becomes translucent. Add the mince and garlic, increase the heat and cook, stirring from time to time, until the meat begins to brown. Keep an eye on it to make sure it doesn't catch on the bottom of the pan.
2. Tip in the tomatoes and stir. Add the herbs, salt and pepper and stir again. Cover and simmer over a gentle heat for about 30 minutes, stirring occasionally. If it seems to be getting too dry, lower the heat and add a little water. If it seems too sloppy, increase the heat a little.
3. Boil 1–2 litres of water with ½ tsp salt in a large pan, add the spaghetti and cook at a rolling boil for the time indicated on the packet (about 10 minutes for normal spaghetti, less for Quick Cook and a bit more for wholewheat). Do not overcook the pasta

as it will turn into a sticky mess. You can test a strand by biting a bit off: when there is only a tiny white dot in the middle it's ready.

4. Check the seasoning of the sauce. Drain the spaghetti then return to the pan with a small glug of olive oil and shake around to coat the strands. Serve the pasta and then top with the sauce and Parmesan cheese if required.

THE APPLIANCE OF SCIENCE: HOW TO WIRE A PLUG

Many electrical appliances these days do not have removable plugs. If they do, they can be changed when the fuse blows or if the plug is damaged. Changing a plug is an honest job that shows that you are the master of your domain: all you need is a screwdriver.

First unscrew the screw that holds the two halves of the plug together, then unscrew the screws holding the plastic casing over the wires and loosen the screws inside the plug that hold the wire in place. Remove the wires from the plug casing.

Strip back a couple of centimetres of the plastic wire-covering from the cable attached to your appliance so that you can see the separate coloured wire casings. You also need to strip back a millimetre or two of each coloured casing so that you can see the copper wire that must connect to the points to make the plug work.

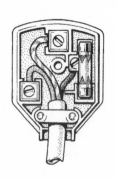

You need to attach the correct wires to the correct points of the plug. The **blue** wire is **neutral** and needs to be screwed into the point marked **N. Brown** means **live** and needs to be screwed into the point marked **L. Green and yellow** means **earth** and needs to be screwed into the point marked **E.**

Finally you need to secure everything neatly inside the plug casing and screw the back of the plug back on. Job done.

CALORIE COUNTER:
RECOMMENDED DAILY ALLOWANCES

	Men (aged 19–50)	Women (aged 19–50)
Calories	2,500	2,000
Fat	100g	76g
Protein	55.5g	45g
Fibre	18g	18g
Water (and other non-alcoholic fluids)	1.5–2l	1.5–2l

ALE ARITHMETIC: ALCOHOL UNITS

Shockingly, scientists have discovered that drinking over 2 pints of beer a day is risky to your health (or, even worse, 1½ pints if you are a woman). No doubt when you read about binge drinkers you think, 'Oh, silly teenagers off their faces on alcopops trying to escape the psychic pain of adolescence,' but in fact you qualify as a binge drinker if you drink more than 4 pints in one go (or 3 pints if you're female).

According to studies, 31% of men say they drink on average more than the recommended 21 units in a normal week and 20% of women say they drink more than their recommended 14 units. This is easy to shrug off as the damage alcohol causes, as with cigarettes, can take years to reveal itself. But when it arrives, it can come in a variety of debilitating hues including liver disease, depression, anxiety, impotence, osteoporosis, pancreatitis, stomach ulcers, infertility, heart disease, high blood pressure, cancer, strokes and dementia. Drinking too much also makes you fat (alcohol is basically a nutrient-free glass of calories, although red wine has been shown in some studies to provide useful antioxidants when consumed in moderation). It can also make you very boring and repetitive.

However, even this litany of terrible possibilities is unlikely to turn the average harassed working mother or stressed-out business executive away from a soothing G & T at the end of the day. Or convince you that friends' birthdays and weddings are best celebrated stone-cold sober. The problem is that, like most things that are bad for us, alcohol can be lovely. So, below are some tips to help you do your best to cut your units down to a healthy level.

- Have at least two drink-free days a week.
- Drink water or soft drinks in between your alcoholic drinks.
- Be sure to have some food when you're on a boozy night out.
- Try to avoid those unnecessary, random odd glasses of wine or beer on weekday evenings and only have them when you really, really want them.
- Go for small glasses of wine rather than large ones and halves instead of pints. You'll save money in the long run by drinking less and you'll soon get over being called a pansy by your mates. If the peer pressure is really that bad, you can get away with pretending a tonic water has gin in it simply by asking for ice and lemon.

Drink	Approximate units
A large glass of red wine	3
A large glass of white or rosé wine	2.8
A pint of cider	2.5
A pint of ale or stout	2.3
A pint of lager	2.3
A Martini	2.2
A standard glass of red wine	2.1
A measure of whisky or vodka	2
A gin and tonic	1.9
A small glass of Baileys	0.9

AND BEND, AND STRETCH . . . : EXERCISE

It seems us Limeys are a lazy bunch: physical activity levels in the UK are pitiably low. Only 35% of men and 24% of women reach the recommended 30 minutes of moderate physical activity at least five times a week. Some people have genuine health reasons why they shouldn't do any form of vigorous activity, and if you've been out of the game for a long time or are overweight it's worth speaking to your doctor before you suddenly start rock-climbing every weekend, but for the rest of us there are compelling reasons to try to work a little workout into our lives.

Exercise reduces the risk of diabetes, heart disease, colon and breast cancer, osteoporosis and depression. So, if you don't fancy tennis, triathlon, trampolining, volleyball, badminton, cricket, swimming, waterskiing, parkour, kick-boxing, kabaddi or javelin-throwing, at least try walking or cycling to work, taking the stairs, doing a bit of speed-gardening, or running on the spot while you're watching TV. Exercise is not just helpful to your health but also a good way to work out any frustrations you might have accumulated during the day (imagine that punchbag is your boss) and many people find it really does make them cheerier and more balanced, as well as fitter and svelter.

HOW TO DELIVER A BABY

Only doctors and midwives are legally allowed to deliver babies, but in an emergency situation here is what you should know:

- Keep yourself and the mother calm and comfortable – remember that giving birth is a natural process that happens to thousands of people every day. This doesn't mean you should be cavalier about it but there is nothing helpful about running around shrieking.
- Call 999 and ask for an ambulance and, if you have time, call the midwife. The 999 operator can talk you through the labour until the ambulance arrives.
- Encourage the mother to breathe slowly and deeply and adopt a comfortable birthing position.
- Count the minutes between contractions. If they're less than 2 minutes apart, expect the baby to arrive soon.

- Clean your hands and arms thoroughly with soap and hot water.
- When the baby's crown appears, place your hand gently against the head helping it to come out slowly. Do not pull – you are just helping to control the birth.
- As the baby's face appears, stroke downwards gently on its nose to clear the airway.
- Once the baby has been fully delivered, do not cut the umbilical cord. Place the baby on the mother's chest.
- Make everyone a cup of tea and demand the baby is named after you in recognition of your heroic efforts.

HOME ECONOMICS TEST PAPER

1. How long does it take to cook ordinary spaghetti?

a) about 10 minutes
b) about 3 minutes
c) about 5 minutes
d) about 20 minutes

2. Which of the following should a pregnant woman not eat?

a) broccoli
b) custard
c) trout
d) chocolate mousse

3. Who said the kitchen is 'the great laboratory of every household'?

a) Nigella Lawson
b) Mrs Beeton
c) Marilyn Monroe
d) Queen Victoria

4. What percentage of fruit eaten in the UK is imported?

a) 10%
b) 50%
c) 75%
d) 91%

5. What is 'peristalsis'?

a) a process whereby the muscular walls of the gut contract in order to push food along

b)   the interaction between nerve cells
c)   the food inside your digestive system
d)   a school of ancient Greek philosophy

6. What is a macrobiotic diet?

a)   a diet where you only eat baby food
b)   a diet where you only eat fish and vegetables
c)   a diet which includes no meat, eggs, dairy products, white sugar, tropical fruits, potatoes, peppers or aubergines
d)   a diet which includes no jelly, salmon, peas, cream, white sugar, tomatoes or beer

7. What four things do plants need to survive?

a)   fertiliser, water, food, heat
b)   pesticides, moisture, fertiliser, light
c)   heat, light, moisture and food
d)   heat, light, moisture and conversation

8. In the electrical appliances and plugs in your home, unless labelled otherwise, brown-coloured wires mean:

a)   neutral
b)   live
c)   earth

9. If you are a forty-year-old woman what quantity of fat is your recommended daily allowance?

a)   76g
b)   65g
c)   133g
d)   45g

10. Approximately how many units of alcohol are there in a big glass of red wine?

a)   1
b)   2
c)   3
d)   4

11. How often should a healthy adult exercise?

a) 15 minutes, three times a week
b) 5 minutes, once a week
c) 45 minutes, twice a week
d) 30 minutes, five times a week

12. What is the first thing you should do if you're trapped in a broken lift with a woman who has just gone into labour?

a) panic
b) call 999
c) get her to lie down
d) try to climb out through the roof

13. How many units of alcohol are there in a gin and tonic?

a) none
b) 3.3
c) 1.9
d) 8

14. What is a pescatarian?

15. Which of the following has NOT been associated with excessive alcohol consumption?

a) impotence
b) stomach ulcers
c) deafness
d) heart disease

16. How long is it safe to keep cooked rice in the fridge before reheating it?

17. What should you eat more of if you find yourself constipated?

18. Which organ releases the enzyme pepsin to help break down food?

19. Which of the following is NOT a traditional ingredient of spaghetti Bolognese?

a)   tomatoes
b)   chicken liver
c)   beef stock
d)   cabbage

20. Which of the following is the most useful ingredient to keep in your pantry?

a)   fresh trout
b)   canned tuna
c)   swordfish steak

21. Which of the following is NOT a type of food poisoning?

a)   campylobacter
b)   salmonella
c)   tachycardia
d)   listeria

22. What is the most environmentally friendly way to remove limescale from your shower head?

23. Pick the odd one out in this list: marjoram, parsley, pepper, pancetta, basil, dill, mint

24. What do dust mites eat?

25. What causes dry rot in timber?

26. What is a Braxton Hicks?

a)   a fermion
b)   a type of watermelon
c)   a herb
d)   a preliminary contraction that occurs before labour

27. Where would you find your pyloric sphincter?

28. Niacin is also known as vitamin:

a) B_1
b) B_2
c) B_3
d) B_4

29. Pellagra and beriberi are both:

a) diseases caused by vitamin deficiency
b) lovely girls' names
c) rare varieties of strawberry

30. What lifestyle change increases your life expectancy and fertility and decreases the likelihood of you developing gangrene, cancer and heart disease?

⊙ PHILOSOPHY ⊙
AND
PSYCHOLOGY

THE UNIVERSAL QUESTION:
WHAT IS PHILOSOPHY?

Since time immemorial, men and women have been trying to answer the big questions: who are we, what are we doing here, how should we live, what is beauty, or truth, or morality? We humans have a remarkable capacity to reflect on ourselves (some might call it the ultimate navel-gazing). Here we'll give you a handy philosophical chronology, a tour through time, from Socrates to Aquinas, Locke, Spinoza, Hume, Kant, Kierkegaard, Nietzsche and Sartre all the while bearing in mind what that wise old savant Confucius has to say about people who haven't read *Advanced Homework* – 'Ignorance is the night of the mind, but a night without moon and star.'

Moving on from philosophy we'll trace the roots of psychology and examine how to apply it to human behaviour (and explaining why Pavlov was so obsessed with dog saliva). We'll look at the father of psychoanalysis, Sigmund Freud and give you a list of things to watch out for in your dreams (giant spiders and old men are not so good). We'll examine the many schools of thought, from Gestalt to Behaviouralism, the Cognitive Approach, and Evolutionary Psychology. And if you need further proof that we humans are a dark and dastardly lot, we'll examine one of the most shocking (literally) psychological experiments ever carried out. It's guaranteed to make your blood run cold.

PHILOSOPHY TIMELINE

Sages in what would later become India produced a series of texts in *c.*1500 BCE called the *Vedas* which in turn gave rise to many Eastern religions. They concluded that the answer to the question, 'Who Am I?' was that we are not simply individual souls but rather part of the One.

Confucius (551–479 BCE)
Confucius was one of the earliest philosophers to ask the question, 'Who am I and what am I doing here?' He believed the answer lay in our relationships with others. In what is now modern China, Confucius strove to be virtuous by following '*dao*' (the way), or the path to virtue. For him, that meant that we should depend on our humanity, we should adhere to rules of community, always defer to our parents and try to be good citizens. Not everyone felt the same: a group calling themselves (rather confusingly) **Daoists** also believed in *dao*, but that the way to goodness lay in being as honest to nature as possible, rejecting customs and social pretensions and instead relying on our instincts. Key text: Avalects.

Socrates (469–399 BCE)
Born in Athens, Socrates devoted himself to gaining self-knowledge and wisdom through rigorous questioning instead of accepting the

majority's beliefs – this method of enquiry would later be known as Socratic dialogue. One of the most pleasing quotes attributed to him is 'I know nothing except the fact of my own ignorance'. Key text: Plato's *Socratic Dialogues*.

Plato (429–347 BCE)

Plato was a pupil of Socrates who devoted his life to furthering his teachings, founding the Academy in Athens, which existed for nearly a thousand years. Plato believed that the world could be thought of in two realms, the visible (that which we understand with our senses) and the intelligible (that which we understand with our minds). In addition, he proposed the idea of Forms – that truth, beauty and goodness exist as unchanging entities parallel to the visible world and that we are only capable perceiving them as imitations of the Forms. In his *The Republic*, Plato explains his theory with an allegory narrated by Socrates.

Aristotle (384–322 BC)

Aristotle forged an education at Plato's Academy and later set up his own school, the Lyceum. He wrote on many subjects but most famously on logic (known as the *Organon*) where he attempted to develop a method of reasoning that could be applied to a greater understanding of everything. His method was concerned with syllogisms, whereby a conclusion is reached by linking two propositions e.g. All men are mortal: Socrates is a man: therefore, Socrates is mortal.

Thomas Aquinas (1225–74)

Building on the work of the ancient Greek philosopher Aristotle (384–322 BCE), Aquinas managed to reconcile faith and experience by showing that some truths, such as the mystery of being, can only be known through spiritual revelation, and others, such as the physical composition of things, can only be known through sensory experience. Key text: *Summa Theologica*.

Michel de Montaigne (1533–92)

Montaigne's philosophy was a generous one: he accepted that we humans tend to be hysterical rather than serene, and wanted us to learn to accept ourselves and our bodily functions. He was remarkably progressive –

one of the first sceptics – often asking the question, 'What do I know?' His advice on impotence is also still relevant today (the key is to not think about it too much . . .). Key text: *Essays.*

Thomas Hobbes (1588–1679)

Hobbes was a political philosopher and is most famous for his idea of the social contract – that life in nature, without government, is 'solitary, poor, nasty, brutish, and short'. According to Hobbes, we need governments and nations to form social order and prevent chaos. Key text: *Leviathan.*

Benedict (Baruch) de Spinoza (1632–77)

The Spanish-Portuguese Jewish Dutch thinker Spinoza's moral philosophy was based on the idea that the secret to virtue and happiness lay in controlling human passions. He believed that God and nature are the same thing (**pantheism**), and he was deeply critical of sectarian religion. Key text: *Ethics.*

John Locke (1632–1704)

Locke insisted that we humans are defined by deeply personal memory. He is one of the three significant British **empiricists**, along with Berkeley and Hume, who argued that knowledge arises from experience, and that our own perception is paramount. Key text: *An Essay Concerning Human Understanding.*

George Berkeley (1685–1753)

Berkeley was an Irish bishop and follower of Locke who argued that nothing exists outside of our minds. His catchphrase was 'To be is to be perceived'. His position gave rise to the question: 'If a tree falls over and nobody is there to witness it, does it actually fall?' Berkeley was religious, so his answer was that omnipresent God perceives the toppling timber. Key text: *An Essay towards a New Theory of Vision.*

David Hume (1711–76)

A Scottish philosopher and probably the most famous of the modern sceptics, Hume was also a master empiricist, believing that because we can never be outside of our own experience, it is impossible to prove that there is, in fact, a reality outside of our own experience. Key text: *A Treatise of Human Nature.*

Voltaire (1694–1778)
Key figure of the Enlightenment, Voltaire was imprisoned in the Bastille for his devastatingly witty lampooning of the aristocracy. His morality was based in the rational, and he rejected the irrational and the superstitious, and was, unsurprisingly, a fan of religious tolerance, *Candide* examines the devastating effect of religious fanaticism on the world. Key text: *Candide* (1759).

Jean-Jacques Rousseau (1712–1778)
Botanist, musician, novelist, and *serial ménage à trois*-er, the philosopher Jean-Jacques Rousseau was another key figure of the Enlightenment. His most famous work of philosophy is probably *The Social Contract* (1762) which opened with the dramatic proposition that man is born free, but everywhere is in chains. He put forth the idea of civil liberties and the might of the will of the populus as opposed to the divine right of kings, and laid the intellectual foundations for the French Revolution. Key text: *The Social Contract* (1762)

Ludwig Wittgenstein (1889–1951)
A sensitive soul, prone to depression, Austro-British Ludwig Wittgenstein made huge contributions to analytic and linguistic philosophy – proposing the idea that we all play a 'language game': using words and propositions to serve different functions, and moreover because words are flexible and contextual, a scientist and an artist may play different 'language games'. Key text: *Philosophical Investigations* (1953).

Immanuel Kant (1724–1804)
The celebrated German intellectual Kant believed it was necessary to separate nature's **determinism** (the fact that every event has a causal explanation) from human freedom and choice, and that we should focus on the rationality of choice. A large part of Kant's work asks, 'What can we know?' and he concludes that our knowledge is limited to mathematics and the science of the natural, empirical world. Key text: *Critique of Pure Reason.*

Georg Wilhelm Friedrich Hegel (1770–1831)
The ambitious Hegel wanted to create a whole philosophical system that could take into account the ideas of his predecessors so that both the past and the future could be philosophically understood. Hegel saw the accumulation of all human knowledge in terms of the pattern of dialectics, whereby forms of consciousness change through history, moving from **thesis** to **antithesis** to **synthesis**. Key text: *The Phenomenology of Mind*.

Arthur Schopenhauer (1788–1860)
Gloomy Schopenhauer was famously pessimistic, believing the human condition to be essentially painful. He identified in people a 'will-to-life': a life force that drives us into existence and towards propagating the next generation. Only through a constant awareness of this can human beings become fulfilled. Key text: *The World as Will and Representation*.

Søren Kierkegaard (1813–55)
The brooding Danish genius was primarily concerned with individual existence, choice and commitment, and is known as the father of **existentialism**. Kierkegaard regarded philosophy as the result of the individual life, as opposed to the Hegelian view of philosophy as reality as a whole. Kierkegaard believed the human condition could only ever be conflicted, paradoxical and ambiguous: we make our own choices, and these choices can only ever be viewed subjectively. Key text: *Either/Or*.

Friedrich Nietzsche (1844–1900)
Impressively moustachioed Nietzsche did not believe in absolute right or wrong and suggested instead that individuals forge ideas of morality based on their place in the world and, more specifically, their dominance. For Nietzsche, there are two types of morality: master morality (as demonstrated by the ancient Greeks) and slave morality (as demonstrated by Christians) – and he had no truck with the sappy Christian idea that the weak should be protected. Key text: *Beyond Good and Evil*.

Bertrand Russell (1872–1970)
Russell was a famous and at times controversial Welsh philosopher. He was the founder of **analytic philosophy**, which tries to clarify, through logical analysis, the meaning of statements and concepts. For Russell, language was key – he held that terms like 'the average woman' should be handled with extreme caution. Key text: *The Principles of Mathematics*.

Jean-Paul Sartre (1905–80)
The rock star of modern philosophers, Sartre was a **phenomenologist** – an analyst of the structures of consciousness. He was also an **existentialist**, and borrowed from Kant the idea that we focus on the rationality of decision rather than the causal influences acting on us. Sartre went even further, insisting that our freedom must be absolute: if we are conscious we have choices, which means we must bear responsibility for the choices we make. Key text: *Being and Nothingness*.

Albert Camus (1913–60)
Nobel Laureate, writer, existentialist and brilliant goalie, Camus' position was that we are not absurd and the world is not absurd, but because we want nothing more than an order and clarity the world can never provide, our existence in the world is an absurdity. So, alas, the human condition is always a troubled one. Key text: *The Myth of Sisyphus*.

DOUBTING DESCARTES: RENÉ'S THOUGHT EXPERIMENT

Not content with being the father of analytical geometry, René Descartes, a Frenchman who spent much of his life in Holland, is also known as the father of modern philosophy. Born in 1596, he studied widely – in Law, Mathematics and Physics – and published many works, the most influential being *Meditations on First Philosophy* (1641).

Descartes insisted we should doubt absolutely everything: so, the questions to ask yourself are 'Are we here right now?', 'Is there a God?' and 'Does the world actually exist?' By doubting everything, Descartes believed you could whittle life down until you found out what you really knew to be true and absolute. This thought experiment became the foundation of modern philosophy. Descartes' position was that the one thing he could be completely certain of was his own consciousness, as the very fact of doubting must allow for an act of conscious thought: he summed this up with the phrase '*cogito ergo sum*' or 'I think therefore I am'. From this starting point, other truths can be established, e.g. if your consciousness exists than there must be a place for it to exist in, and so on. One of the problems that Descartes' argument throws up, and which philosophers have debated endlessly, is that if the only certain thing is our own consciousness, logically we must doubt the existence of our bodies. Take a quiet moment and try your own thought experiment; like philosophy in general, it's mind-bending, but lots of fun.

WHAT IS PSYCHOLOGY?

The word psychology comes from the Greek words '*psyche*', meaning 'mind' or 'spirit', and '*logos*', meaning 'study'. Psychology is the investigation of the behaviour and experience of human beings. Although many of us consider ourselves brilliant armchair psychologists, we're not – true psychologists develop theories and test them rigorously, they don't rely on intuition or feelings. Psychology is scrupulously scientific and, like any academic discipline, there are different schools of thought that you should be aware of.

WONDROUS WILHELM WUNDT AND INTROSPECTION

Wilhelm Wundt (1832–1920) was a physiologist who set up the first experimental psychology laboratory at the University of Leipzig in Germany in 1879. There, he and his colleagues studied their own conscious mental processes in a system called **introspection**. They showed visual stimuli to subjects under controlled conditions and asked them what they experienced. Unfortunately Wundt's method proved unreliable: other researchers, using other subjects, turned up different results, but he still deserves lionisation for his role as a bold pioneer.

ON THE COUCH: PSYCHOANALYSIS

Created by world-famous shrink Sigmund Freud, the term psychoanalysis refers to both the theory that most human behaviour stems from unconscious thought processes, and also the therapy that Freud developed to treat various psychological conditions. By accessing the unconscious mind, psychoanalysts believe that the origins of conflicts can be laid open and resolved. Psychoanalysis involves various techniques, from free association to dream interpretation.

-IATRY OR -OLOGY: DO YOU NEED A PSYCHIATRIST OR A PSYCHOLOGIST?

Psychiatry is the diagnosis and treatment of mental disorders.

Psychology is the study of the human mind and its functions.

BEHAVIOURALISM

American psychologist John B. Watson (1878–1958) argued that the science should focus on the behaviour of human beings rather than their mental processes (which can only ever be subjective). Following his theory, behaviour is observed and analysed using methods that biologists and chemists employ in their studies. Behaviouralism's roots stretch back to Pavlov's famous 1889 dog experiments and it is still influential today.

PSYCHOLOGY IN ACTION I: DROOLING DOGS AND THE PAVLOVIAN RESPONSE

Born in 1849 in Ryazan, Russia, Ivan Pavlov abandoned his original idea of a religious career to follow a scientific path, changing the landscape of physiology with his work on the digestive system in mammals, for which he won the Nobel Prize in 1904. As part of this research he turned his attention to conditioned reflexes, and his almost accidental discoveries laid the foundations for an objective science of behaviour.

While mining the secrets of the digestive system, Pavlov observed that when a dog is served food, it begins to salivate (saliva is an essential part of a dog's digestion as it makes its dinner easier to swallow). He also noticed the odd fact that the dogs drooled even before the food was in front of them. It turned out they were reacting to the lab coats worn by the assistants doling out their canine collations. Pavlov then tried ringing a bell when the dogs were fed. Sure enough, after a while, the dogs dribbled at the sound of the bell alone.

Pavlov's discovery that reflexes can be conditioned has been invaluable in various fields such as anti-phobia treatments, where patients are taught to fight their fearful responses by a process called **extinction.** Pavlovian response has also been used in advertising: when you're next slobbing out in front of the telly watch out for adverts attempting to train you to associate a brand's name with feelings of well-being.

THE COGNITIVE APPROACH

Cognitive psychology developed in the 1950s and 60s as a backlash against the view of psychology as the purely scientific study of behaviour, which was felt to be restrictive. Instead, the cognitive approach re-examined mental processes, focusing on the study of the cognitive (knowing or perceiving) ways in which human beings process information or knowledge they have about the world. Cognitive behaviouralists are particularly interested in perception, memory and problem-solving.

GESTALT PSYCHOLOGY

'Gestalt' means 'configuration' and this field of psychology is all to do with imagery and the processes of perception. It began as a protest against associationism, which states that the mind learns by associating simple images and then building a picture. Gestalt Psychology instead understands that images have a context, i.e. our minds will make sense of a round shape in a seascape differently to our viewing it in a cityscape. This view is extended to therapy in that it takes a holistic approach in which mind and body are not separated, and instead of the psychoanalytic reliance on unlocking childhood memory and experience, present experiences are key, as is directly confronting one's fears.

THE PHYSIOLOGICAL (BIOLOGICAL) APPROACH

The physiological approach insists that behaviour is linked to human biology. In its therapeutic practice, drugs can be used to affect different parts of the brain to alleviate stress, anxiety or psychosis. This physical focus gave rise to electroconvulsive therapy (ECT) for people with severe depression. ECT is a controversial treatment in which a patient has an electrical current passed through the brain for around half a second. It's not quite clear how ECT works, but it seems to be linked to hormone secretion. Another dramatic treatment, now banned, was pre frontal lobotomy, where surgery was carried out on the brain in order to diminish violent behaviour.

THE EVOLUTIONARY APPROACH

This school of thought takes Darwin's theory of evolution as its starting point. It holds that human beings have evolved through a process of natural selection, and everything, including our mental processes and behaviour, is shaped by this. Our behaviour can be seen as a reflection of the adaptations that helped our ancestors survive, such as the common, and sensible, phobia of snakes and spiders. More controversially, evolutionary psychology highlights the differences between men and women in terms of how they select their partners. Studies have shown that since women have shorter periods of fertility, men will favour a younger partner, while women opt for a mate with more resources who'll give her children the best chance of survival, rather than someone young, fun and full of... Jealousy is also said to have its roots in our evolutionary background – the idea is that once a woman is impregnated then her job in terms of furthering her genetic material is done, while for the male of the species there is no such certainty. The idea is that men respond to this uncertainty by exerting sexual control. It follows on that men are more inclined to be threatened by sexual infidelity, while women are threatened by emotional infidelity. Slightly more tenuous is the suggestion that little girls' preference for pink may have its roots in our hunter-gatherer days, when women foraged for red-hued roots and berries.

PSYCHOLOGY IN ACTION II: A SHOCKING LESSON: MILGRAM'S OBEDIENCE EXPERIMENT

Stanley Milgram's infamous experiments on obedience and authority began in 1961, just a few months after the trial of Adolf Eichmann for war crimes. Milgram wanted to know how ordinary Nazis had come to carry out the Holocaust and set up a simple experiment at Yale University to test how much pain an ordinary citizen would inflict on a fellow human if under orders from a figure of authority.

Participants were told that the study would look at the relationship between punishment and learning and that one person would be the teacher and the other would be the learner (in fact the learner was an actor). The learner was then strapped into a chair, and electrodes were attached to his or her arm. Both the teacher and the learner were told that the electrodes would deliver electric shocks that would serve as punishment for incorrect answers. They were also both told that while the shocks would be painful, they would not cause any permanent tissue damage (in reality no shocks would actually be received). The teacher and learner were then put into separate rooms.

The shock generator had thirty switches, ranging from 15 to 450 volts, labelled from 'slight shock' to 'danger: severe shock', with a last switch labelled 'XXX'. The teacher was told to punish the learner for incorrect answers by increasing the shock by 15 volts each time. When the experiment began, the learner (remember he's an actor) made various mistakes. As the volts got higher, the teacher heard the learner in obvious pain and by 150 volts the learner would be screaming. When the teacher hesitated, as he invariably did, the experimenter encouraged him to carry on. At 300 volts the learner began to pound on the wall and demand to be let out, and at 330 volts he was silent. The experimenter then told the teacher that his lack of response was to be considered an incorrect answer, and shocks were to still be administered. The experiment concluded when the highest shock level was reached.

Frighteningly enough, 65% of participants gave out shock levels of 450 volts. Even more frighteningly, in the post-experiment interview, Milgram asked participants to rate how painful they thought the shocks were, and the typical answer was extremely painful. So next time your boss tells you to do something you're not sure about, remember this chilling tale.

THE DREAMING DOCTOR:
SIGMUND FREUD (1856–1939)

Born in Austria to an affluent Jewish family, Sigmund Freud's brilliance showed from an early age. He trained as a doctor in Vienna and worked as a neurologist before moving into academia. Central to Freud's thinking is the idea that all human beings have an unconscious in which forces (especially sexual) struggle against each other for supremacy. He proposed that erotic desire starts in infancy, and that many patients' problems stem from sexual dysfunction or imbalance. He encouraged the idea that all men are afflicted by the **Oedipus complex**, which means they love their mothers and hate their fathers, and developed the 'talking cure' in which a patient talked through his or her own problems in an attempt to reveal previously repressed feelings that explain current behaviour. As part of this cure Freud explored various techniques: **free association**, in which uncensored thinking was encouraged; **transference**, in which the patient was invited to transfer feelings or thoughts onto the analyst; and **dream analysis**, in which the patient's dreams (where Freud believed the unconscious roamed free) were analysed for symbolic importance. He also paid close attention to **parapraxis**, or the Freudian slip (such as a man calling his wife by the name of another woman), and nonsensical speech patterns. Freud's influence has been enormous and his ideas have repeatedly gone in and out of fashion since his death in 1939 in England, where he had fled to escape the Nazis.

WHAT TO WATCH OUT FOR IN YOUR DREAMS

Freud called dreams 'the royal road to the unconscious' and believed that they symbolically revealed the fears and anxieties that we refuse to confront in conscious, waking thought. He also saw dreams as wish-fulfilment (nightmares are about wishing that a scenario will not occur). Freud divided the subject of dreams into two types: **manifest** – those we remember as soon as we wake up which do not necessarily reveal the dreamer's true anxieties; and **latent** – the forbidden thoughts and desires which we suppress and so don't recall. Here's a simple Freudian guide to what to watch out for in your dreams, and what they really represent:

- Tree trunks, ties, weapons, sticks, umbrellas, balloons, rockets and any elongated objects: erection/the penis.
- Boxes, cases, chests, cupboards, ovens, suitcases and cave-like objects: the female genitalia.
- Baldness, teeth falling out and hair being cut: castration.
- Playing of instruments or games, climbing trees: masturbation.
- Dancing, riding, climbing or descending a ladder or stairs, brandishing a weapon: sexual intercourse.
- Going in or out of water: birth.

Sweet dreams!

Carl Gustav Jung (1875–1961)

Born in Switzerland, as a child Jung showed a passion for dreams and fantasy which would inform his later work. Jung believed that the human psyche was essentially religious, and that it could be understood by exploring dreams, fantasy, myth and religion. For him, the goal was a harmony of the soul, and he thought a too heavy reliance on science or indeed art would lead to imbalance. Instead, the conscious and the unconscious should be integrated in the process of **individuation** – a key concept of analytical psychology. He developed word association tests in which a patient's response to terms such as 'water', 'to marry', 'to prick', would reveal 'complexes'. He worked closely with Freud, but he disagreed with his narrow view of sexuality (though he did coin the term Electra Complex as a counterpart to Freud's Oedipus Complex, in which girls feels romantically drawn to their fathers and resent their mothers). Jung defined the personality types of **introvert** and **extrovert**, and also the idea of the personal unconscious, which referred to an individual's thoughts and feelings, and the **collective unconscious**, which are thoughts and feelings shared by all humanity. To further investigate these ideas he lived among the Pueblo Tribes of New Mexico, travelled to Egypt and India, and studied alchemy and phenomenology.

∽ PHILOSOPHY ∽ AND PSYCHOLOGY TEST PAPER

1. Which of the following is the odd one out?

a) Sigmund Freud
b) Friedrich Nietzsche
c) David Hume
d) George Berkeley

2. Who pioneered the study of psychology as a stand-alone discipline?

a) Pamela Stephenson
b) Wilhelm Wundt
c) Thomas Aquinas

3. Who wrote *Meditations on First Philosophy?*

a) Albert Camus
b) Jean-Paul Sartre
c) René Descartes
d) Socrates

4. Jean-Paul Sartre was a:

a) epidemiologist
b) pathologist
c) phenomenologist
d) biologist

5. Psychiatry is:

a) the diagnosis and treatment of mental disorders
b) the study of the human mind and its functions

6. What is the name of Albert Camus' key philosophical work?

a) *The Myth of Cicero*
b) *The Myth of Platypus*
c) *The Myth of Sisyphus*
d) *The Myth of Sicily*

7. Who invented behaviourism?

a) John B. Watson
b) Confucius
c) Stanley Milgram
d) Søren Kierkegaard

8. What was George Berkeley's answer to the question of whether a tree has actually fallen over if no one is there to perceive it?

9. Who is considered the father of existentialism?

10. Which famous philosopher's first names were Georg Wilhelm Friedrich?

11. Who wrote the teachings of Socrates that we still have today?

a) Socrates
b) Plato
c) Aristotle
d) Zeno

12. What was Stanley Milgram investigating through his famous experiments at Yale University?

a) Nazi actions in the Holocaust
b) people's attitudes to risk
c) the subconscious
d) sailors' responses to stress at sea

13. Who said 'I think therefore I am'?

a) Confucius
b) Ivan Pavlov

c) Immanuel Kant
d) René Descartes

14. According to Freud, if you dream about getting into a swimming pool what are you really dreaming about?

a) castration
b) the penis
c) birth
d) death

15. What is another term for a Freudian slip?

a) parenthesis
b) parallel
c) paradigm
d) parapraxis

16. Who described life as 'solitary, poor, nasty, brutish, and short'?

a) Benedict de Spinoza
b) Thomas Hobbes
c) Julius Caesar
d) John Locke

17. What does '*dao*' mean?

a) the light
b) the sky
c) the edge
d) the path

18. Berkeley, Hume and Locke were all:

a) imperialists
b) empiricists
c) vegetarians
d) realists

19. **Who wrote the famous Latin philosophical poem *De Rerum Natura (On the Nature of Things)*?**

a) Lucretius
b) Epicurus
c) Leucippus

20. **What does ECT stand for?**

a) energy capacity tablets
b) environmental candour technician
c) electroconvulsive therapy
d) electrical capacitive topography

21. **What is the name of the philosophical belief system that identifies God with the universe and nature?**

22. **Which political philosopher said 'It is safer to be feared than loved'?**

23. **Who is the ancient Greek philosopher associated with scepticism?**

a) Pyrrho
b) Plato
c) Pythagoras
d) Thales

24. **The Persian prophet Zoroaster gave his name to which famous nineteenth-century philosophical work?**

25. **Who came up with the concepts of extrovert and introvert personality types?**

a) Immanuel Kant
b) Kurt Koffka
c) Carl Jung

26. **Pavlov carried out his famous experiments on:**

a) children
b) dogs

c)   cats
d)   squirrels

27. What does the ancient Greek word '*psyche*' mean?

a)   soul
b)   helicopter
c)   leaf
d)   soup

28. Arthur Schopenhauer held that the human condition was essentially:

a)   painful
b)   absurd
c)   happy

29. Which thirteenth-century philosopher wrote *Summa Theologica*?

30. Epistemology is the study of:

a)   dreams
b)   religion
c)   knowledge

ADVANCED HOMEWORK FOR GROWN-UPS

ANSWERS

⬳ ENGLISH LANGUAGE AND LITERATURE ANSWERS

1. b)

2. b)

3. a)

4. b)

5. a)

6. c)

7. d)

8. gin

9. d)

10. b)

11. c)

12. b)

13. Like 'th' in 'thin'

14. a)

15. c)

16. c)

17. b)

18. a)

19. *Tristram Shandy*

20. c)

21. c)

22. b)

23. c)

24. a)

25. a)

26. c)

27. d)

28. 'i' before 'e' except after 'c'

29. b)

30. b)

31.
a) girls'
b) Smiths' and they're
c) it's (**It's** unwise to give the baby whisky in its bedtime bottle)

32.
a) whom
b) whom

∽ MATHEMATICS ∽
ANSWERS

1. $7\sqrt{5}$

$\sqrt{20} = \sqrt{5} \times \sqrt{4} = 2\sqrt{5}$
$\sqrt{125} = \sqrt{5} \times \sqrt{25} = 5\sqrt{5}$

$2\sqrt{5} + 5\sqrt{5} = 7\sqrt{5}$

2. 3/6 (or 0.5 or 50%)

3. 4.95

4. 4/52 (or 0.08 or 8%)

5. c)

6. Isabel. Each apple in the bag cost Isabel 32p but each individual apple cost Pat 33p.

7. x = 3, y = 27

8. a)

9. 0.33

10. 1.4. The mean is a way of expressing an average by dividing the total number of bottles by the total number of people.

11. −8

12. 1,000

13. they are all prime numbers

14. 2

15. a parallelogram

16. An isosceles triangle has two sides of the same length. An equilateral has all three sides the same length.

17.

First shopping trip:
$2b + 3s + 8.99 = 15.86$
If you remove the flax seeds from this equation you get:
$2b + 3s = 6.87$

Second shopping trip:
$2b + s = 4.29$

If you multiply the second equation by 3 you get:
$6b + 3s = 12.87$

You can now subtract your first equation from your second to give you:
$4b = 6$

If you divide both sides of this equation by 4 you get:
$b = 1.5$

Now you know b you can work out s by putting your newly discovered b value into either equation:
$3 + 3s = 6.87$
$3s = 3.87$
$s = 1.29$

So each pack of blueberries cost you £1.50 and each pack of spinach cost you £1.29.

18. an angle that exceeds 180° but is less than 360°

19. 54

20. 20m²

21. 75%

22. 6

23. Patty

24. ³⁄₁₄

25. 36cm²

26. 8

27. 4

28. 39

29. 180°

30. £12.50

∽ GEOGRAPHY ∽
ANSWERS

1. a)

2. b)

3. b)

4. a)

5. d)

6. d)

7. c)

8. Lancashire

9. b)

10. c)

11. d)

12. b)

13. a)

14. b)

15. b)

16. force 6

17. c)

18. Antananarivo

19. d)

20. a)

21. a)

22. b)

23. the winter solstice

24. b)

25. b)

26. b)

27. The Atlantic Ocean is larger and deeper.

28. b)

29. b)

30. a)

HISTORY AND POLITICS ANSWERS

1. Emperor Constantine

2. b)

3. the attack on Pearl Harbor

4. d)

5. b)

6. c)

7. Haile Selassie

8. d)

9. b)

10. b)

11. c)

12. d)

13. b)

14. d)

15. c)

16. c)

17. a)

18. c)

19. a)

20. c)

21. c)

22. a)

23. It is an illuminated manuscript of the four Gospels of the New Testament, created by Celtic monks in around 800 CE.

24. c)

25. b)

26. a)

27. b)

28. b)

29. c)

30. a)

∽ ECONOMICS ∽
ANSWERS

1. d)

2. a)

3. c)

4. c)

5. a)

6. b)

7. b) Because demand is so high, passengers are willing to pay much higher prices for these tickets than for tickets at other times, when they don't need to get to work

8. d)

9. a)

10. c)

11. b)

12. b)

13. c)

14. a)

15. c)

16. c)

17. a)

18. d)

19. a)

20. c)

21. b)

22. c)

23. a)

24. a)

25. b)

26. b)

27. b)

28. It is money that has no intrinsic value as an object. Its only value comes from the fact that the government recognises it as currency.

29. It is money that has an intrinsic value as an object – for example a gold coin, rather than a banknote.

30. d)

❦ ART AND DESIGN ❧
ANSWERS

1. d)

2. c)

3. d)

4. c)

5. c)

6. a)

7. c)

8. d)

9. d)

10. It means 'wild beasts', and was used to describe the group of painters we call the Fauvists.

11. b)

12. a)

13. b)

14. c)

15. b)

16. d)

17. b)

18. b)

19. c)

20. a)

21. d)

22. c)

23. a)

24. c)

25. b)

26. a)

27. d)

28. b) Drying paintings in the dark can cause the paint to yellow.

29. b)

30. b)

Dot-to-Dot solution

Mona Lisa – Leonardo da Vinci

⚭ BREAK TIME ⚭
ANSWERS

1. 15
    tequila, beer, whiskey, schnapps, perry, lager, bitter, cider, pastis, porter, gin, stout, Martini, wine, ouzo

2. cassoulet, frogs' legs, fruits de mer, crêpe Suzette, crème caramel, steak frites, bouillabaisse, foie gras, profiteroles, tarte Tatin

3.
a) a stamp
b) a sponge
c) a towel
d) the letter 'm'
e) your name
f) a hole
g) the letter 's'
h) the moon
i) your word
j) read the label

∽ SCIENCE ∽
ANSWERS

1. They are all moons of Saturn

2. b)

3. a)

4. d)

5. d)

6. horse chestnut

7. a)

8. a)

9. the pancreas

10. a)

11. b)

12. c)

13. a)

14. a)

15. c)

16. c)

17. b)

18. in chromosomes in the nuclei of our cells

19. c)

20. c)

21. a fermion

22. a)

23. a badger

24. the four chemical bases of DNA

25. c)

26. a)

27. roughly every seventy-six years

28. d)

29. d)

30. c)

∽ CLASSICS ∽
ANSWERS

1. Ceres

2. c)

3. d)

4. c)

5. d)

6. A graphologist studies handwriting

7. b)

8. a)

9. senator

10. b)

11. Augustus

12. a)

13. Jocasta

14. It comes from the ancient Greek words 'psyche', meaning 'soul', and 'iatros', meaning 'doctor'

15. a)

16. by the gods, as punishment

17. house

18. b)

19. light

20. c)

21. b)

22. d)

23. b)

24. blood – sanguine; yellow bile – choleric; black bile – melancholic; phlegm – phlegmatic

25. b)

26. Because her elopement with the Trojan prince Paris from her Greek husband Menelaus' house led the Greeks to set off in their ships to get her back

27. c)

28. Daphne turned into a laurel tree, Arachne into a spider, Io into a cow and Philomela into a nightingale

29. a)

30. d)

∞ DRAMA AND ∞ FILM STUDIES ANSWERS

1. b)

2. *Citizen Kane*

3. a)

4. a)

5. a)

6. c)

7. c)

8. d)

9. b)

10. d)

11. Clark Gable

12. c)

13. d)

14. a)

15. b)

16. c)

17. Frances Gumm

18. c)

19. d)

20. c)

21. d)

22. Woody Allen

23. a)

24. François Truffaut

25. a)

26. commedia dell'arte

27. b)

28. Aristophanes

29. a)

30. *Othello*

✺ MUSIC ✺
ANSWERS

1. d)

2. G, B, D, F, A

3. a)

4. c)

5. that the piece should be played at a walking pace

6. James Paul McCartney and John Winston Lennon were the main songwriters for the Beatles

7. c)

8. d)

9. b)

10. it's a flat, a showing that a note must be dropped by a semitone.

11. bhangra

12. c)

13. d)

14. a)

15. b)

16. b)

17. d)

18. c) (it's by Rossini)

19. soft-loud

20. d)

21. a style of piano jazz from the 1930s, involving virtuoso right-hand playing and complex runs

22. c)

23. a)

24. a treble clef

25. b)

26. c)

27. d)

28. d)

29. b)

30. a)

⌘ MODERN ⌘
LANGUAGES
ANSWERS

1.

a) *Je voudrais une table pour deux*
b) *Est-ce que je peux avoir le menu?*
c) *Je veux une bouteille de champagne, s'il vous plaît*
d) *Je prends les huîtres pour l'hors d'oeuvre*
e) *Je voudrais le bifteck saignant avec des pommes frites, s'il vous plaît*

2.
a) *Apocalypse Now*
b) *Silence of the Lambs*
c) *Dirty Dancing*
d) *Jaws*
e) *Gone With the Wind*
f) any James Bond film
g) *The Godfather*
h) *Die Hard*
i) *Star Wars*
j) *Terminator*

3. b)

4. *Mann*

5.

Hallo, Ich komme aus Großbritannien
Bonjour, je viens de Grande Bretagne

6.

les livres
des chapeaux

7.

8. four: Galician, Basque, Castilian and Catalan

9. *Amo-te*

10.
a) oysters
b) grapefruit
c) frogs' legs

11.
> *I libri*
> *gli ucelli*
> *le biciclette*

12. *Sláinte!*

13. *Dydd Sul*

14. 1822, after the decipherment of the Rosetta Stone

15. St Cyril

16.
a) *fils*
b) *bateau*
c) *livre*

17.
a) I finished the book.
b) She will ask for the necklace.
c) They wait for the bus.

18. Any of the following:
devenir, revenir, monter, rester, sortir, venir, aller, naître, descendre, entrer, rentrer, tomber, retourner, arriver, mourir, partir

19. Herr

20.
a) *le gâteau*
b) *le jambon*
c) *la fraise*
d) *le melon*

21. *Je vous prie d'agréer, monsieur, l'expression de mes sentiments distingués*

22. approximately four

23.
a) masculine
b) feminine
c) feminine
d) masculine

24. <u>Banken</u> *brechen zusammen, an den* <u>Börsen</u> *herrscht* <u>Panik</u>

25. She's not keen. '*Schrecklich*' means 'disgusting'.

26. eating his cake

27. san

28. a)

29. c)

30. c)

❧ HOME ECONOMICS ANSWERS

1. a)

2. d. Chocolate mousse can contain raw egg

3. b)

4. d)

5. a)

6. c)

7. c)

8. b)

9. a)

10. c)

11. d)

12. b)

13. c)

14. a vegetarian who eats fish

15. c)

16. one day

17. fibre

18. the stomach

19. d)

20. b)

21. c)

22. Either scrub it off or tie a bag full of vinegar around it to soak overnight

23. pancetta

24. dead skin

25. fungi

26. d)

27. between the stomach and the duodenum

28. c)

29. a)

30. giving up smoking

⊙ PHILOSOPHY ⊙
AND PSYCHOLOGY
ANSWERS

1. a) Freud was a psychologist and the others were philosophers

2. b)

3. c)

4. c)

5. a)

6. c)

7. a)

8. God perceives it

9. Søren Kierkegaard

10. Hegel's

11. b)

12. a)

13. d)

14. c)

15. d)

16. b)

17. d)

18. b)

19. a)

20. c)

21. Pantheism

22. Niccolò Machiavelli

23. a)

24. *Thus Spake Zarathustra* by Friedrich Nietzsche

25. c)

26. b)

27. a)

28. a)

29. Thomas Aquinas

30. c)

☞ ACKNOWLEDGEMENTS ☜

We are very grateful to:

Rosemary Davidson, Cherrell Avery, Gemma Avery, Tom Avery, Isabel Barter, Marcus Bates, Jamie Bebb, Oliver Bebb, Kate Blad, Emma Buttle, Peter Chetwynd, Yen Chong, Lyndsey Clegg, David Coates, Geraldine Coates, Jo Coates, Monique Corless, Rachel Cugnoni, Suzanne Dean, Tom Drake-Lee, Eleanor Foley, Isabel Foley, Thomas Foley, Dan Franklin, Kathy Fry, Greg Heinimann, Dr Anthony Hippisley, Jane Kirby, Francis Lambert, Lucy Luck, Chris Lyon, Patrick Mackie, Peter McAdie, Robert McDowell, Ross Milne, Clare Murphy, Jack Murphy, Katherine Murphy, Esther Mustchin, Ian Pindar, Rosalind Porter, Simon Rhodes, John Salter, Rowena Skelton-Wallace, Jonathan Smith, William Vann, Ed Wallace, Kyra Watkins, Philip White-Jones, Stuart Williams, Claire Wilshaw, Christopher Wormell